Southern Living
2003 Garden Annual

Welcome to a glorious Lowcountry garden (See pages 178–183.)

Southern Living
2003 Garden ANNUAL

Oxmoor House®

Southern Living
2003 Garden ANNUAL

Book Division of Southern Progress Corporation
P.O. Box 2463, Birmingham, Alabama 35201

ISSN: 1048-2318
Hardcover ISBN: 0-8487-2715-0
Softcover ISBN: 0-8487-2716-9
Printed in the United States of America
First Printing 2003

SOUTHERN LIVING
Executive Editor, Homes and Gardens: Derick Belden
Garden Editor: Gene B. Bussell
Senior Writer: Stephen P. Bender
Associate Garden Editors: Ellen Ruoff Riley, Charles Thigpen
Associate Garden Design Editor: Glenn R. DiNella
Assistant Garden Design Editor: Troy H. Black
Senior Photographers: Jean M. Allsopp, Van Chaplin, Allen Rokach
Photographers: Tina Cornett, William Dickey, Laurey W. Glenn, Meg McKinney Simle
Production Manager: Katie Terrell Morrow
Editorial Assistant: Lynne Long
Production Coordinator: Jamie Barnhart

OXMOOR HOUSE, INC.
Editor-in-Chief: Nancy Fitzpatrick Wyatt
Executive Editor: Susan Carlisle Payne
Art Director: Cynthia R. Cooper
Copy Chief: Catherine Ritter Scholl

SOUTHERN LIVING 2003 GARDEN ANNUAL
Editor: Susan Hernandez Ray
Copy Editor: Jane Gentry
Editorial Assistant: Diane Rose
Contributing Designer: Rita Yerby
Contributing Indexer: Katharine R. Wiencke
Director, Production and Distribution: Phillip Lee
Books Production Manager: Larry Hunter
Production Assistant: Faye Porter Bonner

To order additional publications, call 1-800-765-6400.

Oxmoor House®

For more books to enrich your life, visit
oxmoorhouse.com

Cover: Cosmos, page 62
Back Cover: Sunflowers, page 160

Contents

Foreword 6

January 8
houseplants • side yard makeover • violas and pansies • garden fragrance • small winter bulbs

February 20
African violets • lawn care • Okame cherry

March 30
azaleas • bluebonnets • butterfly plants • Southern garden makeovers • Bok Tower

April 60
shared vegetable garden • wall garden • blue blooms • Texas Mountain Laurel • transplants • houseplant helper • caladiums • strawberry jar planters • mosaic table • heart rot • Southern roses • a Charleston garden

May 82
courtyard redesign • 'Tangerine Beauty' crossvine • backyard update • impatiens • new front path • Florida lawn care • Jerusalem sage • blooming Louisville garden

Sugar snap peas *page 23*

Maple leaves page 190

Zinnias page 132

June 106

crepe myrtles • landscaped pool • tiger lilies • new pergola • vegetable supports • dwarf morning glories • delightful deck • easy flower arranging • brick edging • little-known herbs • hanging baskets • beautiful blooms in Rome, Georgia

July 128

South Alabama blooms • Phillipine lilies • inviting bench • Clemson University garden • blooming in the pines

August 142

garden candlelight • firebush • garden treasures • coleus • potpourri • tropical oasis • sunflowers

September 162

fall perennials • Texas courtyard • kitchen garden • azalea for fall • exotic orchids • Delta gardener • colorful Lowcountry landscape

Mexican bush sage page 162

October 184

Japanese maple • autumn arrangements • pot of daffodils • front walkway • easy-to-grow grasses • Halloween treat

November 202

sasanqua • fall benchmark • pyracantha • lenten rose and dwarf iris • pumpkins • tulips • stylish parking • fall decorations • Bromeliads

December 220

wreaths • Jackson vine • festive flowers • winter containers • shining decoration • glass-covered garden • Christmas cactus

Snowdrops page 19

Index 236

Plant Hardiness Zone Map 240

Often, the seasons pass a bit faster here at *Southern Living*. Either we are writing a story that is due to the copy desk, or we are on the road looking for that next great garden or gardener. When we do get our hands back in the dirt of our own gardens, we are frequently surprised at what is blooming, without any coaxing of our own. From the first bulbs of winter that thrust yellow beacons toward the blue skies of a sunny day, to the soft shades of azaleas which echo spring's promise, the garden voices proclaim beauty. The vibrant colors of zinnias shout praise to the heat of summer, and before their song is over, the orange leaves of fall have joined the chorus. The days pass quickly.

So consider *Southern Living 2003 Garden Annual* a celebration of our year. Here are all the wonderful people, places, and plants we came to know in 2002. While you are thumbing through these pages, we hope you will find inspiration in creating your own garden. The monthly checklists and letters to the editor will provide timely guidance and answers to your gardening questions. Also included is a plant hardiness zone map for regional planning.

Remember to take time and enjoy the seasons. Smell the roses, trade plants with your friends, or plant a tree with your family. Go play in the garden! Enjoy.

Gene Bussell
Garden Editor

Black-eyed Susans and daisies dominate the slope of this Rome, Georgia garden in the summertime

(See pages 124–127.)

'Harmony' iris mixes with the white blooms of Lenten rose
(See pages18–19.)

January

Garden Checklist 10

Big Looks for Under $10 12
these houseplants are an inexpensive way to brighten a winter room

A Side Yard Makeover 14
a reflecting pool inspires a garden retreat

Viola and Pansy Rescue 15
tips to keep your plants thriving all winter

Garden Fragrance for the Seasons 16
select flowers to enhance your garden's perfume

Small Signs of Spring 18
warmer winter days bring out bright little blooms

garden checklist
JANUARY

Editor's Notebook

The holidays are a hectic time. In between such heartwarming events as having the oven break right before Christmas dinner and driving 500 miles to visit relatives you don't like, it's easy to overlook the little things, such as planting those tulip bulbs you bought in October. Should you toss them out along with Aunt Jen's chickpea-and-sauerkraut dressing? Not so fast. They can still bloom for you this spring. But you have to chill them for at least eight weeks before planting. There is a right and wrong way to do this. The wrong way is to shortcut the process by shoving the bulbs in your freezer. They look fine when frozen, but thaw them out and they turn into disgusting mush—kind of like that dressing. The right way is to place them in the vegetable crisper, making sure there's no fruit in there (fruit gives off a gas that damages bulbs). After eight weeks in the fridge, the bulbs can go into the ground—which, come to think of it, is a good way to dispose of Aunt Jen's dressing.

—STEVE BENDER

Fruit

It's a great time to plant fruit trees and vines such as apples (blossoms shown at right), peaches, pears, citrus, mangoes, and grapes. Local nurseries and county Extension offices can tell you what types will grow well in your area. Most fruit trees need full sun, but some of the cold-sensitive fruits receive better protection when sheltered by larger trees.

TIPS

- **Birds—**Attract feathered friends by providing high-energy foods containing suet and high-quality seeds.
- **Citrus—**In the Coastal and Tropical South, these fruits ripen until early spring, and most get sweeter as they mature on the tree. Kumquats are hardy to 18 degrees. Satsumas are more cold hardy than oranges or grapefruit and usually don't need protection. The least hardy are lemons and limes; keep them in large pots that can be sheltered.
- **Garden journal—**A notebook of monthly observations throughout the year will prove invaluable in your future plans. Record when things bloom, weather conditions, what you plant, combinations you like (or don't), your successes, and your failures.
- **Lawns—**If you want a greener lawn during winter, you should overseed your turf with annual ryegrass now. Use 5 to 10 pounds of seed per 1,000 square feet. Mow weekly until the ryegrass dies out in April.
- **Seeds—**Send for mail-order flower and vegetable seed packets now. This is especially important if you plan to start seeds indoors for transplanting after your last frost.
- **Soil preparation—**Begin getting your vegetable garden ready for planting. On dry days, till the soil. Add organic matter to loosen the soil and hold in moisture.

PLANT

- **Flowers—**In the Lower, Coastal, and Tropical South, there is a large selection of flowers you can plant now for cool-weather color in full sun. Consider alyssum, calendula, dianthus, lobelia, nasturtiums, pansies, petunias, snapdragons, and sweet peas. Plant them in areas with good drainage. The foliage of dusty miller and ornamental cabbage or kale can also add interest to the garden. In the Tropical South, tender flowers such as impatiens, gaillardia, marigolds, and geraniums can generally be added to the list.
- **Fragrant shrubs—**Introduce fragrance

Camellia

Camellia japonica are blooming in the Middle, Lower, and Coastal South. As long as the ground isn't frozen, now is a good time to add these shrubs to your garden. Container-grown plants transition easier into the garden. Camellias prefer moist, well-drained soil that is high in organic matter. Selections such as 'Debutante,' 'Kramer's Supreme,' and 'Nuccio's Pearl' will brighten your landscape during the winter months. Remember to cut blossoms and bring them indoors to enjoy when the days are too cold to be outside.

in your garden. Winter honeysuckle *(Lonicera fragrantissima),* winter daphne *(Daphne odora),* and wintersweet *(Chimonanthus praecox)* will make treasured additions to your landscape and are available at garden centers now. Plant these shrubs near entryways.

■ **Leafy vegetables**—In the Middle and Lower South, plantings of spinach, lettuce, mustard, turnips, and mesclun may be made from now through March. Start early tomatoes from seeds indoors. Set out kale, cabbage, broccoli, chard, parsley, and dill as transplants.

■ **Trees and shrubs**—Any tree or shrub that normally overwinters in the Coastal and Tropical South can be planted now. It will get off to a better start than if you wait until spring to plant.

■ **Windbreak plantings**—In the Upper South, evergreen shrubs and trees such as Eastern red cedar, Arizona cypress, and 'Fruitlandii' or 'Bonita' Oriental arborvitae planted in staggered rows and spaced 6 to 8 feet apart can significantly reduce wind velocity and its drying effects on plants.

■ **Winter beauty**—For cool-weather interest in your yard, include crepe myrtles such as 'Natchez' and 'Basham's Party Pink' with attractive trunks; multiple-stemmed river birches with their peeling, papery bark; and sycamores for their chalky, mottled limbs.

PRUNE

■ **Fruit trees**—Prune fruit trees now in order to produce a quality crop. Apples and pears benefit from a cutting that tips the main stem and main branches to create an oval-shaped tree. Tipping slows the stem growth and strengthens the branches to hold the heavier fruit. Peaches and plums benefit from pruning that trims the central leader and opens the canopy to create a flat-topped tree. This allows the branches to spread out, providing more airflow and helping to prevent rot. If you don't have fruit trees, this is the best time to add them.

■ **Liriope and mondo grass**—Rejuvenate these plants by cutting them back now before new leaves can be seen. Trim small plantings by hand; for larger ones, use your lawnmower with the blade set 2½ to 3 inches high. Don't cut too severely to avoid damaging new shoots.

■ **Maintenance**—Now is the time for pruning many dormant trees and shrubs. Start by removing any dead, crossing, or wayward limbs. Prune back to the branch "collar" (a slightly raised ring of bark where the branch is attached to the trunk). In the Coastal and Tropical South, take this opportunity to prune most ornamental and shade trees, shrubs, and fruit trees and vines. Hold off on pruning spring-flowering plants, such as azaleas or spirea, until they have finished blooming. If you prune them now, you will remove any future flowers.

FERTILIZE

■ **Lime**—Now is the time to test your soil to see if it needs lime. Your local Extension office can provide you with the mailing kit for submitting a soil sample. Never add lime without testing the soi to ensure that it's needed.

Berries

Winter berries brighten the landscape this time of year. Nandina (right), hollies, yaupon, and pyracantha are among the favorites for our area. The structures and fruits of these plants are best displayed against a background of dark green foliage such as that of 'Nellie R. Stevens' hollies, cherry laurels, and Southern magnolias.

January notes:

Tip of the Month

I recycle aluminum piepans as saucers under my flowerpots to keep water off the floor. They are inexpensive, lightweight, and rustproof. CAROL W. ADAMS
BOWLING GREEN, KENTUCKY

GARDENING
PLANTS AND DESIGN

big looks for under $10

BY JOHN ALEX FLOYD, JR.
PHOTOGRAPHY VAN CHAPLIN
STYLING ROSE NGUYEN

These plants may be steals, but their decorative touches and easy care pay off.

Houseplants, with their green and colorful foliage, are a quick way to brighten a winter room. The ones presented here yield big impact for mere dollars. We purchased these plants from a variety of places, including nurseries and home-improvement centers. In our local market, the prices ranged from $3.33 to $8.99, depending on the variety and the type of plant. All those shown here are simple to grow and can thrive in low-light situations. Plus, to keep costs down, we made sure to limit the price of containers to less than $20.

There are a couple of tricks to getting the most decorating impact from these kinds of plants. The easiest thing to do is pair them by putting two small plants in a single container or clustering two or more of the same type. Elevating a small plant on a base or in a tall container also increases its presence.

Indoor plants in small containers have special needs, especially during cold months. Because home heating systems tend to dry out the air, be sure to water the plants often, generally at least once a week. Their small container size makes for a compact root system, and that, combined with the dry environment, means that damp soil is their friend. One of the neatest and simplest ways to keep plants moist—and at the same time protect your furniture—is to place the container inside a plastic bag that fits snugly around the rim of the pot. Make sure the bag's bottom isn't too tight; it should leave room for drainage into the bag so that the plant's roots will not be sitting in water.

Of the plants presented on these pages, the one that dislikes moist soil is mother-in-law's tongue *(Sansevieria trifasciata)*. All the others—parlor palm, pothos, peace lily (*Spathiphyllum* sp.), and arrowhead vine—don't mind a little dampness.

Finally, if you have a brown thumb and the plants you buy rarely last long, don't worry. Remember that the cost of these selections won't bust your budget. These tough and inexpensive plants are just right for adding warmth and life to wintertime interiors. ◆

top, left: Two variegated peace lilies occupy one blue-and-white porcelain bowl. **top, right:** Golden pothos, paired on this mantel, trail dramatically over their containers. **bottom, left:** The strong leaf textures of mother-in-law's tongue accent this coffee table. Keep the soil dry to the touch, and they will thrive with little light for months. **bottom, right:** A 4-inch variegated arrowhead vine and a 6-inch parlor palm share identical containers. Both plants can take low-light situations. **far left:** Two pots of trailing pothos and three pots of variegated arrowhead vines complement each other in a copper tray. We splurged a bit on this combination. The five plants cost about $15.

PHOTOGRAPHS: VAN CHAPLIN

top, left: A brick-and-bluestone terrace brings new life to this garden. **top:** The home's windows were the inspiration for the terrace wall. **above:** The pierced-brick wall, along with plants such as mondo grass, Lenten rose, and variegated yucca, provides maximum textural appeal in a minimum amount of space.

A Side Yard Makeover

Inspired by a forlorn reflecting pool, an Atlanta couple created a vital new garden retreat.

It's one of those quirky, warm winter afternoons as Norman and Sally Harbaugh gather on the new terrace that surrounds their renovated water garden. As they chat about their day in the peaceful company of croaking frogs and darting iridescent goldfish, it's hard to believe this was once their least favorite part of the garden.

In the past, Norman and Sally never spent much time gathered around the small reflecting pool alongside their Atlanta house. "It was just kind of stuck out there with nothing but grass surrounding it," Norman says.

"It was a nice little pond, but we never used it because the area around it was just a mess," Sally agrees. Local landscape architect Diane Dunaway changed all that.

When she took in the view of the small pool from the three arched windows of the upstairs sunroom, Diane immediately knew she had found the inspiration she needed to bring effervescence to the Harbaughs' side yard. "It's more like a reflection garden because it's over on the side of their house," Diane says. "I thought the repetition of those beautiful windows across the courtyard would tie the whole space together. Sally has such a reverence toward history, architecture, and the landscape that I wanted to dovetail the garden to the home."

Diane's plan called for a triple-arch, solid-brick wall that mirrored the windows and afforded a bit of privacy. The reflecting pool and surrounding brick coping were cleaned up, and brick-and-bluestone paving was installed around it in a checkerboard pattern.

The pool now brims with iris, variegated sedge (*Carex* sp.), parrot's-feather *(Myriophyllum aquaticum),* and goldfish. A shelf provides hospitable conditions for bog plants, such as callas, arrowhead, and creeping Jenny (*Lysimachia nummularia* 'Aurea'). Norman has adopted the pond maintenance as a labor of love.

Other than a few blooming 'Gumpo' azaleas and Lenten roses, the plants are basically shades of green. The two large existing fortunes osmanthus that flanked the French doors were trimmed back, and harbour dwarf nandinas, cast-iron plants *(Aspidistra elatior),* English boxwoods, a Japanese maple, and yaupon hollies were added. Standard mondo grass carpets the ground beneath a small concrete bench, and as the crowning touch, the spitting-frog fountain was cleaned and repaired.

Now Norman and Sally reap the benefits of their renovated pool any time of year—whether they are outside taking in the sights, sounds, and scents of their new garden or perched in the sunroom above and gazing down below. GLENN R. DINELLA

left: Violas and pansies bounce back in a big way with a little tender loving care. **bottom, left:** Cut back lanky stems near the plant's base, and trim damaged leaves. Snip above a healthy leaf for strong new growth. **bottom, right:** Feed plants with a liquid fertilizer once every 10 days to 2 weeks.

PHOTOGRAPHS: JEAN ALLSOPP

Viola and Pansy Rescue

Help is on the way with these quick-and-easy tips.

Winter's biting winds and fickle weather can wreak havoc with violas and pansies. Plants become spindly with discolored foliage and few flowers regardless of whether they reside in beds or containers. It would be easy to think these tough troopers have bailed out on you, but all they need is some TLC to sail into spring. The treatment is identical for both plants—but to simplify our instructions, we'll call them all violas.

Courageous Cutbacks

Heavy-duty pruning can cause apprehension, and that first cut takes confidence. In the case of violas, timid trimming is helpful, but a fearless approach is most beneficial.

Look closely at your plants to spot new growth emerging from their center or crown; this is your sign they're determined to survive. Take scissors or small clippers in hand, and remove all leggy stems. Cut each one close to the plant's crown, directly above a healthy leaf. Snip dingy and damaged leaves, placing all cuttings in the trash or compost. Your plant should look refreshed, neat, and tidy.

Eager Eaters

Violas require food to bloom abundantly, and their appetite is man-size. Any timed-release granular fertilizer applied in the fall has already been consumed, so they need an immediate energy-boosting meal.

- Water violas thoroughly prior to feeding. Fertilizers contain salts that burn roots and cause damage when applied to dry soil.
- Mix a water-soluble all-purpose fertilizer (20-20-20) according to label directions, and water each plant generously.
- Feed the violas every other week. You may alternate between a blossom-boosting type (15-30-15) and the all-purpose blend.

Maintenance

As your violas flourish, keep them fat and flowering with an occasional pinching. In garden language, deadhead spent blossoms every few weeks to encourage new flower production.

Deadheading can be approached as a chore or a pleasant task with appreciable rewards. Violas produce plenty of flowers to bring indoors, and their tiny bouquets carry a welcome splash of spring to a windowsill, desk, or breakfast tray. Give a bunch, tied with a satin ribbon, to a friend. The more of them you pick, the more new buds quickly follow. ELLEN RILEY

FERTILIZER FACTS

A healthy diet produces hearty annuals. Here's the skinny on plant food.

- **20-20-20 all-purpose fertilizer:** This balanced blend addresses the entire plant—plenty of nitrogen (the first 20) to feed foliage, a nourishing dose of phosphorus (the second 20) for roots and flower production, and a good measure of potassium (the last 20) to ward against winter's stresses. Apply as a liquid every 10 days to 2 weeks.
- **15-30-15 fertilizer:** A little menu variation is a good thing for blooming annuals. This plant food contains a larger amount of phosphorus (the middle number) than the previous blend and increases flower production. Once pansies and violas have a lush, healthy crown of foliage, alternate this blossom-boosting type with the all-purpose fertilizer to kick flowers into high gear.

Garden Fragrance for the Seasons

Add another dimension to your garden's collage.

PHOTOGRAPHS: JEAN ALLSOPP, VAN CHAPLIN, TINA CORNETT

Fragrance, at the slightest invitation from the breeze, weaves gently through the garden and finds our noses. Each sweetly scented flower has the potential for a bouquet of memories, reminiscent of a special time and season. And it reminds us that gardening feeds all of the senses.

Plan your garden's perfume the same way you choose your own scent: Find the aromas that suit your personality, and then take a seasonal approach. Choose selections for each time of year, designing them into the garden as you would color and texture. Place aromatic blossoms carefully to avoid a collision of fragrances or an overwhelming headiness. Plant flowers to cut, so you can bring the essence of your garden indoors or share with a friend. ELLEN RILEY

Winter

Your cold-weather choices are not abundant, but winter honeysuckle's sweetness is perhaps the happiest surprise. Its delicate scent on a warm January day will take the chill from your heart, and the trace of perfume from yellow primroses is an unexpected discovery. Forced hyacinths on a windowsill are more overt—one bloom can saturate an entire room.

- winter daphne
- winter honeysuckle
- pansies (yellow ones are the most fragrant)
- paperwhite narcissus
- hyacinths
- primroses

sweet William

ginger lilies

Spring

Fragrance kicks into high gear this season, with heavenly perfumed peonies just begging to be arranged in a simple clear vase or your grandmother's cut-glass bowl. Clove-scented dianthus are a colorful sight as they ramble saucily down a front walkway. Nostalgia is the essence of the oft-invasive Japanese honeysuckle; its sweet nectar has delighted children for generations.

- sweet William
- sweet alyssum
- dianthus
- sweet peas
- peonies
- lilies-of-the-valley
- Japanese honeysuckle
- Florida flame azaleas
- bearded iris

yellow pansy

Summer

Careful planning becomes imperative in these warm and humid gardening months. Scents linger heavily in the air, and each fragrant selection should have its own space to stretch out. White and purple petunias come into their own as the sun sets, and moonflowers grace the evening with their light aroma. A garden without a gardenia is lonely, and an Oriental lily in a pot on a terrace is divine.

- petunias, heat tolerant
- Oriental lilies
- roses
- flowering tobacco
- four o'clock
- moonflowers
- gardenia
- Confederate jasmine
- Southern magnolia
- harlequin glorybower

Fall

Autumn's scents often appear in surprising places. Pristine white ginger lilies grow on plants that resemble corn. The blooms, evocative of angel or butterfly wings, waft their fragrance into the garden's corners. Usually taken for granted, the perfume of elaeagnus' discreet fall flowers fills the air.

- 'Royal Standard' hosta
- ginger lilies
- osmanthus, all types
- sweet autumn clematis
- elaeagnus
- common witch hazel

Oriental lilies

SMALL SIGNS *of* SPRING

Seasons don't change with the ringing of a bell. Spring undermines winter at a slow, measured pace. The erosion begins in the earth's depths, where bulbs come to life and push through the frigid soil.

The smallest seem to be the toughest of all, bursting into the sun on a warm day and daring the inevitable cold to return. Because flowers are few this time of year, these beauties are more welcome than the blooming boughs of April. Many a gardener kneels nearby to enjoy these gifts more fully, and among them is Douglas Ruhren, whose garden of little bulbs in the front of his Durham, North Carolina, home has been known to stop traffic when most other plots are just beginning to awaken.

Warmer winter days bring forth welcome flowers.

This garden demonstrates that, while each flower is small, the impact of hundreds can be big. Although he has planted many, Douglas builds on that success. "The reward of growing these small bulbs is that they multiply," he explains.

It all began in 1987 with a Christmas gift of four types of hardy cyclamen from garden friend Nancy Goodwin. From that, he came to love *Cyclamen coum,* which blooms from Christmas to March.

But this garden is made up of more than just cyclamen. Usually there are crocus and snowdrops. Douglas recommends giant snowdrop *(Galanthus elwesii),* which blooms in December and January; 'S. Arnott' snowdrop for flowers in late January and early February; and common snowdrop *(G. nivalis)* for a late February show.

For early daffodils Douglas recommends 'Golden Bells' (*Narcissus bulbocodium* 'Golden Bells'), a recent introduction. Also, try 'Mite,' which looks like a badminton shuttlecock frozen in flight. 'W.P. Milner' is "200% charm and grace, my absolute favorite hybrid," Douglas says. And don't forget the popular 'February Gold' for flowers that live up to their name.

Others that complete the early show include Greek anemone *(Anemone blanda).* The selection 'White Splendour' is the most vigorous. *Iris reticulata* joins in and is easy and perennial, unlike *I. danfordiae.* To complement the bulbs, Douglas adds Lenten roses, variegated Solomon's seal, and Japanese roof iris.

Because Douglas is head gardener at Daniel Stowe Botanical Garden, it's easy to understand why his summer garden is quiet. "A garden of green is nice to come home to," says Douglas of the warm-weather carpet beneath a huge oak tree. He doesn't let the blanket of English ivy there grow too deep for the little bulbs. About the time the bulb foliage starts to yellow, he mows the ivy and removes the Lenten roses and Japanese roof iris that have grown into the bulbs.

Then, as summer becomes a bit too secure in its verdant cloak, Douglas's fall bulbs push through the soil, and the edges of the seasons melt one into another in a seamless progression of blooms.

BY LINDA C. ASKEY / PHOTOGRAPHY VAN CHAPLIN

clockwise from top, far left: It all began with a simple gift of hardy cyclamen. Douglas enjoys the small bulbs in his garden. 'Harmony' iris mixes with the white blooms of Lenten rose. 'Little Beauty' daffodils bloom when only 5 to 6 inches tall. Snowdrops add small, crisp white flowers. Douglas has many crocus in his garden, including this vibrant 'Ruby Giant' (*Crocus tomasinianus* 'Ruby Giant').

Okame cherry paints the winter landscape (See pages 28–29.)

February

Garden Checklist 22

Easy and Colorful African Violets 24
some creative arrangements for these
bright little flowers

Give Your Lawn a Good Start 27
a little care now will make for great summer grass

Pretty and Pink 28
vibrant blooms of Okame cherry can
transform the winter blues

garden checklist
FEBRUARY

Editor's Notebook

Of all our native Southern trees, I can't think of any more praiseworthy than beeches. As a kid, I remember snaking through winter woods and being awestruck by a massive trunk that suddenly appeared before me. Later, I admired the tree's silvery-gray bark, which when lit by the setting sun seemed to extend the afternoon by hours with its glow. But the beech's best feature, I've since decided, is the leaves. Unlike other deciduous trees that drop their foliage in autumn, the beech holds its withered leaves all winter, lending a golden-tan color to an otherwise barren landscape. Beech trees don't transplant easily, so they're seldom available at garden centers except in small sizes. They grow slowly, too, so patience is required. If you encounter a beech in the wild, please refrain from the bohemian practice of carving your initials in the bark. Such action is proof of an ignoramus at work. Why, just last week I came upon an ancient beech with "C. Columbus, 1492" carved into it. I haven't the faintest idea who this Columbus guy was, but I can guarantee he never did anything of note. —STEVE BENDER

TIPS

■ **Forcing branches**—To push spring forward and warm your winter days, try forcing a few branches. Forsythia, flowering quince, and flowering cherry are easy to force. Cut the stems at an angle, and place in a container of water. To get a consistent bloom, choose stems whose flowerbuds have begun to swell. Also, consider the overall shape of the plant while cutting, because you are, in effect, pruning your plant. Once indoors, recut the stems, and place them in tepid water. Keep the container in a cool spot, and let the blooms begin.

■ **Soil preparation**—The South is blessed with many mild days in winter. These are perfect for getting your garden soil ready for this season's vegetables. If you haven't already done so, till the ground, and incorporate organic matter. Add lime if necessary.

PLANT

■ **Apricots**—Now is the time to plant in the Upper South. Apricots are small, handsome landscape trees and reward their owners with an abundance of fruit. 'Moor Park' has excellent medium to large fruit on a vigorous tree.

■ **Fruit**—Pears, persimmons, peaches, plums, grapes, and blackberries can provide welcome color and tasty fruit. Choose selections carefully as recommendations vary across the South. Consult your county Extension agent or nursery for the best choices in your area.

■ **Roses**—Bare-root roses are available now at garden centers. Soak roots overnight in water before planting. Add organic matter to help the soil retain moisture as new roots become established.

■ **Seed**—Start the seeds of peppers, tomatoes, and eggplants indoors now. Once the danger of frost has passed, you can set the plants out in your garden. Try 'Karma' and 'Valencia' peppers, 'Sungold' and 'Sweet Million' tomatoes, and 'Neon' eggplant.

■ **Trees and shrubs**—It is a good time to add trees and shrubs to your garden. While the weather is still cool, they can establish roots to transition into spring and be better prepared for the summer heat. If you wait until March, the garden centers will be packed, and the choices will be picked over. Set out container or balled-and-burlapped trees at about the same depth they were growing at the nursery. Stake the first year, and wrap trunks with tree paper to prevent sun scald.

■ **Vegetables**—In the Lower and Coastal South, set out onions, potatoes, and garlic now; also seed turnips, mustard, spinach, carrots, beets, and lettuce. Herbs to set out include dill, parsley, arugula, rosemary, and French sorrel.

Flowers

If you're in the Upper, Middle, or Lower South, regardless of any mild weather, it's best to resist the urge to plant tender flowers until April. For quick color until then, plant cool-weather flowers such as snapdragons, petunias, dianthus, and sweet alyssum. In South Florida, though, after mid-February, it's fairly safe to plant warm-weather flowers such as impatiens, wax begonias, marigolds, coleus, cosmos, gaillardia, gomphrena, salvia, verbena, and zinnias.

Annuals

Set out pansies (below), alyssum, snapdragons, calendulas, ornamental kale and cabbage, and petunias now for instant color. These should last until hot weather in June. For an immediate effect, select well-developed plants in 4- or 6-inch containers, and arrange them in elongated masses of five or more of the same kind or color. Spacing at 8- to 10-inch intervals allows room for plants to develop. These annuals are good companions for spring bulbs such as tulips, daffodils, hyacinths, and Dutch iris.

PRUNE

■ **Overgrown plants**—For plants that are overgrown or need shaping, now is the best time of year to do it. For fruit trees, remove crossing or rubbing branches; then shorten the main branches to a desired form. Roses should be pruned back to a few strong canes about knee-high. An exception to this would be climbing roses; prune these lightly after blooming. Begin by removing any dead or weak wood; then shorten three to five of the healthiest canes to 18 to 24 inches. Prune antique tea, China, and other classes of old roses less drastically, leaving the natural shape of the plant intact. Don't prune spring-blooming and climbing roses until after they flower.

■ **Spring flowering shrubs**—Wait to prune plants that flower in spring, such as azaleas, until after they finish blooming, too. Overgrown broad-leaved shrubs, such as hollies or ligustrums, that need a complete rejuvenation can be cut almost to the ground. Don't use this technique on evergreens with needles, though. They don't have latent buds beneath the old wood, and pruned branches will remain bare.

Peas

Sow English peas or sugar snap peas in your garden. Seed now while the weather is cool to give the plants time to grow, flower, and set fruit before the weather turns too hot. Try 'Maestro' English peas and 'Super Sugar Snap' peas.

FERTILIZE

■ **Lawns**—Hold off on fertilizing your turf in the Coastal South, which would feed winter weeds, too. Instead, keep grass mowed to discourage weeds from spreading. To prevent summer weeds, apply a pre-emergence herbicide in late February or early March. Follow label directions carefully.

■ **Trees and shrubs**—In the Tropical South, feed trees and shrubs as needed late this month or early next. Mature shrubs growing in a well-mulched bed probably won't need fertilizer; likewise, large trees won't either. Focus on the smaller plants. Roses, because of their repeating bloom, will benefit from a monthly feeding through summer. A 15-0-15 product is a good all-purpose landscape fertilizer for most Florida soils.

February notes:

Tip of the Month

Whenever you boil eggs, let the water cool, and then use it to water your houseplants. The calcium in the water will make them healthy and strong.

ANNA VICTORIA REICH
ALBUQUERQUE, NEW MEXICO

EASY AND COLORFUL

african violets

Take a fresh approach with this enchanting houseplant.

Once associated with grandmother's windowsill, African violets nowadays boast a new look, one that's as fresh and exciting as the 21st century. Imagine a houseplant cloaked in glittering gem-toned flowers nestled among elegant cashmere leaves. The spectrum of shades, shapes, and sizes teases the imagination, but these beautiful new selections have been developed to be tough, reliable, and affordable.

"I think people love African violets because they're so easy to keep, and there are so many types," says Reinhold Holtkamp, Jr., vice president of Holtkamp Greenhouses and Optimara, in Nashville. "I've not actually seen a violet bequeathed in a will, but a lot of times we hear people will get them from their grandmothers." While this plant family may be the ultimate pass along, the new types are sensational. "African violets are so inexpensive," he continues, "you can buy a nice quality violet for between $2 and $4. There are so many types and sizes—a super miniature grows in a 1½-inch pot and can be put almost anywhere. You don't need much space to have African violets."

top, left: The new EverFloris violets' green leaves support heavy-blooming flowers, each one edged in chartreuse. **top, right:** Years of hybridizing have produced a marvelous selection of flower colors, types, and sizes. **above:** These plants' flower colors and velvety leaves offer an easygoing elegance that befits silver's rich patina. **right:** Mix different shades of violets to make interesting displays.

BY ELLEN RUOFF RILEY / PHOTOGRAPHY RALPH ANDERSON

plants every time you water. The Holtkamps recommend a well-balanced fertilizer, such as 14-12-14. "There are some fertilizers with a very high middle number," Reinhold says. "That number represents phosphorus, which stimulates flower production. With our violets that isn't necessary," he states. In fact, high-phosphorus plant food causes some flowers to diminish in size and quality.

Without the proper nutrition, an African violet will cease flower production and become frail. If your plant comes to this point, you have two options. "When this happens you must repot the plant, place it in better light, and feed it on a regular basis. It may slowly recover, or you can just pitch it and buy another one," Reinhold says. "It's really okay to throw the old ones away and buy new ones. Then you have the opportunity for new colors and flower forms."

It's So Easy

The formula for success with African violets is simple: Provide the correct light exposure and a foolproof watering technique, and you're in business. Their tender leaves prefer light from an eastern or northern exposure window; if you have a western or southern location, protect the violet from the sun's harsh rays.

"African violets die from overwatering," Reinhold says. "When excess water is not removed from the saucer, they become soggy, and roots decay." Many violets come with a self-watering system that consists of a cotton wick extending from the pot's bottom into a water reservoir. Liquid is absorbed into the soil as the plant requires, so oversaturation is impossible.

The old-faithful method is to place the plant in a saucer of water for about 20 minutes; the violet will absorb sufficient moisture during this time. Empty the remaining liquid from the saucer, and the plant will be content for about a week.

Stay Strong or Say Goodbye

A vigorously flowering violet requires fuel to remain healthy. To maintain top-notch blooming energy, feed your

SITTING PRETTY

Look to your violets for cues on how to display them. Here are a few ideas for fresh looks.

- Violets look great in silver. Place small selections in a cream pitcher or sugar bowl, a compote, or the tiniest ones in napkin rings at each place setting.
- Purchase colored pots, or paint pots to complement flower colors.
- Place petite plants in egg cups on a windowsill.
- If you're tight on display space, purchase violets in suction cup holders, and decorate a window or refrigerator door.

If overwatering concerns you, try a self-watering system. In one, a cotton wick dips into a water well; in another, a pad keeps the plant moist.

Space-age Violets

The Holtkamps' research and development division is constantly working to provide interesting and sturdy African violets. "We're trying to overcome the fear of 'Oh, I can't grow these plants' with new and improved selections," Reinhold says. Their most exciting recent introduction is the EverFloris.

This new series comes with a fascinating story: As part of a NASA program, African violet seeds were sent into space to test the effect of long-term exposure to cosmic radiation and weightlessness. Back in Nashville, after their space journey, the seeds produced many mutant plants. One unusual characteristic quickly became apparent—the violets never ceased blooming. Besides an enormous number of incessant flowers, plants grew large and strong. After 10 years of development, EverFloris violets, with their frilly, lettuce-like leaves; sturdy stature; and free-flowering nature, have become rising stars in the Holtkamps' Optimara line.

"If you give it the right light, the right fertilizer, and water it correctly, you'll be more successful with an EverFloris than you will with other violets," Reinhold says. ◆

PHOTOGRAPH: ALLEN ROKACH

Give Your Lawn a Good Start

Even now, your grass needs you. So give it the attention it deserves.

Back in Maryland when I was a kid, my father used to outrage the whole family by gazing out of our dining room window on a cold February day and announcing, "Yep—won't be but another week or two and I'll be out there cutting that grass." February is *still* winter, we would protest. Truth is, February is spring in much of the South, but even where it isn't, the lawn still needs your attention. Here are some things you should think about now to guarantee the prettiest lawn on the block this summer.

Mowing

Mow actively growing cool-season grasses when they get too tall, never cutting more than one-third of the grass's height. Mow dormant warm-season grasses low, down to a ½ inch or so. Removing the dead topgrowth gets rid of thatch and debris and exposes the grass crowns to sunlight. This helps the lawn green up faster.

Aerating

Somewhere, someone is growing a lawn on soft, fertile, alluvial soil. But probably not at your house. Most of us are saddled with hard-packed clay, which is tougher to grow grass on than the interstate. That's why aerating at least once a year is essential to a thick, green lawn. Aerating reduces compaction; helps get water, fertilizer, and air to the roots; and speeds the decomposition of thatch. Aerating with a core aerator (you and your neighbors can rent one for about $75 a day) temporarily disfigures the lawn, but the grass recovers quickly. February is a great time to do this.

Fertilizing

Cool-season grasses, such as Kentucky bluegrass, tall fescue, perennial ryegrass, and various blends, need feeding in spring and fall. Use a slow-release fertilizer that's high in nitrogen, such as 29-3-4 or 31-2-4. (The first number represents nitrogen.) It's still too early to fertilize in the Upper South (March is better), but go ahead and feed elsewhere. As for warm-season grasses, such as Bermuda, buffalo grass, centipede, St. Augustine, Zoysia, wait until they fully green up before feeding. Use only centipede fertilizer on centipede, as it doesn't like a lot of nitrogen.

Weed Prevention

Hey, you people with warm-season grass! Notice all those green weeds cropping up in your brown lawn? That's because you didn't apply a herbicide last fall to keep weed seeds from germinating. It's too late to control major infestations now, although you can spot-treat grassy weeds with atrazine (Purge) and broadleaf weeds with 2,4-D (Weed-B-Gone, Weed-Stop). To stop crabgrass and other summer weeds from sprouting, put down a weed preventer containing benefin (Balan), trifluralin (Preen), dithiopyr (Dimension), benefin plus trifluralin (Team), or pendimethalin (Halts), depending upon what types of weeds plague you. Apply per label directions just as your earliest spring shrubs start blooming.

Seeding and Sodding

It's okay to be seeding and sodding cool-season grasses now, except in the Upper South (again, you should wait until March). Use a starter fertilizer that's relatively high in phosphorus, such as 18-24-10 or 20-28-6 (the second number represents phosphorus), rather than the high-nitrogen fertilizer used on established lawns. Don't apply a weed preventer if you're seeding, or the grass seed won't germinate. Wait to seed and sod warm-season grass until the weather warms into the 70s and 80s.

STEVE BENDER

Pretty and Pink

Okame cherry is the tree to plant if you're tired of the winter blues.

below: Before other trees stir from their winter sleep, Okame cherry opens into a cloud of pink blooms. **right:** Blossoms appear in January in the Coastal South, February in the Lower and Middle South, and early March in the Upper South.

OKAME CHERRY

At a Glance

Height: 20 to 30 feet
Light: full sun
Soil: moist, fertile, well drained
Growth rate: moderate
Pests: borers, scale, aphids
Range: everywhere except the Tropical South

If you're one of those people who can't wait for spring, here's a tree that can't wait either. Okame cherry is so impatient, it often blooms before Valentine's Day.

A hybrid between Taiwan flowering cherry *(Prunus campanulata)* and Fuji cherry *(P. incisa),* Okame cherry seems to have inherited the best qualities of both. From the first parent, it received gorgeous rosy pink blossoms that open early and need little winter chill. In fact, it blooms reliably as far south as Central Florida. From the second, it acquired extra cold hardiness, making it a good choice for the Upper South, too.

How early is early? Well, in the Coastal South, expect blooms in January. Mid-February is about right for the Lower South, late February for the Middle South, and early March for the Upper South.

But there's more than showy flowers to this tree. It also boasts handsome, reddish brown bark and leaves that turn orange and bronzy red in autumn. Growing 20 to 30 feet tall with an upright, spreading shape, it makes an excellent lawn, street, or patio tree. You can also plant it on either side of the front steps to accent your entry.

Though relatively new to the South, Okame cherry is available at many garden centers. Don't worry if you forget its name. Just visit the nursery sometime this winter and look for a tree that's pretty and pink. STEVE BENDER

White azaleas in bloom
(See pages 34–36.)

March

Garden Checklist 32

The ABCs of Azaleas 34
how to grow these glorious signs of spring

Bluebonnets Lose the Blues 37
a maroon version of this annual that pops with individuality

A Penchant for Plants 38
the pleasure of a butterfly garden

The Southern Gardener 39
a special section of three different makeovers

40 **First House Fix-Up**
makeover on a budget

42 **Quick and Easy Color**
start with seeds

43 **Framed With a Fence**
a simple structure adds interest

44 **Don't Ignore Your Door**
paint adds personality

45 **Tree Planting 101**
make a vertical impact

46 **Plants Make the Difference**
enhance a landscape

48 **A Little Color on the Side**
no more wasted space

49 **Small Lawn, Big Impact**
a garden's centerpiece

50 **Color in the Shade, Color in the Sun**
suggestions for great results

51 **Staying Put**
a conversion gives a house new life

53 **Keep 'Em or Cut 'Em?**
tree removal tips

54 **The Entrance Experience**
an inviting front porch

55 **Creating a Beautiful Border**
a perennial combination that packs a punch

Spirits Soar at Bok Tower 56
beautiful gardens surround this gift to America

garden checklist
MARCH

Editor's Notebook

What is the purpose of a lawn? To grow crabgrass, of course. And from the looks of my lawn, I've succeeded masterfully. My builder left me with this crummy Bermuda, which is the sole grass I know that manages to be invasive and sparse at the same time. The sparseness leaves plenty of openings for crabgrass to germinate in spring, and because a single crabgrass plant can produce up to 8,000 seeds, every opening gets filled. But no lawn needs suffer such intrusion if you'll only watch the forsythia this spring. When it starts to bloom, crabgrass seeds are about to sprout. Quick—apply a granular crabgrass preventer such as Scotts Halts or Sta-Green Crab-Ex. Then you can go back to using the lawn as it was meant to be used—as a place to park your RV. —STEVE BENDER

Vines

For an extended bloom time, plant two different vines at the same location. In the photo at right, clematis *(Clematis jackmanii)* and gold flame honeysuckle *(Lonicera heckrottii)* work well together on the wooden fence. The gold flame honeysuckle blooms in spring and continues through frost, while the clematis blooms from midsummer into early fall. For a porch or trellis in partial sun, try evergreen clematis *(Clematis armandii)*; it sports white fragrant blossoms in early spring. Add tropical 'Pink Parfait' mandevilla for pink blossoms throughout summer and fall.

TIPS

■ **Houseplants**—Clivia, also known as kaffir lily, is an easy, dependable houseplant that will last for years. These plants love to be pot bound and prefer bright light, but they can take low-light conditions. Water every two weeks, and fertilize with a general-purpose, water-soluble fertilizer from spring till autumn. In late fall, reduce watering, and allow plant to rest in a cool room through the winter. Spring blooms will follow.

■ **Soil preparation**—The South is blessed with many mild days in winter. These are perfect for getting your garden soil ready for this season's vegetables. If you haven't already done so, till the ground, and incorporate organic matter. Add lime if necessary.

PLANT

■ **Color**—For sunny areas in the Coastal and Tropical South, brightly colored flower choices include angelonia, gomphrena, melampodium, pentas, annual salvia, vinca, narrow-leaf zinnia, firebush, gaillardia, lantana, ornamental sweet potatoes, and sun coleus. For shade, try impatiens, jacobinia, caladiums, coleus, and torenia.

■ **Flowering trees**—Now, while many of our small, native flowering trees are in bloom, is a good time to select types for planting. Consider American plum, native crabapple, dogwood, silver bell, hawthorn, and fringe tree *(Chionanthus virginicus)*.

■ **Perennials**—Select plants for a summer and fall display. Daylilies, hardy hibiscus, purple coneflowers, gaura (pink and white), yarrow in many shades, and cannas all may be set out this month. Arrange them in elongated masses of three or more of each kind.

■ **Roses**—You can plant bare-root roses during the first part of this

Pentas

Common pink pentas *(Pentas lanceolata)* are almost foolproof for very light shade to sun. Butterflies love the flowers, which are borne throughout the year. The plants will be killed to the ground in winter where there are freezes, but usually resprout the following April to May. There are also pink and white forms of pentas, as well as cultivars with a more compact growth form.

Salvias

These plants afford months of color and easy care. *Salvia greggii* now comes in shades of pink, white, purple, red, yellow, and peach. Choose *S. farinacea* for blue and white selections. 'Indigo Spires' salvia is an easy plant that blooms almost continuously from spring till frost. Each plant fills a 3- to 4-foot space with long spikes of violet blue. For color later in the summer and fall, consider Mexican bush sage *(S. leucantha)* for its spikes of violet purple contrasting with dusty green foliage. 'Powis Castle' artemisia with its 3- to 4-foot mounds of gray foliage can bind these combinations together.

month. For roses already in your garden, prune any dead or damaged canes now. For repeat-blooming roses, prune by one third. Thin out older canes on climbing roses, leaving newer ones for more blooms. Feed, water, and mulch plants well.

■ **Shrubs**—In the Upper South, now is the time to plant flowering shrubs such as quince, snowball viburnum, or flowering almond. Some of the newer althaeas have showy flowers and fewer seedpods. Winter honeysuckle *(Lonicera fragrantissima)* provides flowers for late winter and may be used for hedges.

■ **Vegetables**—After danger of hard frost has passed but while the weather is still cool, set out transplants of broccoli, cabbage, cauliflower, onions, kale, turnips, and radishes. Always plant in a sunny, well-drained area. Set out tomatoes and peppers when the soil is warm.

PRUNE

■ **Azaleas**—Prune immediately after they finish flowering in the Coastal South, cutting out dead wood. If the plants are too large, shorten branches to the desired length. If they have healthy tops but are completely bare at the bottom, you may cut the stems to within a foot of the ground. This will regenerate growth from the base of the plant until October if the plants receive at least 2 inches of water per month.

■ **Shrubs**—Prune early-flowering shrubs, such as quince, spirea, and forsythia, once they have finished blooming. If you wait until summer to prune, you will remove next year's flowers.

FERTILIZE

■ **Azaleas and camellias**—In the Middle and Lower South, small applications of fertilizer three to four weeks apart beginning in mid-March will encourage flower production for next year. Choose azaleas while they are in bloom; consider planting the Encore series, which is known for multiseason blooms.

■ **Lawns**—Wait and fertilize warm-season lawns, such as St. Augustine, Zoysia, and Bermuda, until after they have turned green. If you have centipede, use a product that contains iron and is especially formulated for that type of grass. Cool-season lawns, such as Kentucky bluegrass, tall fescue, and perennial ryegrass, grow rapidly at this time. Feed with a slow-release, high-nitrogen fertilizer such as a 29-3-4 or 31-2-4. Ask your county Extension agent or local nursery about obtaining a soil test to fine-tune your fertilizer needs. Most turf grasses need nitrogen at this time of year. Slow-release nitrogen sources will last at least three months with one application.

March notes:

Tip of the Month

Every March, I prune the tallest canes of my nandinas almost to the ground and trim off the leaves. The canes are woody and firm and make excellent supports for iris, gladioli, phlox, and mums. They last several seasons and cost nothing! MRS. J. DAN LANE
DECATUR, GEORGIA

The ABCs

These popular plants rank right up there with moonlight and magnolias. Here's how to grow them.

DESIGN: NAUD BURNETT, DALLAS

HOMEOWNERS: HAMP AND COLLETTE GREENE, BIRMINGHAM

# of Azaleas

Take a look around your neighborhood this spring. If you live in a warmer section of the South, chances are you won't have to travel very far to spot confectionery clouds of pink, white, red, or lavender blooms surrounding a home.

Evergreen azaleas are not native here, but they've been welcomed with open arms since they arrived in the early 1800s. It's easy to see why the South overflows with these plants. For starters, they're evergreen, which is always a nice quality. Second, they offer a mind-boggling variety of flower form, color, and size.

Whether you're contemplating a new landscape plan, adding to your existing garden, or just looking for tips on caring for the azaleas you already have, here are some guidelines offered by Hank Bruno, trails manager at Callaway Gardens in Pine Mountain, Georgia. This 14,000-acre garden, nestled in the southernmost foothills of the Appalachian Mountains, could be called the Super Bowl of azaleas. It features hundreds of types of azaleas that can be grown in the Southeast. Hank conducts workshops teaching visitors how to grow them. As it turns out, this is not astrophysics. Actually, growing azaleas is as easy as A-B-C.

Begin With Good Design.

A "What I'm seeing in the home landscape is a lot of people are not being very judicious in their use of color," Hank says. "When you've got the vibrant colors that azaleas have, I recommend people select different hybrid groups with different bloom times so they aren't blooming side by side at the same time. Either that or try to harmonize the colors, which is what we're doing here with our plantings. But what I worry about is that people start clashing colors, and the yard looks like a cacophony instead of a concert."

If you want to put together a first-rate symphony, a conductor can tell you that you need to group your instruments; scattering everything randomly would not lead to harmonious music. It's the same with azaleas. Mass plantings of a single color will lend a graceful

DESIGN: NAUD BURNETT, DALLAS

left: Plant azaleas in graceful sweeps rather than spotting them here and there. Keep combinations to no more than two colors, such as these 'Pink Pearl' and white 'H.H. Hume' azaleas. **top, left:** Shop for azaleas in the spring to get the bloom color you want. **above, left:** This low border of 'Hershey Red' azaleas makes a big splash by the front door without obscuring nearby windows. **above, right:** No matter what color your home, white azaleas are always a good match.

BY GLENN DINELLA / PHOTOGRAPHY VAN CHAPLIN

above: Before planting your new azalea, water it thoroughly. **top, right:** Measure the dimensions of the hole before planting. Dig the hole two times as wide as the container. **right:** The top of the root ball should be slightly higher than the soil surface. Mound the soil around it, and mulch. Thoroughly water at least once a week for the first year.

appearance to your garden. (If you're into heavy metal music, you might not be afraid of mixing lavender and orange blooms.) Pastels are easier to work with because the colors tend to harmonize well.

Another design strategy that keeps Hank awake at night is alternating red and white azaleas as a foundation planting, especially against a redbrick house. "If you want to use two colors, put them in blocks rather than alternating them," he says. "We try to encourage a color scheme that appeals to the individual homeowner. We're not trying to dictate the color; we just try to emphasize a little bit of discretion."

Plant It Right.

B If you want your azaleas to enjoy a long and healthy life, you need to give them a good start. "Soil is the key, as with any plant," Hank says. "They like acid soil with a pH of 5.5 to 6. You have to plant them in well-drained soil with lots of organic matter. Drainage is paramount."

Hank recommends preparing a raised bed for your azaleas, tilling or forking in aged pine bark, leaf mold, and compost. This is particularly important if your soil has a lot of clay. "Individual holes usually end up acting like sinks in our clay soils, and you pay the price," he cautions. "You get water held in the bottom of the hole and that sends root rot right on up to the crown." Once the soil has been properly prepared, add fertilizer before planting. Work in a slow-release variety such as cottonseed meal at the rate of 1 cup per plant. You can also use one specifically formulated for azaleas. Apply at the rate recommended on the label.

When planting azaleas, Hank leaves about 2 inches of the root ball above the ground. He then mounds soil up to (but not on top of) the root ball and finishes up with 2 to 4 inches of mulch to hold in moisture, prevent weeds, and protect the tender new plants from cold. They'll need a thorough soaking at least once a week for the first year while they get established. They also appreciate highly filtered shade, such as that from tall pine trees, to protect them from the full brunt of the sun's rays.

below: You can use paint chips to select azaleas that don't clash with the color of your home. First, find a chip that matches your exterior. Then, take it with you as you shop for azaleas to select a bloom that complements your home.

Maintain Your Azaleas.

C Once your azaleas are on their way, they are relatively easy to maintain. "Azaleas are not heavy feeders," he says. "As they're sending out those new roots, if they come in direct contact with fertilizer it will burn them." In spring after the plants have flowered, he adds a slow-release fertilizer such as a 12-5-9.

To keep your azaleas blooming and to maintain their shape, prune them after they've finished blooming. "I usually tell folks if you haven't done it by July 4th, it's too late," Hank says. "If you prune later than that, you're going to lose flowers next year." The only other time to prune is to remove dead or diseased wood, which can be done anytime. Simply prune back the dead branches until you find green wood. If you suspect a disease, sterilize your pruner blades with rubbing alcohol or a 10% bleach solution between each cut to prevent spreading the disease. The caution is worth the time, because anything you can do to keep your azaleas happy means a few more jubilant blooms hailing springtime in the South.

To see the efforts of Hank Bruno and his garden staff, visit the Callaway Brothers Azalea Bowl at Callaway Gardens in Pine Mountain, Georgia. For information call 1-800-225-5292, or visit www.callawaygardens.com ◆

PHOTOGRAPHS: MARY-GRAY HUNTER, SYLVIA MARTIN

Bluebonnets Lose the Blues

Do not attempt to adjust the picture. There is nothing wrong with your book. For the duration of this article, maroon bluebonnets are the right color.

That's right, maroon bluebonnets. "Bluebonnet" is all one word, so any adjective, such as "maroon," has to be added separately. Plus, because all species of bluebonnets in Texas are lumped together as the state flower, *Lupinus texensis* 'Texas Maroon' is included as well. How could this have happened to a decent, God-fearing blue flower known and loved by all? It's kind of a strange story.

It could only have happened in Texas, where Dr. Jerry Parsons, a professor and horticulturist with the Texas Cooperative Extension, has spent the last 20 years trying to persuade bluebonnets to bloom in the colors of the Texas flag. White bluebonnets are reasonably common, and blue is a no-brainer; it was the red flowers that were giving him trouble.

Jerry had gotten as far as increasing the numbers of naturally occurring pink bluebonnets he had found; then he was inspired to show his work to fellow horticulturist Greg Grant. Greg happens to be a graduate of that well-known university in College Station, and as Jerry describes it, his reaction was intense. "Greg leaped from the truck, humming the Aggie war hymn, tears in his eyes. He ran across the field of pink bluebonnets. Dropping by one that was a little darker than the others, he yelled, 'We can get a maroon from this color!' "

Greg was right. Within the blue bluebonnets lurk subtle shades that naturally allow both pink and, with careful selection, maroon bluebonnets to shine forth. In no time at all, with Jerry doing all the work (as he explains it) and Greg making visits to guide the color selection ("because," Jerry says, "only an Aggie can truly see maroon"), the maroon bluebonnet became a reality. They settled on a name for their achievement and persuaded a wildflower seed company to grow it for them. Thanks to these two and their many helpers, we can now enjoy 'Texas Maroon' bluebonnets in our gardens.

Within a few years, Jerry expects us to be able to plant seeds for the red, white, and blue bluebonnet Texas flag, his original project. Does he plan any other digressions? "Well," Jerry says, "we are sort of looking out for a burnt orange bluebonnet. But Greg isn't helping with that project. He's got kind of an attitude."

LIZ DRUITT

'TEXAS MAROON' BLUEBONNETS
At a Glance

Type of plant: annual
Planting time: Sow seeds in the fall, transplant in winter and early spring.
Bloom season: approximately 6 weeks between March and May if deadheaded
Soil: Good drainage is required.
Light: full sun
Water: extremely drought tolerant—don't overwater
Fertilizer: not necessary but will increase bloom and plant size
Nice to know: Bluebonnets are fragrant, and deer don't like them.

top: 'Texas Maroon' bluebonnets: winner of Texas Superstar status. **above and right:** The source of all the colored bluebonnets is the blue bluebonnet itself.

A Penchant for Plants

A butterfly garden serves up the right mix of work and pleasure for this busy homeowner.

PHOTOGRAPHS: VAN CHAPLIN

Within Marian's sculpted planting beds, pentas (above) make up the bulk of the border while verbena and angelonia (left), intermingle with assorted annuals for a relaxed look.

Marian Phalin is a self-professed plant addict. Her compulsion began several years ago when she and her husband, Larry, purchased their Orlando home.

"I just have a plant love-sickness," Marian says. "On Saturdays, I go and buy a few plants and stick them in here and there. I can't help myself. I even visit garden centers when I am out of town."

Although she modestly claims to know little about design, Marian's thriving sense of style is evident in her lush front garden. Choosing a variety of colorful plants for an area can be intimidating. Marian simplifies the daunting task with a single, unbendable rule: "I use only the cooler versions of the color spectrum—cool yellows, pinks, purples, and also cool reds. That way, plants don't clash with one another."

Marian's love for plants has taken her into the world of butterfly gardening. Bright pentas, lantana, butterfly bush (*Buddleia* sp.), spiky porterweed (*Stachytarpheta* sp.), and numerous salvias draw the delicate winged creatures to her garden.

"Pentas are my favorite plants because there are so many colors, and they are easy and dependable," Marian says. Quick-spreading verbena and other plants help soften the entry steps by hugging the stair risers and spilling over onto the walkway. Wear-tolerant St. Augustine grass blankets the foreground.

The long Florida growing season means she gets to enjoy something blooming year-round. A variety of seasonal annuals adds pockets of bright color to the beds. Her cool-weather favorites are pansies and snapdragons, while dianthus and African bush daisies *(Gamolepis chrysanthemoides)* come into play in the hotter months. Not much maintenance is required, but she does a bit of "haircutting" in the fall and early winter, pruning back her roses and pentas. She also uses a slow-release fertilizer about three times a year.

"I'm not a Master Gardener or anything—I just love the vibrant profusion of color." LINDA DUNN SMITH

THE southern GARDENER

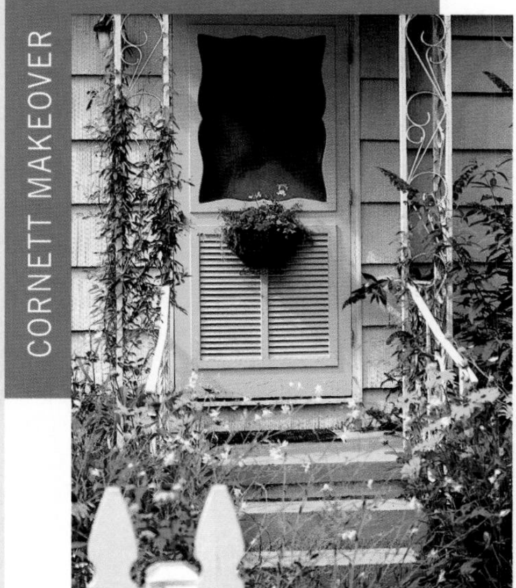

CORNETT MAKEOVER

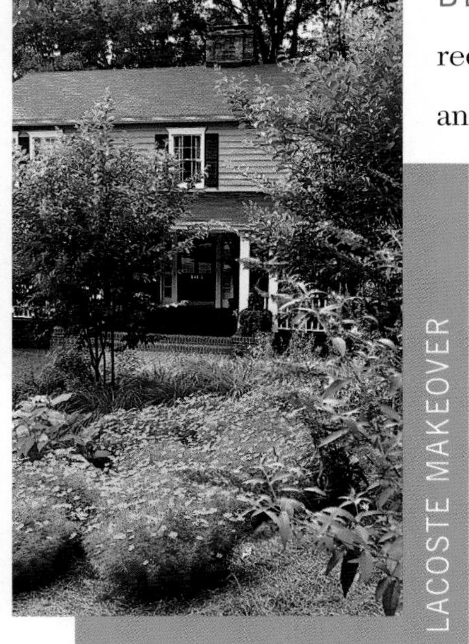

LACOSTE MAKEOVER

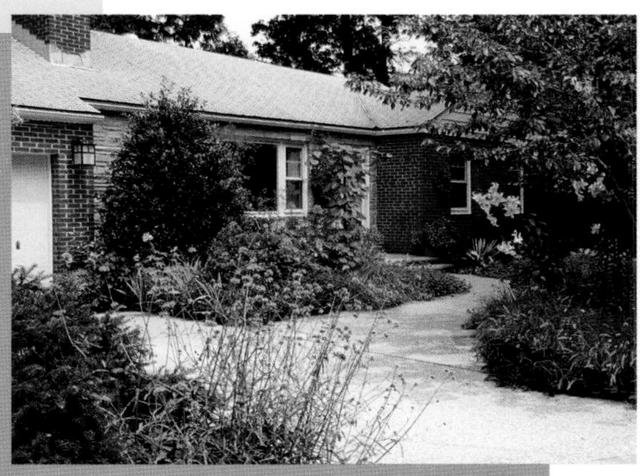

MANNION MAKEOVER

YOU WANT YOUR HOME TO LOOK ITS BEST. New flowers, redesigned plantings, and a little love might just do the trick. In this year's SOUTHERN GARDENER special section, LEARN HOW a combination of IMAGINATION, THOUGHTFUL PLANNING, and a desire for change helped THREE HOMES of different sizes, styles, and price ranges put their BEST FEET FORWARD.

Whether you're enjoying your first home or your dream home, you'll find lots of EASY IDEAS for adding COLOR and CURB APPEAL while decreasing maintenance.

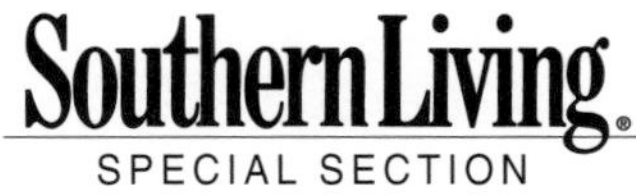

Southern Living®
SPECIAL SECTION

The Southern Gardener Special Section was written by Steve Bender, Glenn DiNella, and Charlie Thigpen; photographed by Van Chaplin, Tina Cornett, and Sylvia Martin; designed by Jennifer Allen; and edited by Linda Dunn Smith.

“I was amazed at all the flowers that filled the front yard. Every season more blooms appeared.”

Tina Cornett

First House Fix-Up

WITH A $1,000 BUDGET, A YOUNG COUPLE SETS OUT TO LANDSCAPE THEIR FRONT YARD.

After Jeff and Tina Cornett bought their first house, they quickly realized that it came with a yard. Few plants grew in the front, and those that did were abused from years of neglect and overpruning. They removed all the old shrubs across the front of the house and relocated them to the backyard. That gave the young couple a clean slate. With the help of a friend, they drew up a landscape plan for a new front yard. (See plan on opposite page.)

The Cornetts had a limited budget and wanted to do all the work themselves. Tina, a photographer, took pictures to document the garden's progress. The yard was small, so it wasn't overwhelming. A landscape plan helped give them the direction they needed.

First they dug all the grass and weeds out of the newly designated beds. A small dump truckload of soil was delivered and tilled into the new planting beds. A low fence was designed to wrap around the front door, creating a small courtyard or

A newly married couple and a fresh landscape give this old house a new life. Jeff and Tina Cornett fixed up their front yard by adding a new fence, setting out plants, and seeding flowers.

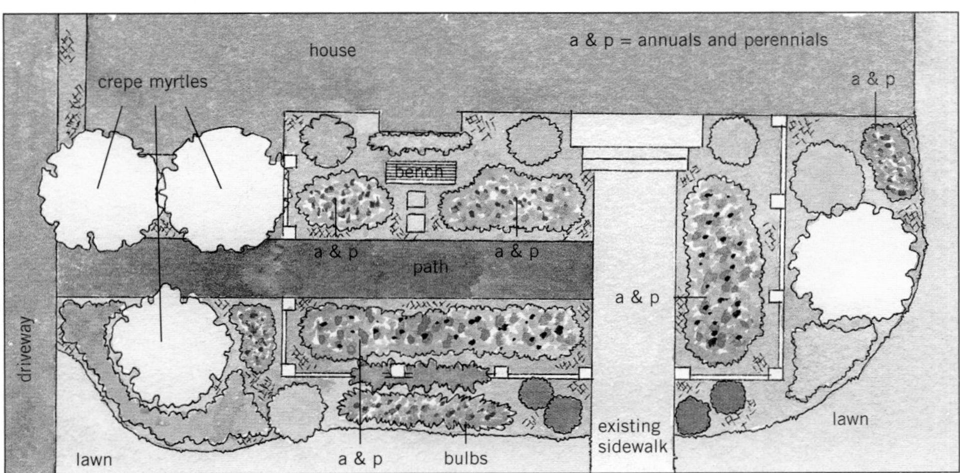

entry garden. To simplify the project, they purchased prefab panels at a home-center store. The low pickets gave the yard structure and helped tie the house to the landscape. After the fence was complete, Tina immediately planted a rose to ramble across the top. Its blooming pink flowers soften the structure and lend the garden a relaxed cottage look.

Three crepe myrtles planted along the path leading from the driveway to the front door help define and frame the little walk. (For tree planting tips, see page 45.) Several clumps of liriope were dug up from the backyard, divided, and planted in the front. The ground cover quickly grew together, making large sweeps of green under the little trees.

The Cornetts received a few passalong plants to incorporate into their garden. Tina's grandmother supplied mums and daylilies, and her father sent a few bunches of gaura. A good friend also shared several different irises from her garden. Such free plants can help quickly fill a garden with blooms and memories.

It took several trips to local nurseries to get everything they needed. Tina and Jeff planted whenever they had any spare time on weekends or after work. When the planting was complete, they spread a thick layer of mulch across the ground. The 3 to 4 inches of pine straw gave the beds a groomed look, and the straw helped keep out weeds. Organic mulches, such as pine straw, add humus and attract beneficial organisms to the soil as they break down. Mulch also helps gardeners by reducing evaporation and keeping roots cool, so plants need less water. It should be replaced once or twice yearly.

During the first year, Tina and Jeff's two biggest maintenance tasks were weeding and watering. In a new garden, weeds should be hand pulled as they come up. Stay on top of them; don't let them become established.

after

New plantings require regular waterings—the soil should stay evenly moist, allowing the plants to root in and adjust to their new surroundings. (Plants that are dry and stressed will often decline or die.) An oscillating hose-end sprinkler covered the rectangular garden well.

The Cornetts were vigilant about the garden's maintenance. As they weeded and watered, their plants grew. This landscape involved lots of little projects that made a big impact."I was amazed at all the flowers that filled the front yard. Every season more blooms appeared," Tina says. The results show how a landscape plan and hard work can affordably turn an ordinary yard into a

before

gardener's delight. Jeff and Tina think it was well worth the effort they made to see the incredible flowers that now come up around their home. (For more on how this couple transformed their yard, turn the page.) ◆

Quick and Easy Color

CREATE BLOOMS ON A BUDGET BY SEEDING YOUR GARDEN.

FAR LEFT: Packs of inexpensive seeds provide plenty of blooms and lots of color. **LEFT:** The Cornetts seeded perennial coneflowers in the fall. The first summer, they bloomed just a little, but the second season, thick blankets of healthy flowers formed.

If you want flowers on a budget, direct seeding is the cheapest way to go. Just ask the Cornetts. They needed to fill some spots in their new landscape and discovered that a few seed packs could fill those places with a quick bounty of blooms.

Getting Started

First, look at the area you intend to seed. See how much sun it receives throughout the day. Don't try to grow sun-loving plants in the shade and vice versa. Make sure the plants you'll be seeding are height appropriate for the space. Also, make sure the flower colors will work together and that the seeds you select are seasonally correct. Many plants—such as bachelor's buttons, black-eyed Susans, coneflowers, daisies, hollyhocks, and poppies—should be seeded in the fall. Plants such as cosmos, cleome, zinnias, sunflowers, and Mexican sunflowers can be seeded in the spring and early summer.

Seed Packets

Carefully read the seed packets. They have information to help you choose the right plants for your garden. Make certain that the packet bears a current date; seeds lose viability after a year. If you can't find your choices locally, use a mail-order source.

Soil Preparation

Once you've selected the seeds, prepare the soil. Kill any weeds or grasses by digging them or spraying with a nonselective herbicide. Use a shovel to turn the soil in a small bed. Large areas should be tilled. If you don't own a tiller, rent one from a garden center. Organic matter, such as sphagnum peat moss, should be mixed into sandy or clay soils. Avoid tilling when the ground is wet—it's best to till when the soil is slightly moist and crumbly. Once the dirt is loose, use a hard rake to smooth the surface and remove any rocks or roots.

Sowing Seeds

Scatter seeds by hand for a small bed; large areas may require a seed spreader. Distribute the seeds evenly.

Moisture is needed for germination, so water frequently the first couple of weeks, keeping the garden soil damp. Begin feeding with 20-20-20 water-soluble fertilizer at half strength when seedlings first appear. To keep your plants healthy, feed once a month with a full-strength solution after the first true leaves appear.

If some areas come up sparse, transplant seedlings from thicker areas. Use a hand trowel to move small plants. Scoop under them deep enough to avoid disturbing their roots. Never pick up the delicate seedlings by their stems. Water immediately after transplanting.

While They're Growing

Pull weeds at first sight. They are unwanted guests that will rob your plants of water and nutrients. Also watch for any pests.

As your plants mature and begin to bloom, sit back and enjoy this gardening adventure. The little seeds turn into beautiful flowers, allowing you to witness one of Mother Nature's many miracles. ◆

EASY FLOWERS FROM SEED

- bachelor's buttons
- cleome
- cosmos
- hollyhocks
- poppies
- zinnias
- daisies
- coneflowers
- sunflowers
- Mexican sunflowers
- marigolds

Annuals such as sunflowers and zinnias are seeded in the spring for summer blooms.

Framed With a Fence

A SIMPLE FENCE CAN DO WONDERS FOR A FLAT, HO-HUM YARD, ADDING STRUCTURE AND INTEREST.

The flat yard around the front of the Cornetts' house needed some type of structure. They chose a low picket fence to create a small enclosure and add a nice vertical element to the garden. The white wood fencing also provides an excellent backdrop for all their flowers.

Tina and Jeff purchased prebuilt, prepainted panels from a home-improvement center to simplify the project. After they determined where the posts would go, they used a posthole digger to dig each hole. Pressure-treated 4 x 4 posts were inserted into each hole and set in concrete. The next day, Jeff screwed the panels into the posts, and the fence was complete.

The Cornetts immediately began gardening around the enclosure. The premade pickets are spaced far enough apart to allow air to flow through the garden, which is beneficial to the plants. Now, roses, shrubs, and flowers wrap the fence with seasonal color, making their front yard look like a well-tended cottage garden.

Fence Facts

Many home and garden centers offer a variety of fencing panels. When selecting a fence, consider the desired use, and choose one that complements the style of your house. For example, an unpainted split-rail fence would look better than a white picket fence in front of a rustic log cabin.

When purchasing premade fence panels, inspect each one, making sure the pickets are uniform and firmly attached to the frame. During manufacturing or shipping, panels may become loose or misshapen.

For posts, select only wood that is treated for ground contact. Handpick each one, making sure that the wood is straight, not warped or crooked.

Determine where each post will be placed. If you need to dig only a few holes, use a posthole digger. If you know you'll have lots of holes to dig, consider renting a gas-powered auger.

For maximum stability, one-third of the post should be set underground. For example, if you have a 5-foot post, 1 foot, 8 inches should be below ground and 3 feet, 4 inches above ground. To make sure posts don't become shaky, it's best to set them in concrete. When using concrete, always use a gravel mix, not a sand mix.

Position the post in the center of the hole, and use a level to make sure it's vertical. Temporary wooden braces can hold the post in place until the concrete sets. Use a metal rod to tamp the concrete around all four sides, and completely fill the hole.

Once the concrete has hardened, you can attach the fence panels. Drill pilot holes slightly smaller than the diameter of the screws you're using in the panels; then screw the panels into the posts. Check to make sure the panels are level before you set the screws. ◆

TOP, LEFT: The fence makes a pretty backdrop for spring daffodils. **TOP:** To make sure the fenceposts are secure, set them in concrete. **CENTER:** Set the corner posts first. Then run a string from corner post to corner post. The string acts as a guide, helping to keep the center posts in line and straight. **ABOVE:** A drill comes in handy for attaching fence panels to the posts.

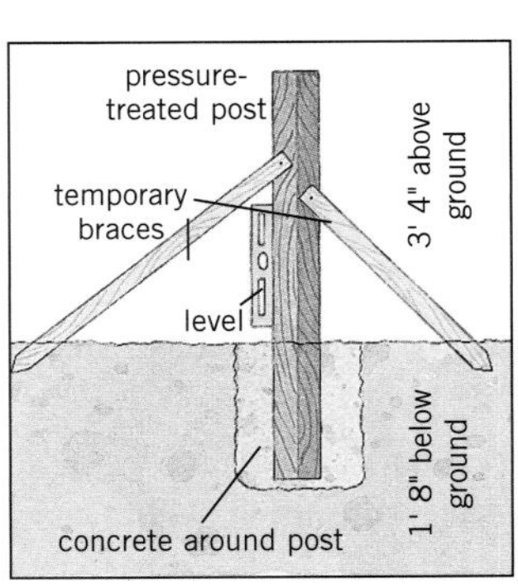

Don't Ignore Your Door

This home's front door and small stoop were rather ordinary. Jeff and Tina Cornett wanted to liven up the area and make the door more prominent. To do this, the sterile entry needed paint, plants, and a little personality.

Paint First

It's amazing how a fresh coat of paint can create a clean, new look. The small, unfinished concrete porch and steps were stained from age. Two coats of gray paint, matching the color of the house, were brushed onto the concrete to cover the old stains. That dressing up gave the porch a more manicured look. Then the front door was painted a soft yellow. The color is eye-catching against the gray house, making the door an obvious focal point.

Plant Second

The old metal railing provided a great trellis for climbing vines. The first spring, morning glory seeds were planted on both sides of the porch. The vines quickly began to twist and turn as they climbed up the railing. In an effort to make the vines grow faster, Tina fertilized them heavily—she probably overfertilized, because the vines practically consumed the front porch but never bloomed. Although no flowers appeared, the Cornetts loved the large green leaves draping their entry.

Fall's first frost killed the warm-weather morning glories, and Tina and Jeff decided to plant an evergreen climber on the railings so they would have green foliage over the doorway year-round. They chose Carolina jessamine *(Gelsemium sempervirens)*. This Southern native thrives in partial shade to full sun, and its yellow spring flowers are very fragrant. Annuals and perennials planted around the porch surround it with colorful blooms.

After frost killed their morning glories, the Cornetts planted an evergreen climber. A small basket filled with plants makes a great addition to the screen door they found at a flea market.

Add Personality

The Cornetts had been looking for a screen door but couldn't find exactly what they wanted. They ended up buying a $5 flea market find that was in keeping with the style of their house. It was painted yellow to match the front door behind it. On pretty days the couple opens the front door to let fresh air flow through the screen.

A small wire half basket filled with plants and attached to the screen door serves as an attractive planter and gives the porch color and flair.

Your front porch and door should welcome guests, not scare them away. Adding a little paint, a few plants, and some personality can go a long way. ◆

RIGHT: Even during the first summer, morning glories gobbled the newly painted porch, creating a lush green entry. When choosing a vine, select one carefully so as not to engulf the entry.

Tree Planting 101

LITTLE TREES MAKE A BIG DIFFERENCE.

Planted correctly, trees can enhance the look of your yard, benefiting it for generations to come. Just look at these three newly planted crepe myrtles. They add an upright element to the landscape and help soften the lines of the house.

When selecting trees, always consider the space you have to fill, and think about a tree's mature size. This will help determine if you need a small, medium, or large tree (see chart at left). Take into consideration any overhead lines, and make sure plants won't eventually interfere with them.

Before digging any large holes, take time to contact your local utility companies to mark gas lines, water pipes, or underground cables.

Once you select the perfect tree and site, dig a hole as deep as the tree's root ball and twice as wide. A mattock and round-point shovel are essential for planting, and an ax comes in handy if the hole has lots of roots. Mix organic matter, such as sphagnum peat moss or soil conditioner, with the excavated soil.

Gently set the tree into the hole, placing the top of the root ball a couple of inches higher than the ground. If your tree was container-grown and the roots are matted together, use a pocketknife to loosen the roots.

Shovel half the amended backfill in the hole until the tree stands upright on its own. Step away, and make sure it's straight with the best side facing forward. Make adjustments before shoveling in the remaining backfill. While filling, occasionally stop to pack the soil down against the root ball with your foot.

TOP, LEFT: When planting a tree, always dig a hole as deep as the tree's root ball and twice as wide. **CENTER:** Use soil to build a small circular mound around the base of your tree. **LEFT:** The circular soil mounds trap water, allowing it to slowly seep around the base of the tree.

Using your hands, shape loose soil into a circular mound around the tree. The bowl shape helps pool water, which trickles down onto the roots with minimal runoff. After planting, water thoroughly, allowing a hose to slowly drip at the tree's base for an hour or two. For the first few weeks, new trees need several soakings.

The ideal time to plant a tree is in the late fall or winter when they're dormant, but they can be planted any time. If temperatures are high and trees are actively growing, they require much more water and care.

New trees benefit from 3 or 4 inches of mulch to keep moisture in. Rings of mulch also provide a buffer to keep string trimmers away from the trunks.

Plant a tree correctly, and it will flourish. Besides being aesthetically pleasing, trees are sure to increase your property value. ◆

GOOD LANDSCAPE TREES: SMALL, MEDIUM, AND LARGE

SMALL
- **Japanese maple**—delicate foliage, nice fall color
- **flowering dogwood**—white blooms, fall color
- **crepe myrtle**—varies in size depending on selection, summer bloom, many different colors

MEDIUM
- **'Little Gem' magnolia**—white summer blooms, evergreen
- **Chinese pistache**—good fall color
- **Chinese elm**—beautiful shedding bark, nice shade tree

LARGE
- **tulip poplar**—fast growing, nice fall color
- **Southern magnolia**—evergreen, fragrant summer flowers
- **pin, live, and willow oak**—Pin and willow are deciduous, live oak is evergreen. All are nice, stately shade trees.

"All you need are a few well-chosen and well-placed trees and shrubs. Then just fill in the beds beneath them...."

Tom Mannion

Plants Make the Difference

TURNING A MODEST HOME INTO SOMETHING SPECIAL MEANT COLOR, PRIVACY, AND SOME FRIENDLY PERSONALITY.

He may be a professional garden designer, but Tom Mannion faces the same challenges average homeowners do. His modest brick ranch in Arlington, Virginia, was shoehorned into a narrow lot between nearby neighbors. Cars buzzed by on the busy adjacent street. A barren asphalt driveway looked like a parking lot in front of the garage. And to get to the front door, you had to negotiate a narrow stone walk that meandered from the street to the front steps (see "before" photo on opposite page).

Inspiring, it wasn't. Welcoming, it wasn't. Private, it wasn't. So Tom decided to change some things.

"My partner, Doug Mearns, and I wanted a new path that could accommodate two people walking side by side, plus a mixture of plantings to provide a little privacy between the street and yard," he recalls. "I also wanted a small lawn that I could cut quickly with a push mower, and

ABOVE: Softened by lush groupings of verbena, ornamental grasses, lilies, and other plants, a wider new walk guides visitors to the front door.

Even though it spans only 35 feet from the front door to the street, this garden enjoys plenty of privacy. Carefully placed trees, shrubs, and perennials limit the view while also creating a handsome composition.

I wanted a flower border in which I could enjoy gardening."

Obviously, he met his goals. Today, a new exposed aggregate walk, edged in Tennessee crab orchard stone, leads from the front steps to a resurfaced driveway and out to the street. Azaleas, Japanese yews, doublefile viburnums, Leyland cypress, and a crabapple help screen the house from the street and neighbors. Vines growing on an iron post add extra privacy for the front door, while a new coat of paint provides a subtle, but significant finishing touch for the garage door.

Just off the walk, a delightful, semicircular lawn serves as the garden's centerpiece. Beyond it lies a mixed herbaceous border that runs all the way to the street. The garden's rich mélange of colors, textures, shapes, and heights includes river oats *(Chasmanthium latifolium),* Lenten rose *(Helleborus orientalis), Verbena bonariensis,* Siberian iris *(Iris sibirica),* Oriental fountain grass *(Pennisetum orientale),* 'Blackie' sweet potato vine, 'Casablanca' lilies, and 'Evergold' variegated Japanese sedge (*Carex hachijoensis* 'Evergold'). The grasses and perennials put long-lasting color right out front and clearly distinguish Tom's yard from those of his neighbors.

Tom thinks his yard proves that even small unfenced yards can be private. "All you need are a few well-chosen and well-placed trees and shrubs," he says. But to keep a garden from becoming a hodgepodge, construct its backbone (the large plants that define shape and extent) out of only a few different kinds of trees or shrubs. The crabapple, viburnums, yews, osmanthus, and a large holly in front of the house serve that purpose here. "Then just fill in the beds beneath them with masses of annuals, perennials, ground covers, grasses, or bulbs," Tom says. ◆

before

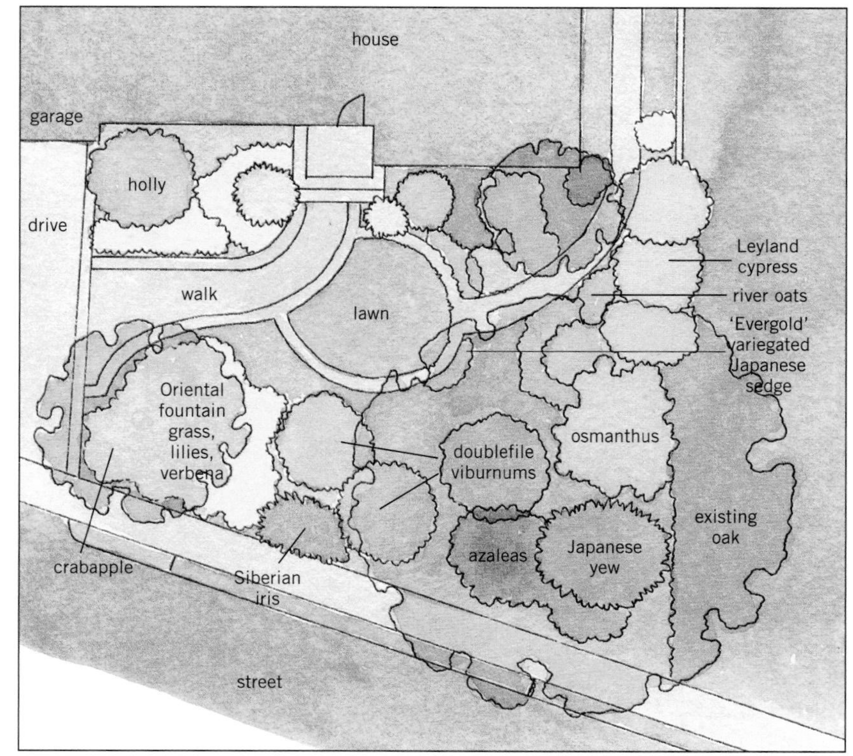

A Little Color on the Side

A LOVELY LITTLE GARDEN PUTS AN END TO EMPTY, WASTED SPACE.

Take a look at any 10 houses in suburbia with a narrow strip of ground between the driveway and the neighbor's yard. What do you see? A basketball goal? Garbage cans? Bare dirt?

Tom Mannion could have left his yard like that, but as a designer, he knows better. So he dressed it up with more trees, shrubs, and perennials. Now a potential eyesore is a haven of flowers all summer.

A narrow path takes you from the driveway around the garage and house to a gate that opens to the backyard. Along the way, you're embraced by blooming plants and hidden from the world. A trio of lovely white 'Natchez' crepe myrtles frames the walk and establishes an overhead canopy. Evergreen Japanese yews anchor two corners. 'Goldsturm' coneflowers, verbena, rosemary, and petunias form a flowering understory. The plantings focus your eyes on the path ahead and deflect your gaze from the neighbor's house.

Tom's design is a perfect example of how to make a small space live big. As this side yard shows, even minor gardens can do major things. ◆

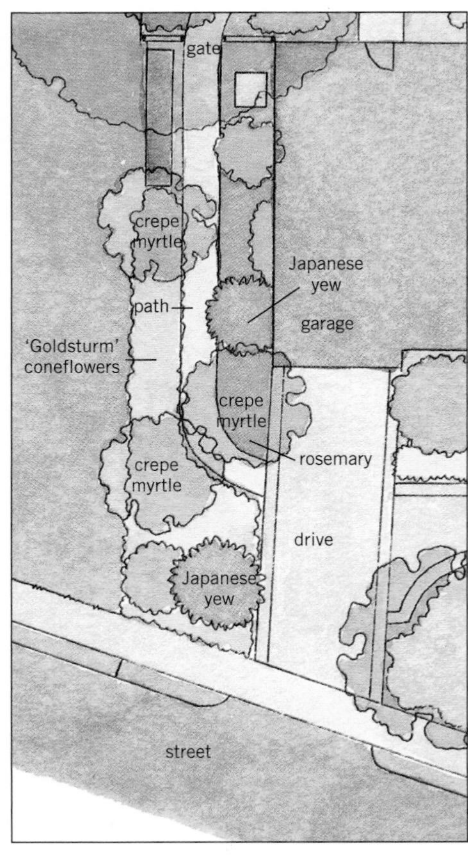

RECIPE FOR SUREFIRE SUCCESS

Several elements make Tom's landscape work.

- The plantings give both privacy and color.
- A new walkway improves access.
- The small lawn has a strong shape.
- A stone mowing edge cuts down on lawn maintenance.
- The side yard planting beautifies an often forgotten space.

ABOVE, LEFT: If you can't imagine what to do with your side yard, take a cue from Tom. Trees, shrubs, and flowers provide nonstop color. **ABOVE:** 'Goldsturm' coneflowers bloom for weeks in the summer.

Small Lawn, Big Impact

MAKE YOUR LAWN THE CENTERPIECE OF YOUR GARDEN. YOU WON'T BELIEVE HOW GOOD IT LOOKS.

Pity the all-green plant. To many gardeners, green isn't a color at all. It's all but invisible, something to be looked past in search of exciting reds, oranges, blues, and yellows found in flowers and ornaments.

Used effectively though, green can be dynamic. Tom's small front lawn proves this—surrounded by exuberant flowers, plumes, and leaves, it still stands out as the garden's focal point. Look out the window from the house, and the lawn is the first thing that catches your eye.

The key to this effect was giving the lawn a bold shape before designing any of the other elements. "The mistake most homeowners make is giving their planting beds a shape first," he notes. "If they'll reverse that, the design will be much stronger. Right away, they'll be creating space."

Tom's fescue lawn acts as a stage for viewing flowers, shrubs, and trees. It also keeps its green color through the northern Virginia winter. Its small size means Tom can cut it in just a few minutes, and the stone mowing border allows him to edge the lawn with a single pass of the mower. ◆

ABOVE: Bordered by cut stone and soft mounds of variegated Japanese sedge, this small lawn gives the garden shape and focus. **LEFT:** Ivory-white 'Casablanca' lilies bloom majestically above a sweep of Oriental fountain grass.

GETTING THE EDGE

A great way to reduce lawn maintenance is the use of mowing edges. In designing them, make sure they either run straight or in gentle (not abrupt) curves. This enables you to run the mower along them without having to stop and change direction. Edges can be made from brick, stone, or poured concrete. If you're using brick or stone, you may choose to mortar them in place, but it's simpler to just lay them in a line atop the soil, level with the lawn, and fill in between with sand or gravel. That way, you can easily adjust the stones later on.

Color in the Shade

YOU *CAN* HAVE RICH COLOR IN THE SHADE. THESE LISTS WILL HELP YOU PICK THE RIGHT PLANTS FOR YOUR GARDEN.

For Months of Flowers
- impatiens—TS or annual
- begonia—TS or annual
- wishbone flower *(Torenia fournieri)*—annual
- peace lily (*Spathiphyllum* sp.)—TS*
- amethyst flower (*Browallia* sp.)—annual

Flowering Ground Covers
- Lenten rose *(Helleborus orientalis)*—US, MS, LS
- carpet bugleweed *(Ajuga reptans)*—US, MS, LS
- common periwinkle *(Vinca minor)*—US to CS
- mazus *(Mazus reptans)*—US to CS
- 'Big Blue' liriope (*Liriope muscari* 'Big Blue')—AS
- golden star *(Chrysogonum virginianum)*—US to CS

Plants With Colorful Foliage
- caladium—TS or annual
- coleus—TS or annual
- 'Mr. Goldstrike' Japanese aucuba (*Aucuba japonica* 'Mr. Goldstrike')—AS
- 'Plum Passion' nandina (*Nandina domestica* 'Monum')—US to CS

Colorful Grasses for Shade
- variegated Japanese sedge *(Carex hachijoensis* 'Evergold')—US to CS
- golden sweet flag (*Acorus gramineus* 'Ogon')—AS
- variegated sweet flag (*Acorus gramineus* 'Variegatus')—AS
- golden Japanese forest grass (*Hakonechloa macra* 'Aureola')—US, MS, LS

Plants for Winter Bloom
- camellia *(Camellia japonica)*—US to CS
- winter daphne *(Daphne odora)*—MS, LS
- tea olive *(Osmanthus fragrans)*—LS, CS, TS
- leatherleaf mahonia *(Mahonia bealei)*—US to CS
- Lenten rose—US, MS, LS

Plants With Colorful Berries
- nandina—US to CS
- holly—zones depend on species
- Japanese skimmia *(Skimmia japonica)*—US
- Italian arum *(Arum italicum)*—US to CS
- Japanese yew *(Taxus cuspidata)*—US, MS

AUCUBA
IMPATIENS

Color in the Sun

WANT EASY IMPACT FOR A SUNNY YARD? THERE'S A VARIETY OF PLANTS TO FIT YOUR NEEDS.

Colorful Plants for Containers
- lantana (*Lantana* sp.)—LS, CS, TS*
- sun coleus—CS, TS*
- purple fountain grass (*Pennisetum setaceum* 'Rubrum')—CS, TS*
- lily-of-the-Nile (*Agapanthus* sp.)—LS, CS, TS*
- angel's trumpet (*Brugmansia* sp.)—LS, CS, TS*

Fragrant Flowering Plants
- gardenia *(Gardenia jasminoides)*—MS, LS, CS
- Korean spice viburnum *(Viburnum carlesii)*—US, MS, LS
- lilac (*Syringa* sp.)—US, MS
- Southern magnolia *(Magnolia grandiflora)*—US to CS
- Armand clematis *(Clematis armandii)*—LS, CS
- confederate jasmine *(Trachelospermum jasminoides)*—LS, CS, TS
- ginger lily (*Hedychium* sp.)—LS, CS, TS
- rose (*Rosa* sp.)—AS

Easy-Care Color
- zinnia—annual
- sunflower—annual
- coneflower—US to CS
- ornamental grass—AS
- daylily—AS
- lantana—LS, CS, TS*
- coreopsis—US to CS

Drought-Tolerant Flowers
- lantana—LS, CS, TS*
- daylily—AS
- coneflower—US to CS
- sedum—US, MS, LS
- yucca—zones depend on species
- narrow-leaf zinnia *(Zinnia angustifolia)*—annual

CHINESE HIBISCUS
FRENCH HYDRANGEAS & DAYLILIES

Long-Blooming Trees and Shrubs
- crepe myrtle *(Lagerstroemia indica)*—US to CS
- butterfly bush (*Buddleia* sp.)—US to CS
- Chinese hibiscus *(Hibiscus rosa-sinensis)*—CS, TS*
- French hydrangea *(Hydrangea macrophylla)*—US to CS

*Can be grown in container where not winter hardy. US=Upper South, MS=Middle South, LS=Lower South, CS=Coastal South, TS=Tropical South, AS=All South

"They had been in the shade for so long, they were excited just to get a little green grass and some sunlight."

Tom Keith, landscape architect

Staying Put

EMPTY-NESTERS JIM AND CYNTHIA LACOSTE TACKLED A PROJECT THAT BREATHED NEW LIFE INTO THEIR FAMILY HOME.

With their two sons now grown and moved away, Jim and Cynthia LaCoste of Greenville, South Carolina, decided it was time to make some changes. Although they were attracted to the idea of building a crisp new home with a bright, welcoming landscape, they were also attached to their family home and neighborhood. They knew they had some difficult decisions to make.

"We were like everybody else," Jim says. "The kids were gone, and we were thinking it was time to downsize. We contemplated building a new home, and we talked about it for several years before finally deciding to stay where we are because we really loved it here. We'd lived in Greenville for 27 years and had been in this house since 1986."

After they resolved to feather their nest rather than build a new one, Jim and Cynthia came up with a few ideas about what they wanted. They knew they wanted a big front porch that would expand their living area as well as give the home a more inviting Southern appearance. They also knew they wanted more light, some foundation plantings, and improved circulation for cars and people. They called in landscape architect Tom Keith, of Arbor Engineering, to generate a plan for the face-lift. After steering Jim and Cynthia to residential designer Jack Thacker for the porch

After 12 years in their Greenville, South Carolina, home, Jim and Cynthia LaCoste decided it was time for major changes. An inviting new porch, a guest parking court, and a few truckloads of plants were the main additions.

A WISH LIST

When Jim and Cynthia approached landscape architect Tom Keith, they had a list of desires in hand. Tom met their every need. Here is what they wanted most for their new dream landscape.

- a roomy front porch
- a welcoming pedestrian entrance
- improved circulation for cars
- guest parking
- sunlight
- colorful plantings
- balanced evergreen foundation plantings
- low-maintenance plantings

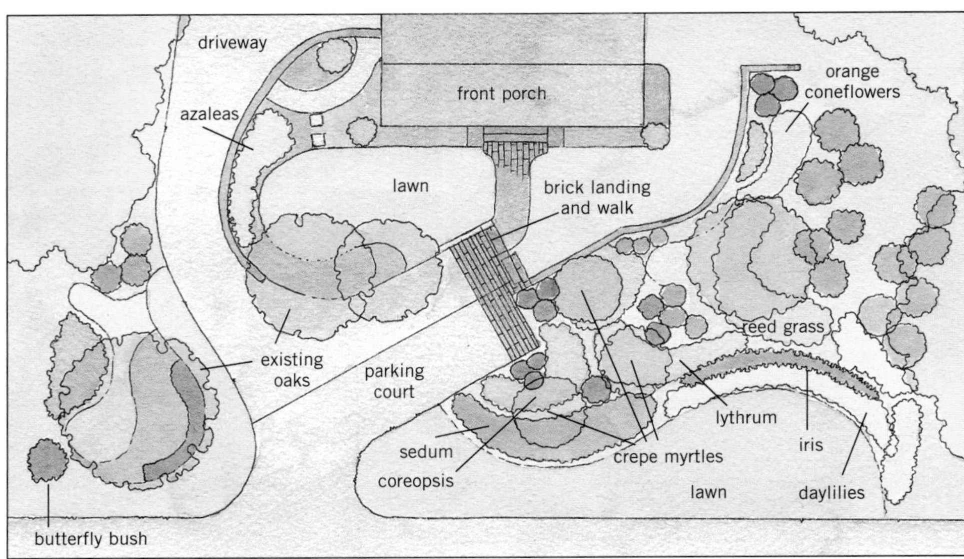

A significant part of the LaCostes' new landscape plan called for creating a little breathing room directly in front of the home.

addition, Tom turned to the front yard.

"Actually, we came up with two different schemes," Tom says. "One was a very symmetrical entrance because they were leaning toward a more formal approach. We tried working off a centerline from the front door with a circular drive. That would have worked if the house had been on a flat lot, but once I explained the problems you get into by forcing that kind of approach on such a sloping lot, I said, 'Let's look at another option.' " Tom's new plan began by shifting the driveway entrance uphill and tucking a guest parking pad near the front steps. Jim and Cynthia agreed that the second plan seemed better suited to their situation.

"Once we got over that hurdle, things just evolved," Tom says. "We had the asymmetrical drive in place, then the question was 'Okay, how are we going to plant this space?' I looked at it and saw an opportunity to introduce some perennials with intensity. I'm sure lots of their friends said, 'You aren't gardeners. Are you crazy?' But they showed a lot of faith in my approach and were willing to venture in that direction."

Knowing Jim and Cynthia's inclination toward a formal style, Tom first designed a basic foundation planting that worked with the straight-forward architecture of the house and provided evergreen color. He planted a narrow 3-foot bed along the porch with 'Big Blue' liriope, and he anchored the corners with taller evergreen cleyeras. Small patches of fescue lawn on both sides of the front walk added a sense of balance to the landscape and provided the green grass that they longed for.

"The foundation planting gave us a base to build from," Tom says. "And it gave them a break from the more chaotic perennial border out front, which was a bit of a stretch for Jim and Cynthia. After all, they were not your typical gardeners. They had been in the shade for so long, they were excited just to get a little green grass and see some sunlight."

After Jim and Cynthia okayed the plan, a number of trees were removed and the front yard was sculpted with a berm of existing soil and a load of topsoil. Next came the construction of the hardscape areas, such as the retaining wall, new driveway, parking pad, front walk, and porch. The hillside perennial border was planted thickly, and in just a couple of seasons had filled out. The whole scheme came together with stunning results. Now Jim and Cynthia take renewed pride in their home and actually enjoy taking care of the landscape.

"I don't know if I'll ever be an avid gardener," Jim says. "But I've bought some books to help with pruning. Cynthia and I both enjoy working in the yard, which I must say I didn't do before the makeover. I hadn't even owned a lawnmower in 10 years. The entire thing has just been a great learning experience." ◆

Keep 'Em Or Cut 'Em?

When Jim and Cynthia LaCoste began discussing designs for their landscape, they realized they needed to cut down some mature trees. They also wanted to preserve a few of their red and white oaks to maintain an established appearance in their yard.

Landscape architect Tom Keith incorporated some older trees into the new landscape plan. He contracted to have trees removed that stood in the path of future retaining walls and paved areas, or that would not have survived the construction process.

Whenever trees are coming out to make room for structural features, Tom recommends taking them out roots and all rather than cutting them down and grinding the stumps.

Although Jim and Cynthia admit the home looked a little naked after the trees were first removed, they knew they had made the right decision when the new plantings began to fill in.

Tom's plan also called for the addition of three tree-form 'Natchez' crepe myrtles, six 'Nellie R. Stevens' hollies, three 'Savannah' hollies, and shrubs and perennials to fill the void left by the trees that were lost. Jim and Cynthia later replaced a dogwood near the front door as well. ◆

TIPS FOR TREE REMOVAL

Fitting mature trees into a landscape makeover might call for professional advice. For tips on hiring an arborist, read the following.

- Make sure the company is insured for personal and property damage as well as workers' compensation. Ask to see their insurance card.
- Ask if they are members of any professional organizations, such as The International Society of Arboriculture (ISA), The National Arborist Association (NAA), or the American Society of Consulting Arborists (ASCA).
- Avoid hiring any arborist that advertises "treetopping." It's an indication that they are not current with proper techniques.
- Clearly mark the trees you want removed.
- Ask for references from clients who have had similar work done, and see it for yourself.

The Entrance Experience

PRIOR TO THE REDO, THIS FRONT YARD DIDN'T PRESENT MUCH OF AN INVITATION TO VISITORS. NOW IT'S ANOTHER STORY.

LEFT: A new parking court and brick walkway direct guests straight to the home's front door. **ABOVE:** Jim, Cynthia, and Marmalade the cat relax in the comfort of their spacious new 10-foot-deep porch.

Every entry creates an expectation. It should set the mood and hint about the space within. When visitors step onto Jim and Cynthia LaCoste's deep front porch and settle on the cushions of the white wicker beneath the whirring ceiling fan, they know they are in for a delightful experience.

It wasn't always like this, though. For the first 12 years Jim and Cynthia lived here, guests were always a little confused when they arrived. They didn't exactly know where to park or which door to enter.

There were simply too many options. They could park on the street and trek down the driveway to the front door. Or they could park in the middle of the driveway, which would get them closer to the front door but blocked everyone else. Or they could pull down to the parking pad, then try to decide between climbing to the back door and hiking around to the front.

"There were several things we needed to address at the entrance," says landscape architect Tom Keith. "For starters, we had to ask, 'How do we get people to the front door and get cars in here?' The other main thing we needed to do was get some breathing space around the front door, particularly after the porch was added."

Sitting Pretty

Residential designer Jack Thacker crafted the spacious new porch. "We have really enjoyed the porch," Jim says. "We decided to make it 10 feet wide so we'd be able to use it for entertaining, and it's turned out to be an extension of the house. We had a party here recently, and we had as many people on the porch as we had inside."

With the porch in place, Tom took it from there. He cut into the slope and added a low retaining wall to create a level area just below the porch for plantings.

Guest Parking

Tom also moved the driveway entrance about 30 feet uphill and created a parking court that delivers guests right to the front door by means of a new brick walkway. "By putting the guest parking on the low side, we framed a nice view of the plantings and porch when you pull in," Tom explains. "And it puts you close to the same grade as the front steps, which makes it easy for guests to enter."

About halfway down the slope, the new section of driveway connects with the old one. The result is a sinewy curve that has romance and consideration for the property's topography.

Another subtle detail that smooths the approach even more is the brickwork Tom wove throughout the design. Combined with luxuriant new plantings and Jim and Cynthia's hospitality, the entrance now makes everyone feel welcome. ◆

FOR KNOCKOUT, LOW-MAINTENANCE COLOR, THIS PERENNIAL COMBINATION REALLY PACKS A PUNCH.

Creating a Beautiful Border

Landscape architect Tom Keith is not shy when it comes to designing perennial borders. He is not one to sprinkle begonias around the trees and add petunias along the edge. His plan for Jim and Cynthia LaCoste's front-yard hillside indicates how he prefers bold strokes of texture and color. He used 180 'Big Blue' liriope under the oak trees, 40 'Goldsturm' orange coneflowers above the retaining wall, and 30 'Stella de Oro' daylilies out front near the street.

Tom even planted 15 'Morden's Pink' lythrum, a clump-forming version of the loosestrife that grows wild throughout the Eastern United States. His mix of 'Gateway' Joe-pye weed (*Eupatorium purpureum* 'Gateway'), spike blazing star (*Liatris spicata* 'Kobold'), Russian sage *(Perovskia atriplicifolia),* and threadleaf coreopsis (*Coreopsis verticillata* 'Zagreb') were not what Jim and Cynthia had in mind. They were interested in Southern signature evergreens. But Tom advised that after many of the trees were cleared, the slope would be more suited to a colorful perennial border.

The plants Tom used have iron constitutions. "He assured me that this would be pretty low maintenance," Jim says. "He said he'd tested them all, and he found some even I couldn't kill." Jim maintains the yard in about an hour a week, plus a few bigger cleanups in spring and fall.

Many landscapes are designed to be viewed from the street, but Tom had to design a border that would be viewed from the porch, the street, and the parking pad. He placed the taller plants, such as the 'Savannah' hollies, 'Nellie R. Stevens' hollies, oakleaf hydrangeas, and miscanthus grasses, off to the side.

He stepped down with drifts of medium-height perennials, such as the Japanese iris, Joe-pye weed, and orange coneflowers. On the outer edge of the berm, he specified plants in the 12- to 18-inch range, such as 'Stella de Oro' daylilies, 'Homestead Purple' verbena, 'Zagreb' threadleaf coreopsis, and mounding lantana. The 'Potomac' crepe myrtles on the lower end of the berm were limbed up so the house and perennials can be seen underneath them.

By using lots of different plants that can be seen from different angles, the entire border cannot be taken in from any single viewpoint; rather, it is revealed gradually as guests arrive. Even more important, Jim and Cynthia are thrilled with the plantings. "It's as pleasing from the porch as it is from the street," Jim says. ◆

TOP: Large sweeps of gold daylilies, purple and white Japanese iris, and pink lythrum help bring a vivid, unified front to the LaCostes' home. **ABOVE (LEFT TO RIGHT):** 'The Fairy' is a low-maintenance rose. 'Stella de Oro' daylilies bloom throughout summer. The foliage of Japanese iris *(Iris ensata)* adds texture to the border. Butterfly bush attracts a host of butterflies and is tolerant of heat.

SPIRITS SOAR AT BOK TOWER

A grateful immigrant's gift to America preaches the gospel of beauty in the heart of Florida.

Bok Tower is a sight you shouldn't miss. In fact, it's a sight you *can't* miss if you're anywhere near Lake Wales, Florida. Together with the hill it sits on, this stunning bell tower soars 503 feet into the air—which is roughly 502 feet higher than the rest of Florida.

The tower and its surrounding gardens are a gift to America from a Dutch immigrant named Edward Bok. He was 6 years old when he arrived in the United States in 1870. A keen mind and tireless work eventually earned him a fortune in publishing. To repay the country that had given him so much, Bok decided to create a bell tower and carillon amid beautiful gardens.

Two questions immediately pop to mind. Why build a bell tower? And why locate it in Lake Wales—a quiet little town in Central Florida that didn't then (and doesn't now) have a beach, canyon, hot spring, zoo, theme park, thousand-room hotel, or even an airport?

First, the tower was inspired by Bok's childhood in the Netherlands. Bell towers had long been the center of community life there; they summoned folks to work, war, feast, and worship. Over time, the towers came to house carillons—huge, complex musical instruments played by carillonneurs sitting at keyboards. Unlike

BY STEVE BENDER
PHOTOGRAPHY VAN CHAPLIN

Captured by the inky waters of the Reflection Pool, the image of the 205-foot bell tower leads you quietly through the gardens.

Victor Hugo's Quasimodo, carillonneurs don't swing bells. Instead, they strike wooden keys and pedals, activating clappers that ring stationary tuned bells.

Second, Lake Wales was Bok's winter home. Citrus groves and logging had not yet conquered the quiet haven he used to escape the stress of business. Bok envisioned a sanctuary of lush gardens centered on a hyperbole of a hill named Iron Mountain. At 298 feet, it was the highest point in peninsular Florida.

Work began in 1923. Bok hired famed landscape architect Frederick Law Olmsted, Jr. to fashion a parklike setting of naturalistic plantings connected by meandering, mulched paths. But while the gardens were lovely, they lacked a centerpiece. Fortunately, Bok had just the right one in mind: a 205-foot bell tower, designed by architect Milton Medary and dedicated by President Calvin Coolidge. Its steel frame is faced with pink and gray marble quarried in Georgia, along with tan coquina stone from Florida.

As massive as the tower is—5,500 tons—it complements, rather than dominates, the gardens. "The tower was made to fit the gardens and the gardens to fit the tower," says David Price, director of horticulture. "Olmsted spent a lot of time looking at the site from 3 to 5 miles away just to see where the tower should go on the hill. So it was sited to look right from a distance and right when you walk through the gardens."

Indeed, it's the monolith that guides you serenely through the gardens. "The tower appears and disappears in the foliage as you walk," David explains. "First, you see its reflection in the pool. Then it's hidden, and you notice all the plants and animals around you. Then the gardens open up around the base of the tower, and your eyes go back to the tower and to the water."

Today, more than 180,000 people visit Bok Tower Gardens each year. Some wander paths lined with azaleas, camellias, magnolias, and palm trees. Others sit peacefully on benches

above, left: This gorgeous angel's trumpet, called 'Ecuador Pink,' is one of many exotic plants whose colors accent the garden's prevailing greens. **top:** "It is the perfect blend of the mixtures of stone," wrote Bok, "that gives the Tower its soft and unbelievable tone of beauty, particularly at sunrise when the rising orb fairly bathes the pink marble...." **above:** Edward

beneath massive, moss-laden oaks. Wildlife abounds, including foxes, bobcats, wild turkeys, raptors, songbirds, and butterflies. At the adjacent Pine Ridge Nature Preserve, visitors observe the area's original sandhill habitat, home to gopher tortoises and other endangered animals. They learn that the preserve's indigenous plants, including longleaf pine, wire grass, and various wildflowers, depend on periodic wildfire in order to thrive and reproduce.

Of course, many come to hear the carillon, played by Milford Myhre. This remarkable instrument is composed of 57 bronze bells. The smallest one measures 7 inches wide and weighs 17 pounds; the largest, called the Bourdon, is 8 feet, 5½ inches wide at its base and weighs 22,300 pounds. From on high, the unobstructed music descends softly upon the countryside, much like the cool mist from a waterfall.

"The purpose of it all?" wrote Bok in his memoir, *America's Taj Mahal.* "Simply to preach the gospel and influence of beauty reaching out to visitors through tree, shrub, flowers, birds, superb architecture, the music of bells, and the sylvan setting."

Edward Bok died within view of his tower on January 9, 1930, less than a year after President Coolidge's dedication. But though he rests beneath a simple marble slab between the tower's brass door and the surrounding moat, his voice has not been silenced. Each day when clappers strike the bells, his spirit sings.

Bok Tower Gardens is located in Lake Wales, Florida, 3 miles north of the historic downtown. It's a little more than an hour's drive east of Tampa and an hour's drive southwest of Orlando. The gardens are open to the public daily from 8 a.m. to 5 p.m. Admission is $6 for adults and $2 for children ages 5-12. Children under 5 get in free. For more information, call (863) 676-1408, or visit www.boktowergardens.org.

Bok rests peacefully beneath a simple marble slab between the Tower's brass door and the surrounding moat. **above:** Thousands of azaleas, camellias, magnolias, hollies, palms, and other plants line meandering mulched paths beneath moss-laden oaks. **top, right:** Tasmanian tree fern **above, right:** orchid tree

A pot of red petunias graces a garden of herbs, perennials, and annuals *(See pages 78–81.)*

April

Garden Checklist 62

Common Ground 64
a vegetable garden shared between neighbors

Beauty By Design 67
a restored wall garden that blooms with color

All Blue 68
blue phlox brightens a springtime garden

The Scent of Purple 70
Texas Mountain Laurel is easy to grow, use, and love

Plant Them Right 71
step-by-step tips for growing transplants

Houseplant Survival Kit 71
refresh your indoor plants

Head Start for Caladiums 72
how to start your tubers indoors

Planters with Pockets 73
creative combinations for strawberry jars

Easy Garden Table 74
a mosaic top for an outdoor table

Watch Out for Falling Trees 75
watch for heart rot

Fabulous Southern Roses 76
Noisette roses delight a new generation of gardeners

Step Inside a Charleston Garden 78
beautiful year-round blooms

Editor's Notebook

Isn't it funny how some of the nicest plants go by the weirdest names? Take fothergilla, for example. It was named for an English physician named John Fothergill. That sounds like an easy name to pronounce, but every time my colleague Charlie Thigpen attempts it, it sounds like he's singing "Frère Jacques." Anyway, fothergilla is a great Southeastern native shrub you ought to try if you have well-drained acid soil. It grows 3 to 5 feet tall and wide, and it combines fragrant spring flowers that look like shaving brushes with bright yellow and red fall foliage. Charlie planted one in his backyard, but don't ask him what it is—he'll just slap on that silly beret and start singing again.

—STEVE BENDER

Seeding Annuals

For easy color in your garden, try seeding annuals. Cosmos (below), marigolds, sunflowers, spider flowers, gomphrena, and zinnias provide quick, long-lasting color for your garden. After all danger of frost has passed, directly sow the seeds. Choose an area that receives at least a half day of full sun and has well-drained soil. Work the soil at least 6 inches deep; then add organic matter and a slow-release fertilizer such as Osmocote or Plant-tone. Sow the seeds, and then gently rake to lightly cover them.

TIPS

- **Perennials**—Black-eyed Susans, purple coneflowers, goldenrods, daylilies, hardy begonias, perennial verbena, and lantana all offer good, long-lasting color and need little maintenance.
- **Trees**—If you add a new tree this month, water weekly if there is no rainfall. Add pine straw or shredded bark mulch around the base of the tree, making sure the mulch doesn't pack up against the trunk. This will reduce water loss and heat stress to the new roots. Choose now while the selection is good, before the weather gets hot. Possibilities for medium to large trees include bald cypress, pecan, oak, ash, maple, Chinese pistache, and lacebark elm *(Ulmus parvifolia).* Allow adequate space for new trees to fully mature. Support with stakes, and wrap the trunks of newly set-out trees for the first two years.

PLANT

- **Annual vines**—Plant scarlet runner beans, moonflowers, morning glories, and hyacinth beans at the end of the month. Soak seeds overnight in water to soften seed coat and speed up germination.
- **Citrus**—In the Coastal and Tropical South, this is a good time to plant citrus trees such as oranges, grapefruit, tangerines, tangelos, lemons, and limes. When planting, remove all grass and weeds from an area 4 to 6 feet in diameter; then thoroughly spade or till the soil to a depth of 1 to 2 feet. Plant the tree in the ground ½ to 1 inch higher than it grew in its container. Water three times a week for two weeks, thoroughly soaking the roots. Then, for the rest of the summer, decrease the waterings to once or twice a week during rainless weeks.
- **Herbs**—Mint, lavender, oregano, thyme, and sage can go into your garden now. Wait until all danger of frost has passed and the soil has warmed before adding sweet basil, fennel, and dill.

- **Jacobinia**—While there are few flowering perennials that perform well in the shade, this is one that actually prefers moderate shade. Jacobinia *(Justicia carnea)* has pink, feather-like spikes of flowers, primarily from July until frost. In areas with winter freezes, the plant should be treated as an annual.

Cut Flowers

To begin a cut flower garden, select a sunny, well-drained location and prepare the soil by tilling in 4 to 6 inches of organic material. Also add an all-purpose fertilizer (such as 5-10-5 or 10-10-10) according to label directions. Select flowers with bright colors and long stems useful for arranging. Possibilities include cosmos, zinnias (below), tithonias, marigolds, sunflowers, celosias (all can be directly seeded into the garden), gladioli, and 'Indigo Spires' salvia.

■ **Lantanas—**For easy summer color, lantanas are available in a wide selection of colors and attract butterflies. Bright yellow 'New Gold' grows 2 feet tall and 3 feet wide and blooms continuously from spring till fall. 'Silver Mound' is similar but has white flowers.

■ **Lawn—**After all danger of frost has passed, plant warm-season grasses such as Bermuda, St. Augustine, centipede, and Zoysia. To totally refurbish a lawn, begin by spraying with Roundup to kill any old grass. Level and till the soil; then decide whether you will seed or sod the grass. Check with a local nursery or your county Extension agent for the best type of grass for your area.

■ **Sky vine—**For a tropical touch, try sky vine *(Thunbergia grandiflora)* with allamanda for an excellent plant combination. After sky vine finishes blooming in spring, allamanda will provide yellow blossoms through the warmest months. Cover an arbor or wall with both vines, thinning and training as needed. Sky vine will bloom again in late fall and winter.

■ **Tomatoes—**When danger of frost has passed, set out transplants of tomatoes. Select sturdy plants that do not have any flowers or fruit. Plant in rich, well-drained soil in a location that gets at least six hours of sun a day. Set plants deep enough so the first two leaves touch the soil. Water well. After planting, provide support with wooden stakes or wire cages. Selections such as 'Better Boy,' 'Celebrity,' 'Beefmaster,' and 'Jolly' will produce an ample supply of fresh tomatoes over the growing season.

PRUNE

■ **Spring-flowering plants—**Shape and prune spring-flowering plants such as azaleas, camellias, Lady Banks's roses, and wisteria immediately after they have finished blooming.

FERTILIZE

■ **Turf—**It should now be warm enough this month to fertilize the lawn in the Lower South. Use a 15-0-15 or 15-5-15 fertilizer that contains slow-release nitrogen. Apply with a spreader at a rate of no more than 6½ pounds per 1,000 square feet of lawn area.

April notes:

Tip of the Month

A piece of an old window blind makes an inexpensive plant label. Cut it to a point on one end, then add the plant's name.

ANNA VICTORIA REICH
ALBUQUERQUE, NEW MEXICO

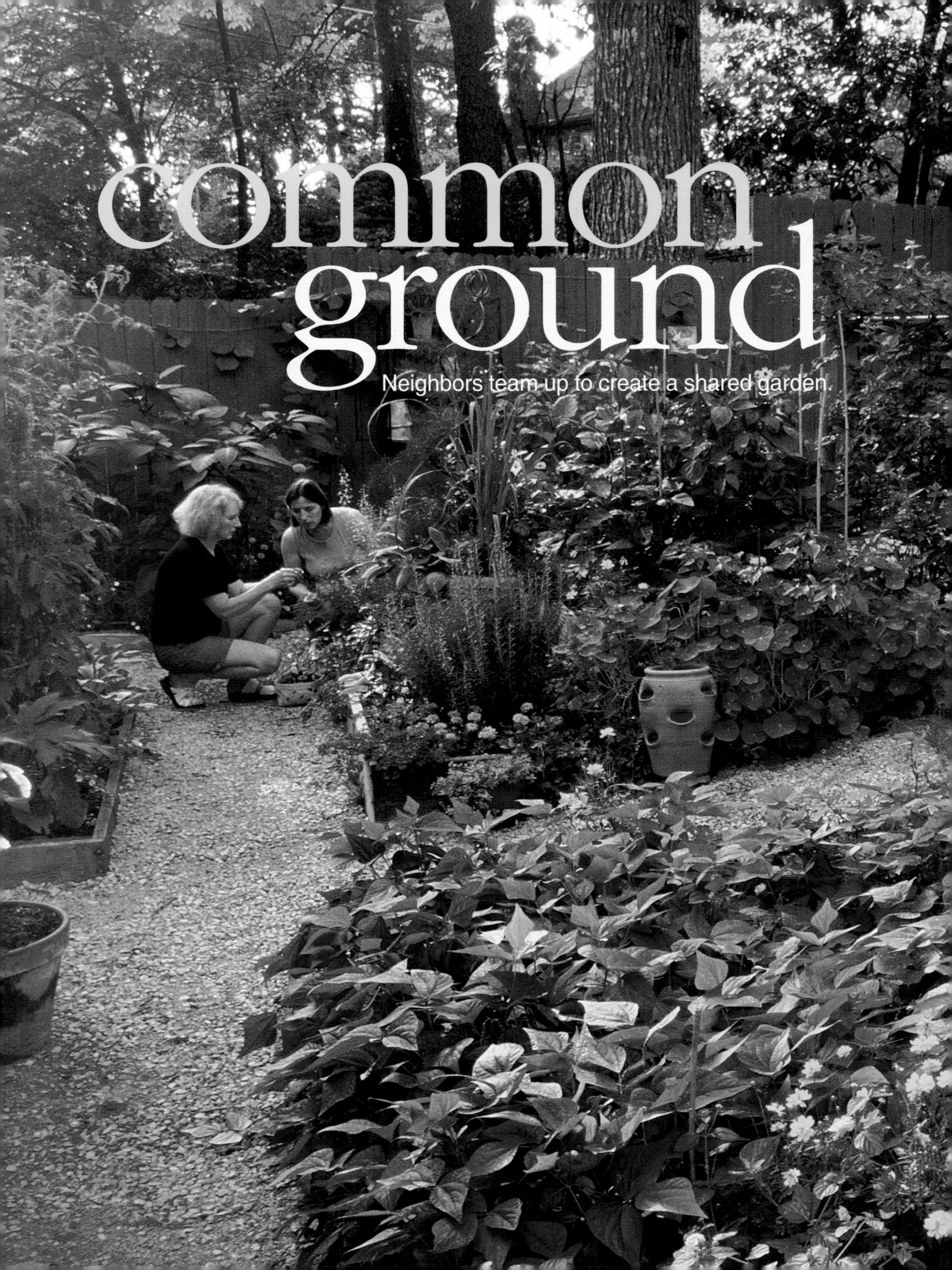
common
ground
Neighbors team up to create a shared garden.

GARDENING

PLANTS AND DESIGN

Allen and Sharon Whittington had a small unused area in their backyard. At the end of the driveway, it sloped away from the house, and, except for an occasional glimpse of it from the deck, the little spot was mostly out of sight and out of mind. A few years before, the couple had built some small rectangular raised beds on its slope in an attempt to use some of this wasted space. Over time, however, they forgot about the backyard project. The neglected beds became overgrown and infested with weeds.

Good friends and neighbors Van and Lois Chaplin asked if they could use some of the Whittingtons' backyard to plant a few vegetables. Their own yard was shady and lacked the amount of sunlight necessary to grow the plants, and Allen and Sharon had that sunny spot that they weren't using. The Whittingtons agreed and, with renewed enthusiasm, joined the Chaplins in helping to reclaim and refurbish the old garden.

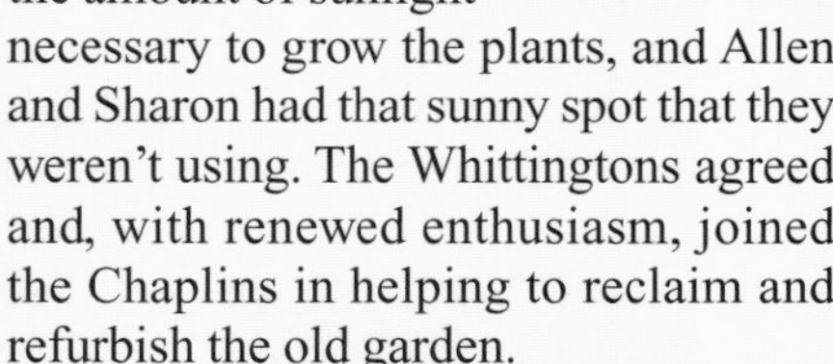

The two families teamed up on weekends and afternoons to create a little patch of paradise. The small piece of ground that was once so sadly neglected quickly took shape. They built additional raised beds to make the hilly ground more usable. Gravel pathways now connect the beds, making it easy to walk through and work around the garden. The paths were purposely made wide enough to maneuver a garden cart or wheelbarrow. After a truckload of stone was delivered to the site, the Chaplins and the Whittingtons carefully stacked them, creating low, sturdy walls.

Allen, who enjoys woodworking

BY CHARLIE THIGPEN
PHOTOGRAPHY VAN CHAPLIN

left: Both families enjoy the basketsful of fresh vegetables. **right:** Zinnias grown from seed add lots of color to the garden.

above: Soil, compost, and manure were mixed into the raised beds. **right:** In the summer the plump, ripe blackberries are easy to pick. **below:** A gate hung on the property line allows the Chaplins to walk into the Whittingtons' sunny backyard.

projects, built a low fence on the front side of the garden and an arched arbor for the entrance. He also made several rustic birdhouses out of weathered lumber to help decorate the garden and make comfortable and attractive homes for local birds. He built a shed close to the beds to house tools. The structure's clear glass roof allows plenty of sunlight to flow inside, making it a good place to start seeds.

The Chaplins cut a hole in the privacy fence that divided the two backyards. Then two posts were set to hang an old iron gate that swings open into the neighbor's yard. The gate makes an attractive entry and provides Van and Lois easy access to the garden.

After construction was finished but before any seeds or plants were set out, they brought in new soil. The dirt in the old beds had settled over the years, and the new ones needed filling. Topsoil, leaf mold, and manure scattered throughout the beds accomplished this. The soil was tilled until it became loose and fluffy; then a hard rake was used to smooth and level the earth.

Lois is a successful garden writer, and her husband, Van, is a photographer for *Southern Living.* Needless to say, the two of them knew how to get the most from the little garden. They started many of the plants from seed, and now bush beans, purple hyacinth beans, moonvines, and zinnias (all grown from seed) cover much of the space. Growing so many plants that way makes the garden more economical.

A few transplants of tomatoes, bell peppers, eggplant, blackberries, and marigolds help fill in the rest of the garden. They trained many of these plants to grow vertically in order to maximize available space. The tomatoes stretch tall in their metal cages, and a simple trellis supports the blackberries. The bell peppers and eggplants stand upright with the assistance of sturdy bamboo stakes.

After the garden was planted, both families kept a watchful eye on the project. They spread a layer of shredded pine bark mulch on the beds. The mulch helps hold moisture in and keeps the weeds out. It also keeps vegetables clean by preventing the dirt from splashing on the produce during heavy rains.

A waterproof chalkboard hung by the garden allows the families to communicate with each other. Before Van would go out of town, he would write the Whittingtons a note telling them when the plants needed water. They also kept track of who watered last so one family wouldn't get stuck with a large utility bill.

The shared garden has been a big success. Both families enjoy lots of fresh produce, and the Whittingtons are amazed at how good their backyard looks. Last summer, Sharon counted 40 moonvine blooms rising from the garden one night. She says the transformation is truly incredible.

Asked if it bothered her that neighbors might be lurking around her backyard, Sharon says no. "Not at all. We've had a great time gardening together. Working on a project is always more fun when friends are involved."

DESIGN TIPS

- When using a wide variety of plants, use walls, arbors, paths, and gates to give the garden structure and form.
- Emulate nature. Plan for more than one season of bloom.
- Native doesn't always mean nice. Some wildflowers (such as golden groundsel) spread rapidly in moist, fertile soil, so you'll need to keep an eye on them.

Beauty by Design

Sometimes even Mother Nature needs a helping hand.

John Gutting is a passionate advocate for native plants. So when this landscape architect from Church Hill, Maryland, was presented the task of restoring a formal walled garden, outfitting it with parterres of tightly clipped boxwoods wasn't an option. He stuck with his passion, and the results are beautiful.

The garden is only 100 feet square. It consists of two equal sections—a sunny upper garden devoted to meadow plants and a semi-shaded lower one for moisture-loving types. A central pathway, sheltered by a handsome wood-and-metal arbor, leads you through a gateway from one section to the other.

The plantings represent a selection of species native to the Chesapeake Bay region. When I visited the garden during the spring, the flowers were glorious. In the upper garden, trumpet honeysuckle *(Lonicera sempervirens)* and crossvine *(Bignonia capreolata)* draped the arbor with bright scarlet blossoms. Dwarf-eared coreopsis (*Coreopsis auriculata* 'Nana'), blue star *(Amsonia tabernaemontana),* golden star *(Chrysogonum virginianum),* and other wildflowers carpeted the ground. In the lower garden, cheery yellow blooms of golden groundsel *(Senecio aureus)* were mirrored in the waters of a perimeter pond.

But this is not a one-season garden—John planned it for a succession of bloom. "From April to November, there's a symphony of colors, flowers coming in and bowing out," he says. "This is what happens in nature all the time." For example, late summer and autumn give witness to joe-pye weed *(Eupatorium purpureum),* goldenrod (*Solidago* sp.), asters, cardinal flower *(Lobelia cardinalis),* and swamp sunflower *(Helianthus angustifolius)* in bloom. Many of the flowers play host to butterflies and hummingbirds.

The trick when using all native plants, John says, is getting people to recognize your creation as a garden. There's a danger that unrestrained masses of blooms, stems, and leaves might simply look wild.

To avoid this, John took advantage of existing formal elements, then added a few of his own. The restored brick walls define the shape of the garden, while the arbor he designed acts as a unifying element. Gravel paths crisscross each other at right angles, edging rectangular planting beds. "All the human-made details give the garden a crisp structure that people respond to," he notes. "I created a botanically diverse community under controlled circumstances." You could call the finished product beauty by design.

STEVE BENDER

PHOTOGRAPHS: ALLEN ROKACH

above: The garden is home to a variety of sun-loving wildflowers planted in rectangular beds connected by gravel paths. Crossvine and trumpet honeysuckle decorate the central arbor. **top, right:** blue star **center, right:** trumpet honeysuckle **right:** Golden groundsel and sensitive fern *(Onoclea sensibilis)* make a splendid pair. They both spread aggressively, so it's best to confine their roots.

Phlox works well planted with green foliage plants, such as hostas and ferns.

All Blue

We'll show you why having a case of the spring blues isn't such a bad thing.

Blue phlox tumbles down the hillside at Weesie Smith's former home like a mountain stream each spring. She first discovered and purchased this plant at the farmers market in Montgomery in the 1950s.

Weesie knew little about plants when she got that first blue flower, but now she is an accomplished gardener and self-trained native plant expert. She rescued many wildflowers from construction sites and relocated them to her wooded Mountain Brook, Alabama, home. She also has ordered plants through numerous catalogs and scrounged around countless nurseries searching for unusual garden treats. She looks after her plants like a trained schoolteacher, grading each one to see if it will pass or fail.

The thousands of plants that grace Weesie's garden are special, but none have prospered like the blue phlox. In spring, flowers carpet almost her entire 3 acres. Many of the numerous native azaleas that Weesie planted bloom at the same time as the phlox. The long, graceful branches of the

native azaleas seem to rise from puffy blue clouds. Early spring is always filled with yellow daffodils and forsythia, so it sure is nice to see blue in the garden. It's an impressive show.

Several flowers cluster atop each phlox stem in March and April. Together they form loose balls of fragrant blooms. The show can last three to four weeks provided the temperatures stay cool and there is sufficient rainfall. They grow in clumps about 12 to 18 inches in height.

Weesie sometimes calls the phlox "weeds" and is constantly pulling them out of areas they don't belong. She doesn't really dislike the plant, but it tends to invade other spaces. Rather than throw out the weeded phlox, she gives it away to friends and fellow gardeners and then relocates a few plants to other areas of her yard.

After the blooms fade, little seedpods form where the flowers once were. These tiny pods eventually pop open, dispersing seeds throughout the garden. The tiny seeds will sprout in almost any soil and are native across much of the South. They like well-drained soil but can sometimes be found growing in boggy areas. They will thrive in partial sun or live in deep, deciduous shade. Don't mulch around them, so the seeds can make contact with the ground. Seedlings will begin to emerge in late spring and early summer but won't flower until the second year.

Once the small, brown seedpods open, the stems should be cut back to the ground. The remaining plant is not much to look at. That is why the phlox works well when mixed with ferns, hostas, and other late-rising perennials. Blue phlox provides strong color early; then it steps aside and lets other plants take over.

This plant sometimes can be found at nurseries or can be ordered from many mail-order catalogs. You should never dig it from the woods and disrupt native stands.

If you need a touch of blue in your garden, plant this wonderful woodland phlox. Like many native plants, it's pretty self-reliant. Although its ability to reseed in the garden is a problem for Weesie, most gardeners will enjoy the invasion of the blues.

CHARLIE THIGPEN

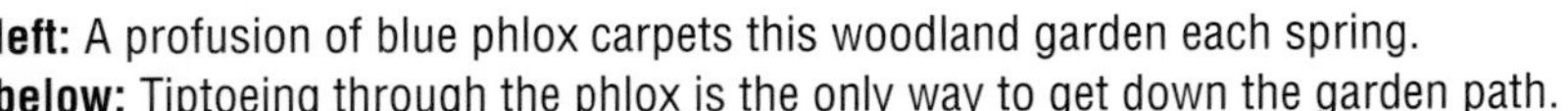

left: A profusion of blue phlox carpets this woodland garden each spring.
below: Tiptoeing through the phlox is the only way to get down the garden path.

PHOTOGRAPHS: TINA CORNETT

The Scent Of Purple

These wisteria-like flowers fill the air with their remarkable fragrance every spring.

Imagine the perfect shrub. Glossy dark evergreen leaves. A handsome shape that blends perfectly with natural and formal plantings. Big, velvety, silver-gray seedpods full of shiny red seeds pretty enough for jewelry. Cascades of purple flowers that rival wisteria in beauty and surpass grape Kool-Aid in fragrance.

Jill Nokes, Austin horticulturist and garden designer, notes that Texas mountain laurel is a remarkable asset in the landscape. "It's a workhorse here," she says. Jill mentions that as a Texas native, it's perfectly adapted to rocky, alkaline soils and needs no supplemental water or fertilizer once established. "Plus," Jill says, "we're so deer infested that we don't have many other choices of shrubs that the deer don't just eat to a nub. For us in the Hill Country, this is an evergreen muscle shrub."

While Texas mountain laurel *(Sophora secundiflora)* can be grown from seed, getting a container-grown plant from a nursery is usually easier. Field-dug specimens are not recommended because the plant's main taproot often doesn't transplant well.

To perform at its handsome best, this shrub needs only strong sun, alkaline soil, and excellent drainage. Under these conditions, just as on the caliche limestone hillsides where it grows wild, it will thrive with no attention at all. Jill suggests avoiding the pine bark-based soil mixes that other plants love, because these hold too much water and are too acid for mountain laurel. She notes that in heavy clay soils, such as those in Houston and parts of Dallas, it's critical to provide good drainage and avoid bark mulches. "For Austin and the Hill Country," says Jill, "the simplest solution is to just plant in straight caliche with no soil amendments at all."

Jill finds that one of its best niches is as a backdrop. "It's so dark green that it makes a terrific background for silvery plants. And," she adds cheerfully, "if your neighbors have a hideous garage, you can use mountain laurel as a screen. It will usually reach about 15 to 20 feet over time. You can even remove the lower limbs and shape it as a tree. Mountain laurel is great with other plants that are compatible with its low water requirements."

Easy to use, grow, and love (unless you *really* don't like grape Kool-Aid), Texas mountain laurel comes as close to perfection as a shrub can. LIZ DRUITT

Texas mountain laurel works as the perfect screen for unwanted views.

PHOTOGRAPHS: SYLVIA MARTIN

Limestone-loving Texas mountain laurel is perfectly sited on a well-drained hillside at Zilker Metropolitan Park in Austin.

TEXAS MOUNTAIN LAUREL
At a Glance

Range: Central, South, and West Texas
Size: usually 15 to 20 feet at maturity, but can reach 25 to 30 feet
Bloom season: March to April
Soil: well drained, not too acid
Light: full sun
Water: Extremely drought tolerant once established.
Fertilizer: not necessary
Nice to know: Deer won't eat Texas mountain laurel.

Plant Them Right

Vigorous roots pushing out of the package are always an unexpected surprise. With a little tough love, this problem can be fixed.

Springtime is decision time when you head to the garden shop. First, there are choices to be made about sun, shade, color, and height. In addition to that, there's the quest to find the healthiest transplants. With a mere glance, you assess foliage, watch for yellow leaves, and look for the most compact new arrivals. None of those overgrown seedlings for you.

But, surprise! At home, when you begin to plant, you remove the cell packs from their tray, only to find vigorous roots growing out the bottom in a tangled mess. This problem wasn't obvious at the nursery. Now, another decision needs to be made—do you plant them this way, or do something about it?

If planted as is, the new transplants will never become well established in the ground. The roots will continue to grow in a tight mass and fail to absorb moisture or nutrients efficiently. Eventually, the plants will die.

The solution is easy, although contrary to a gardener's nature. We know new roots are fragile and should be handled with care. But when they become overgrown and matted, they must be loosened. No longer delicate, they can be handled in a more aggressive manner. Don't panic—get tough. ◆

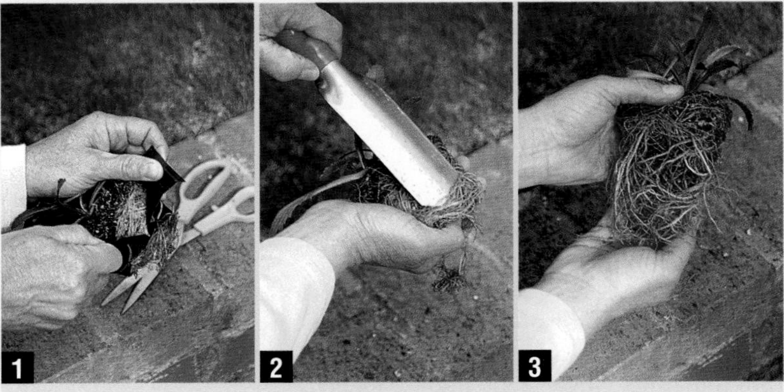

STEP-BY-STEP

1. With scissors, cut away the plastic package.
2. Work the tip of a small pointed trowel into the matted roots, beginning at the bottom of the transplant. Apply light pressure to penetrate the surface, and gently work the trowel back and forth to loosen the roots. Move up the root ball about ½ inch, and repeat the process. Then, turn it over and work on the other side.
3. Once the roots begin to relax, use your fingers to pull them free and straight. They will now be able to grow into the soil and become a well-established plant.

Houseplant Survival Kit

Now that spring has arrived, you may be itching to get outdoors, but don't neglect your houseplants. The winter has probably taken a toll on them. Indoor heat dehydrates foliage and fosters insects, while lower light and drafts add to your miseries. Here's a quick list of items to help perk up your plants.

- **Moisture meter**—This easy-to-use gauge lets you know if a plant needs a drink. Work the pointed probe deep into the soil for an accurate reading. Most houseplants prefer a moderately moist environment, with the gauge reading in the middle of its dry/wet range.
- **Watering can**—A model with a small pointed spout works well. It directs water exactly where you want and dispenses liquid slowly.
- **Mist bottle**—A thin film of water keeps foliage hydrated and clean—dust diminishes light. Also, red spider mites flourish in dry heat indoors and can consume a plant in rapid fashion. A daily dose of clear water on susceptible plants, such as ivy, reduces the risk of these pesky creatures.
- **Insecticidal soap**—When mites and mealybugs get a jump on your leafy friends, it's time for first aid. Clean foliage with water; then apply this spray to leaves and stems, saturating all surfaces. Repeat weekly until insects vanish.
- **Snips**—Small, pointed, and sharp are the pruner qualifications necessary for maintaining most indoor plants.

PHOTOGRAPH: VAN CHAPLIN

Head Start for Caladiums

It's difficult to be patient in spring. Days are balmy and bright, and early flowers are popping into bloom. It's tempting to hurry summer along and begin planting warm-weather plants such as caladiums. But soil temperatures are still surprisingly cool, and these tropical natives prefer a cozier environment.

Planted too soon, caladiums will sit dormant in the damp, cold garden and may rot. Tucked under only a few inches of soil, they easily become damaged or lost in early-spring's gardening frenzy. To prevent these pitfalls and to get a jump on the season, start your tubers indoors. It's easy to do, and you'll protect your investment in this heat-loving foliage plant.

Step 1: Cut a piece of screen to fit the flat's bottom and halfway up the sides. Fill the container with moist potting soil about 1 inch deep.

Step 2: Rest the tubers, buds up, on the soil. Place them close together, but not touching. Cover with additional soil, and put the flat in a warm location. Keep the soil damp but not soggy. In three to four weeks, after any danger of frost has passed, the caladiums will be in full leaf and ready to plant. **Editor's tip:** I place the flat on my warm driveway during the day and bring it indoors at night. If rainy days prevail, I put it on top of my clothes dryer, which also generates heat when in use.

Step 3: When leaves have emerged, slip your hand underneath the tubers, and lift them from the flat onto a piece of newspaper or a worktable. Gently pull them apart, and plant in the garden or containers. Caladiums need only a few inches of soil cover, so don't bury them too deep.

What's Up?

One of gardening's great mysteries is which side of a caladium tuber is the top. The nubby, irregularly shaped tuber gives few clues to this planting dilemma, and many times leaves you wondering if it will grow. The only hints I can give are these.

- Look closely at one of the broad, flat sides. Run your finger lightly over the surface, feeling for tiny points which are new leaf sprouts. If you don't find any, turn it over and check the other side. These raised tips mark the top.
- If that doesn't work, check for remnants of roots. They may be dehydrated and pressed against the surface of the tuber, but they will indicate the bottom.
- When all else fails, plant the caladium on its side. The tuber will sprout, and you won't have to worry about it. Even if you do plant upside-down, chances are good the tuber will grow anyway—it may just take it a bit longer.

ELLEN RUOFF RILEY

Caladiums are a colorful addition to the summer garden. Plan and plant ahead to get an early start on this tropical favorite.

MATERIALS

an empty, undivided flat (garden shops gladly will provide)
fiberglass screen
scissors
potting soil
caladium tubers

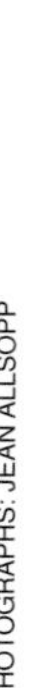

PHOTOGRAPHS: JEAN ALLSOPP

PHOTOGRAPHS: JEAN ALLSOPP

left: Flowers and interesting foliage fill this trio of planters. **below:** 'Elijah Blue' fescue, strawberry begonias, and sedum share strong leaf textures.

above: Japanese roof iris's clear white blooms are a good match with strawberry begonia's cream-colored leaf veins.

Planters With Pockets

Holey pots, Batman, it's a perforated planter. The classic strawberry jar used for years isn't anything to get excited about, unless you plant it with creative combinations. These pots feature a series of pockets that lend vertical interest, allowing you to layer plants. When filled out with foliage or flowers, they also add easy design to a garden or deck.

When I moved into a new house, I wanted to take a little bit of my old garden with me. I used strawberry jars to help relocate a few of my old favorites that suited the jars' well-drained conditions.

Once in my new place, I had little time to garden. Beyond watering occasionally, I paid little attention to the pots till the following spring. Then I discovered that the Japanese roof iris *(Iris tectorum)* I had tucked in the top of the container had multiplied and produced several white butterfly-like blooms. The iris is native to Japan, where it is often planted on cottage roofs. When not in bloom, it displays handsome light green, fanlike foliage.

Strawberry begonias *(Saxifraga stolonifera),* squeezed into the sides of the container, grew beneath the iris. Once the iris quit blooming, the begonias began to flower. Their delicate flowers sprinkle along 8- to 10-inch stems. They also feature nice foliage when not in bloom: round, scalloped, hairy leaves that are grayish green with cream veins.

Other jar pockets were filled with mazus *(Mazus reptans)*, usually used as a ground cover. Its slender stems and small leaves spill down the sides of the container, and small, white, pealike flowers appear in the spring. Above the mazus, the reddish-purple whorled foliage of 'Vera Jameson' sedum (*Sedum* 'Vera Jameson') tops the pot. This sedum produces pink flowers in dome-shaped clusters, but its foliage truly makes it special.

The wall-mounted pot received interesting foliage plants as well. 'Elijah Blue' fescue (*Festuca glauca* 'Elijah Blue') looks like spiked hair rising from the top of the planter. A blue-green sedum *(S. sieboldii)* pours out the bottom, and strawberry begonias fill in the middle holes.

These combinations worked for me, but you can use any plant that needs well-drained soil. Just make sure to use plants that share the same growing conditions. Remember, you can even fill your strawberry jar with strawberry plants. CHARLIE THIGPEN

PHOTOGRAPH: RALPH ANDERSON

Easy Garden Table

Outdoors, glass-top tables seem destined for disaster. If you're in need of a new top, try our can-do solution.

For many of us, outdoor meals are centered around a glass-top table. Inevitably, this dining fixture succumbs to ill fate—shattering from a fallen limb or a misguided baseball. When this happens, you're left with a great table base and no top. Our project combines an easy mosaic design with a unique garden twist.

A pot full of flowers or herbs on the table adds ambience to a meal. The problem is, making eye contact over the contents is often difficult. Our solution is simple: Let the bulk of the container hang below the table's surface. The pot rim rests on the top, and you can see over the centerpiece.

Have fun with your mosaic design. It can be simple or intricate, depending on your imagination, expertise, and patience. Just remember that mosaics take time; a complex pattern can become tedious.

When planning, leave space around the outside border to apply L-shaped finishing pieces called sink rail tiles. Choose a color and texture to complement your design, and it will neatly finish off the table's edge.

ELLEN RUOFF RILEY

Step 1

Step 4

PHOTOGRAPHS: PAUL WATKINS

MATERIALS

½-inch-thick exterior-grade plywood

electric drill with ⅞-inch bit

jigsaw

oil-based paint

tiles, broken dishes, etc., for mosaic pattern

hammer

old towel

tile adhesive

terra-cotta pot

sink rail tiles (to finish outside edge)

grout

STEP-BY-STEP

Step 1 (See photo.): Cut the plywood to the correct size and shape for the table base. Measure the terra-cotta pot's inside diameter, across the ridge where the lip begins. Draw this size circle in the plywood's center, and drill a hole inside the line to make a starting point for the jigsaw blade. Cut out the shape.

Step 2: Apply an oil-based paint to both sides of the plywood and the edges to seal the wood. Allow to dry thoroughly.

Step 3: Prepare the mosaic materials. Cover tiles in an old towel, and use a hammer to break them into small pieces. Wear protective eyewear when smashing tile.

Step 4 (See photo.): Apply adhesive to a small area. Quickly place the tiles in your design, and move on to another small section. Follow directions on the adhesive package regarding drying times. Tile the rim of the terra-cotta pot to match the table. Along the table's outside edges, apply the sink rail tiles. This will create a neat, seamless surface over the edge.

Step 5: Mix and apply the tile grout according to label directions. Finish the terra-cotta pot edge. When both have cured, place the pot in the table, and plant.

TELLTALE HEART ROT

How can you tell if your shade tree has heart rot? Look for these signs.

- a cavity in the trunk that usually starts near the ground
- a wedge of sunken or flaking bark that proceeds up the trunk
- lots of woodpecker holes in the trunk
- carpenter ants entering and leaving a hole in the trunk
- flat, shelf-like mushrooms growing on the side of the trunk
- a dark ooze that drips out of a hole in the trunk after a rain

left: A large strip of sunken, rotted wood running up the trunk of this oak indicates heart rot. As heart rot continues, it can hollow out the trunk, causing the tree to fall in high winds.

Watch Out for Falling Trees

If only trees would tell us when they're planning to fall, our lives would be a whole lot easier. But because trees can't talk, we have to guess. Will it be tomorrow, next month, next year, or 10 years from now? There's no way to tell.

Rest assured, a big tree with a rotten center will fall down sometime. The center of a tree contains a vital core of heartwood—dense, strong wood that supports a tree in the same way steel supports a skyscraper. Though heartwood is dead, it retains strength as long as it's safely encased inside sapwood and bark. But damage those outer layers, and you expose the heartwood to water, boring insects, and fungi. The result is a condition known as heart rot, which progressively hollows out the tree.

Damage occurs in many ways. Broken limbs, lightning strikes, fire injury, and topping can all lead to rot. So can smashing into the trunk with a pickup truck. But heart rot doesn't always result from an outside force. Some large trees naturally form a sort of bowl about 10 to 12 feet up from the ground, where all the main limbs spread out from the trunk. Water collects in this bowl and eventually causes rot.

What should you do if you discover a large tree with heart rot? The safest thing is to cut it down. Remember, heart rot never gets any better; it only gets worse. And if a tree that's known to be dangerous falls and injures someone or damages property, you may be held liable.

Of course, if you resist removing the tree for sentimental, aesthetic, or financial reasons, there are alternatives to the chain saw. In some rot cases, cabling, bracing, or filling the rotten cavity can strengthen the tree. Doing this correctly requires a licensed, bonded arborist who belongs to the American Society of Consulting Arborists or the International Society of Arboriculture.

Don't put this off until after the next big storm. Or you could be calling 911 and pleading, "Help! I've just been hit by a falling tree and I can't get up!"

PHOTOGRAPHS: SYLVIA MARTIN

Fabulous Southern Roses

Bred in the South and perfect for our gardens, historic Noisette roses are delighting a new generation of gardeners with their beauty, fragrance, and ease of care.

Born in Charleston, South Carolina, they were sent to France for that extra bit of polish, then brought back in triumph to fill the South with their charm and beauty. Since that time in the early 1800s, Noisette roses have been the easy, graceful, fragrant fulfillment of everything a Southern rose should be. Their shapely flowers, filled with silken petals in shades of cream, pink, yellow, apricot, or white, are produced with open-handed generosity on big, healthy, amazingly adaptable plants that thrive in the warmth and soils of most Southern gardens. Cherished specimens have been handed down via rooted cuttings for so many generations that they've become genuine living heirlooms. Still, they all originated from one rose.

'Champneys' Pink Cluster' came of a marriage between two great rose families—in the Southern sense of family, that is. Its "people" were the

above: Romance is personified by the glorious performance of Noisette climber 'Claire Jacquier' on a wall in Charleston. The pink rose is the climbing form of 'Old Blush.'
top, right: the creamy yellow blooms of 'Céline Forestier'
bottom, right: 'Natchitoches Noisette'

NOISETTE ROSES
At a Glance

Bloom: heavy in both spring and fall, scattered flowers in summer
Range: all South—though some may be tender in Upper South
Light: at least six hours direct sun
Soil: any well drained
Water: Soak root zone with about 1 inch of water weekly during growing season.
Fertilizer: Apply a slow-release fertilizer (such as Mills Magic Rose Mix) at pruning times (usually February and August). Apply a liquid fertilizer (such as alfalfa tea or fish emulsion) every two weeks when rose is blooming heavily. Do not feed after October.
Nice to know: Noisette roses, while not impervious to black spot, thrive without being sprayed.

modern garden. From spring to fall, these roses prove their lasting worth by producing armloads of fragrant flowers to share and enjoy.

Fortunately, Noisette roses are no longer just pass-along heirlooms. They are now available at many nurseries that specialize in old-fashioned roses, and their beauty is featured in a number of rose display gardens. All across the South this spring, Noisette roses will be coming into exuberant bloom just as they have for nearly 200 years. You can watch and applaud. Or you can join the growing ranks of rose lovers who are inviting these Southern beauties back into their own gardens. LIZ DRUITT

centuries-old, cluster-flowered European musk rose *(Rosa moschata)* and the more recently introduced ancient pink Chinese rose 'Old Blush.' The pair shared two important traits. Both loved warm climates, and, in a day when most roses bloomed just once in the spring and then quit, these prolific roses flowered periodically all summer and again in the fall.

The floral union produced what all families hope for—progeny showing the most attractive traits of their mingled bloodlines. 'Champneys' Pink Cluster' featured myriad dainty bunches of the palest pink, perfumed petals, blossoming in successive waves over a large, sturdy bush. Best of all, the new rose was completely at home in the Southern region, standing up to heat, humidity, irregular winters, and sandy and clay soils with endearing ease.

Only genealogists—or seriously addicted rosarians—will be interested in following the travels of 'Champneys' Pink Cluster' and its seedling, 'Blush Noisette,' across the ocean to rose breeders in France. It's of more interest to the average gardener today that their heavy-blooming progeny returned to us enriched with a broader range of colors, fatter flowers, and some climbing habits. Both the early bush-style Noisettes and the later big, buxom climbers are perfectly adapted to our Southern climate—and perfectly magnificent in the

ONES TO TRY

- 'Aimée Vibert'—white climber, 6-10 feet, thornless
- 'Blush Noisette'—light pink shrub or bushy climber, 4-8 feet
- 'Bouquet d'Or'—soft gold climber, 10-12 feet
- 'Champneys' Pink Cluster'—pink shrub or bushy climber, 4-8 feet
- 'Crépuscule'—apricot climber, 6-12 feet
- 'Madame Alfred Carrière'—blush white climber, 12-20 feet
- 'Rêve d'Or'—tawny yellow climber, 10-12 feet

top, left: 'Rêve d'Or' **top, right:** Ruth Knopf, of Charleston, harvests from her bounty of roses. **center:** 'Blush Noisette' **above, right:** 'Lamarque,' a white Noisette, can climb up to 20 feet.

STEP INSIDE A
Charleston

Garden

In Peg and Truman Moore's garden, beauty stems from careful planning—and hiding Truman's pruners.

When you call Peg and Truman Moore, expect the phone to ring a few times. They're probably out in their Charleston, South Carolina, garden. Maybe they're enjoying a glass of wine on the porch. Maybe Peg is busily clipping spent blooms. Or, maybe Truman is yanking weeds along the walk, trying to impress Peg with his usefulness.

These two own an amazing garden. Though relatively small—just 45 x 100 feet—it abounds with blossoming plants. No season, no month, or no week passes by that does not see something in bloom. Just as impressive as the flowers is the clean, formal framework of lines, vistas, and focal points that reins in this boisterous assembly.

Which noted landscape architect designed the garden? If you're as creatively challenged as I am, you'll cringe at the answer. Peg and Truman leafed through some garden books,

BY STEVE BENDER
PHOTOGRAPHY
ALLEN ROKACH

above: Herbs, perennials, and annuals thrive on the herb parterre at the head of the lawn. A pot of red petunias atop a pedestal serves as a distant focal point, emphasizing the line of the walk. **top, left:** Details, such as this tiny birdbath tucked behind magenta petunias and white serissa, make the difference. **center, left:** The fountain edge was designed at just the right height for sitting. **bottom, left:** Scarlet petunias atop an ornate pedestal provide a dazzling focal point.

grabbed pencil and paper, and did the whole thing themselves.

Newcomers to the Lowcountry, the Moores moved from New York into their historic home (built in 1786) eight years ago. They chose Charleston, says Peg, because "we wanted to live in a sophisticated city, but a smaller city. And because we were very involved in historic preservation, we wanted to live in a place that values its history. Charleston does."

They also coveted a garden. "I wanted a place to garden year-round," she explains. "Our real estate broker understood this. I told her I didn't care about the kitchen or living room—the first thing I wanted to see was the garden."

Or rather, the potential area for a garden. "The yard was pretty much a blank slate," Peg recalls. "Nothing but fire ants and grass." But this did not bother the Moores, who preferred starting from scratch than tearing down an old garden. Truman, noting existing features, carefully measured every inch of the yard to create a base plan. He also studied the area's sun and shade patterns. Then Peg embarked on a series of roughly 30 ever-evolving design sketches. She based the earliest ones on the works of renowned landscape architect Loutrel

"It's a joy to have things growing and blooming year-round. You don't have to endure nine months of nothing, like you do up North."

Briggs, who designed many great gardens in Charleston.

"His gardens were symmetrical and formal," Peg notes. "But it's hard to have a symmetrical garden when one half is sunny and the other is shady, like our garden. Even if the same plants survive in both places, they don't grow to the same size. So I gave half the garden the Loutrel Briggs look—the formal lawn, the brick walks, the loquat hedge, the herb parterre—and then the other half, the sunnier part, I did in the looser cottage garden style."

The color scheme evolved as well. "Like many people, I started out with the whole pink-blue-and-white bit," Peg says. "But here in Charleston with our intense sunshine, that palette tends to be too pale. So I added a lot of reds and oranges." Indeed, at this moment in early May, the bright reds and oranges of verbena, petunias, geraniums, gerbera daisies, daylilies, and pot marigolds catch your eye and carry it throughout the garden.

Peg and Truman live in Charleston all year—they don't flee to cooler climes when the weather gets hot. So their garden, unlike many in the city, needs color beyond the spring. To accomplish this, they grow dozens of flowering plants in pots that Peg keeps along the brick terrace. Some bloom in spring, some in summer, and some in fall and winter. Whenever and wherever she needs color, she plugs them into the garden at an appropriate spot.

Such gardening can be exhausting, but the payback is worth it. "It's a joy to have things growing and blooming year-round," Peg declares. "You don't have to endure nine months of nothing, like you do up North."

Rich, generous soil is key to a garden like this one. "Someone told us that during World War II, the owner here kept chickens," Peg says. "So actually, we started with pretty good soil." To make it even better, she and Truman hauled in many truckloads of compost in the garden's early stages. And they amend the soil with compost and manure every year.

Every successful gardening partnership demands that each partner accept a role. Here, Peg is the master gardener—the planner, the planter, the artist. As for Truman, he's the "under-gardener," a position he has held ever since he committed the cardinal sin of pruning the roses without asking Peg. Truman: "I thought we understood we were going to hard-prune 'em." Peg: "He cut off 45 rosebuds that were just about to open. I couldn't believe it."

With Truman's duties now redefined, all is well at the couple's house. "I'm Doctor Death," he announces proudly. "I get rid of weeds and bugs. I'm good for fungus, Florida betony, dandelions, and stuff like that. If it needs to be killed, I'm the guy."

But that stuff will have to wait. Right now, the only liquidation Truman is contemplating is a glass of red wine with Peg.

Enclosed by walls and a loquat hedge, the garden rests on a long, narrow lot behind the house. Flowering plants bask on the sunnier side (left) while ferns, hydrangeas, and impatiens enjoy the fruiting loquat's shade (right).

Hydrangeas and multicolored annuals bloom in a Kentucky garden *(See pages 100–105.)*

May

Garden Checklist 84

A Little Garden Makeover 86
an easy and inexpensive design for a charming courtyard

Bright Color Now 89
'Tangerine Beauty' crossvine makes a spectacular impact

A Natural Solution for a Slope 90
a waterfall and a landscape makeover saves a backyard disaster

Big Show, Easy To Grow 92
impatiens guarantee long-lasting summer color

A Path With a New Perspective 94
a little trickery makes a lawn look larger

A Family's Guide to Lawn Care 96
secrets to a successful Florida lawn

Two Plants, One Name 99
Jerusalem sage looks great in the border

Beauty in the Bluegrass 100
spring blooms at Oxmoor Farm in Louisville, KY

Editor's Notebook

I know it appears from the glorious photos on these pages that our photographers miraculously arrive at every garden at the absolute peak of color. Sorry to shatter your illusions (step away from that ledge, please), but it seldom works out that way. Despite our best planning, calamities happen—usually the day before we get there. A freeze kills all the blooms, a windstorm strips all the leaves, or a 50-ton brachiosaurus re-created from prehistoric DNA decides to nap on the herb garden. This doesn't make us loony, because we've come to realize that gardening and disasters go hand in hand. Gardens aren't meant to be static paintings you hang on the wall. Rather, gardens are works in progress, dynamic collections of hits and misses, triumphs and disappointments. So next time your garden is struck by a falling Russian satellite, smile. Not only will you be the talk of the neighborhood, but you'll also have the chance to plant something even better. —STEVE BENDER

Caladiums

If you need easy, dependable color, try growing caladiums this summer. The leaves come in a variety of colors and shapes. Place plants or bulbs in a partially shaded bed. For a beautiful, carefree combination, set perennial Southern wood fern in the background, your favorite caladium selection in the middle, and easy annuals such as impatiens or wax begonias in a complementary color in the foreground. You will love the results.

TIPS

■ **Houseplants—**Repot any houseplants that have become overgrown and potbound. Remember that ficus, spider plant, and clivia like to be potbound, so don't repot unless you want to share with friends.

■ **Mulch—**Be sure to apply an extra layer of pine straw or shredded bark mulch around newly planted trees and shrubs. These plants dry out fast as the weather gets hotter, and they will need the extra layer of mulch to help retain moisture.

■ **Repairing a lawn—**Take stock of your grass, and replant areas that didn't survive the winter. If you have recurring dead or weak places in your centipede lawn, plant St. Augustine plugs in trouble spots. St. Augustine is not susceptible to some of the problems of centipede, and the centipede-and-St. Augustine combination blends well together.

■ **Spring bulbs—**Allow bulbs to complete their growing cycles. Foliage of daffodils, hyacinths, snowflakes, and other spring flowering bulbs should begin to yellow before being trimmed or cut back. This will encourage bulbs to store enough energy to produce a bigger and better crop of flowers next year.

■ **Stake—**Remember to support tall-growing flowers such as dahlias, lilies, and gladioli now before they begin blooming. Wooden stakes, bamboo, or wire cages are all suitable and widely available. Tomato cages are an inexpensive, durable option that can be fashioned from concrete reinforcing wire, a sturdy wire mesh that is 5 feet wide and has 6-inch-square openings. You'll need a 6-foot-long section to make a tubular cage about 20 inches in diameter and 5 feet tall.

PLANT

■ **Annuals—** Good choices for sunny areas include angelonia, sun coleus, gomphrena, melampodium, pentas, portulaca, narrow-leaf zinnia, ornamental sweet potato, lantana, ruellia, and verbena. Some of the best choices for shade are impatiens, caladiums, Brazilian plume (Jacobinia), and various types of gingers.

■ **Basil—**Plant basil now, and harvest the rewards all year. Common selections are 'Genovese,' 'Purple Ruffles,' and 'Thai' basil.

■ **Daylilies—**Dwarf, spider, double, ruffled, and repeat-blooming types are available. Daylilies like at least a half-day of sun and sandy, well-prepared soil. Consult a local daylily society or nursery for suggestions.

■ **Perennial salvias—**In the Middle, Lower, and Coastal South 'Indigo Spires' salvia displays its dark blue-violet flower spikes from spring until frost. Autumn sage *(Salvia greggii)* is available in pink, red, raspberry, white, salmon, and magenta; it will bloom until frost. Bog sage *(Salvia uliginosa)* thrives in wet places and rewards the gardener with mounds of sky blue flowers all summer. Mexican bush sage *(Salvia leucantha)* blooms from early to late fall. To keep salvias blooming, cut back spent flowers every three to five weeks.

■ **Vegetables—**Plant okra, squash, Southern peas, and peppers for summer harvest. Favorite okra selections include 'Clemson Spineless' and 'Louisiana Green Velvet.'

PRUNE

■ **Pinch—**To make your chrysanthemums bushier and increase the number of fall blooms, begin pinching them back. With your fingers, just pinch the tips of the branches back ½ to 1 inch. When the plants have grown several more inches, pinch back again. Repeat this process until July.

■ **Thyme—**Cut back leafless mats of creeping thyme stems to the point where new growth has sprouted. Fertilize with liquid 20-20-20.

FERTILIZE

■ **Landscape plants—**If young shrubs and trees were fertilized in late February or March, they can now be given a second application. A suitable general-purpose landscape fertilizer is 15-0-15 with 7.5% slow-release nitrogen. Apply it at a rate no greater than 6 pounds per 1,000 square feet.

■ **Lawn care—**Continue to sod or sprig Bermuda, centipede, St. Augustine, and Zoysia now if you need to repair or establish a lawn. Bermuda, St. Augustine, and Zoysia prefer a fertilizer high in nitrogen, but centipede needs one with minimal nitrogen.

■ **Palms—**In the Tropical South, if you haven't fertilized your palm trees in the past two months, do it now. Use a controlled-release 8-4-12 palm fertilizer containing 4% magnesium, 1% to 2% iron and manganese, at least some sulfur, and trace amounts of zinc, copper, and boron.

■ **Rose care—**Fertilize roses monthly with 2 to 3 tablespoons of 15-0-15 per plant, spread in a 3- x 3-foot area around each plant. Water the fertilizer in through the mulch. If roses develop black spots on the leaves and begin to drop leaves, spray every 7 to 10 days with a fungicide such as Funginex or Immunox. If leaves show a yellowish speckling on the upper surface, the roses probably have spider mites, so use insecticidal soap, horticultural oil, or Di-Syston granules, according to label directions.

■ **Vegetables—**Fertilize squash, tomatoes, and peppers with a 5-10-15 fertilizer to promote root growth and fruit production.

Summer Color

Easy-care choices for the months ahead include celosias (pictured at right) and bachelor's buttons. Celosias are available in both spiked and crested forms (cockscomb). They combine well with moss roses and their cousins, the purslanes, which come in magenta, yellow, orange, and pink. Choose a sunny, well-drained location, and prepare the soil by tilling in 3 to 5 inches of organic material, such as composted pine bark or your own compost. Also incorporate about 5 pounds of all-purpose fertilizer per 100 square feet. Once established, these plants require only occasional shaping and watering.

May notes:

Tip of the Month

To keep squirrels from digging in new bedding plants, I use plant supports with rings at the top to stake out the area and place black plastic netting over the rings. Then I use metal staples to fasten the netting to the ground. The squirrels can't get in, and the netting is almost invisible. The netting can be raised or removed altogether as the plants grow.

DAWN S. MCCALL
FORT MILL, SOUTH CAROLINA

a little garden makeover

This easy project, which cost less than $600, quickly turned a compact courtyard into a backyard oasis.

BY ELLEN RUOFF RILEY / PHOTOGRAPHY BETH DREILING

GARDENING

PLANTS AND DESIGN

When two friends moved into their garden home, the tiny courtyard was anything but beautiful. A crepe myrtle, some straggly grass, a boisterous Lady Banks's rose, and a tiny patio were the only remnants of a fading landscape endeavor. Both Beth Dreiling and Margaret Monroe (now Mrs. William Dickey) longed for an outdoor garden room for entertaining, but they also had a small budget. These young gardeners needed to maximize their dollars and get a big look for their bucks. Walk with us through the process of building this fun, functional, and reasonably priced courtyard garden.

Priorities

A primary issue in any garden design is how the area is going to be used. In Beth and Margaret's courtyard, walls set the parameters. The grass lawn held little interest for them, but additional patio space was important. So they planned flowerbeds to soften the brick walls and frame the remaining area—a planted patio accommodating a table, chairs, and foot traffic.

They also craved the sound of water, so a fountain factored into the scheme. Nestled amid large-leaved foliage on the back wall, it would serve as a focal point in the garden.

Getting Started

After they determined the dimensions for the extended patio, they killed the grass with an herbicide. Beth and Margaret then solicited the help of a strong-bodied, tiller-toting friend to turn the soil and remove turf remnants. Next, they put in steppingstones, leaving 4 inches of growing room between them.

They chose specific plants for their garden based on their desire for herbs, cool color, and a lush, tropical look. To carpet the soil between the new patio stones, they selected thyme and oregano for their fast-growing habit and culinary use. They combined those with creeping Jenny *(Lysimachia nummularia)*; its brilliant chartreuse foliage delivers a contrasting textural punch.

Because the flowerbeds get varying degrees of sun exposure, achieving color continuity throughout required thoughtful planning. The brick's rosy pigmentation called for pink and purple flowers, and the watermelon-hued crepe myrtle sealed the deal on color choices. On the sunny side, different shades of pink and white blooms, along with colorful foliage, established a cool color palette. Beth and Margaret trained moonflowers *(Ipomoea alba)* to climb the wall. These stellar night bloomers bring nocturnal charm and gentle fragrance to evenings in the courtyard. The vines also blanket the solid brick surface with soft foliage, producing the illusion of more space.

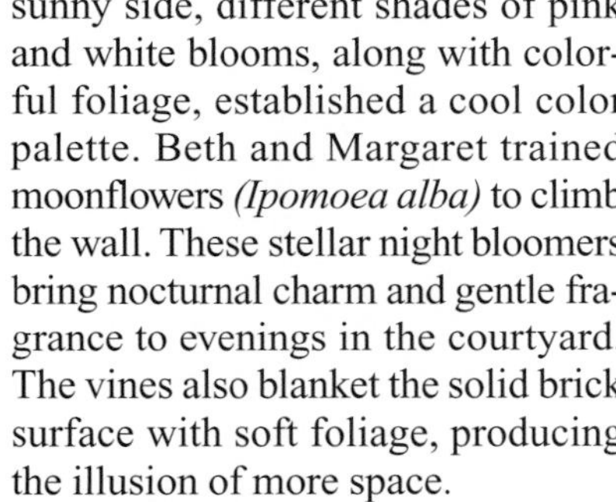

They decided to use similar colors across the courtyard. Shade-loving coleus, in both pink and chartreuse, were teamed with white impatiens. The foliage of 'Illustris' elephant's ear (*Colocasia esculenta* 'Illustris') and white 'Aaron' caladium added texture and filled space rapidly.

Drip, Drop, Splish, Splash

The crowning touch was the cool, inviting sound of falling water. Beth and Margaret chose an old, oval-shaped galvanized tub as the simple base for their fountain. They then

top, far left: Proper planning and a few design tricks transformed this sparse courtyard into a lush garden. **far left:** Moonflower lights up the night. **left, center:** Old mailboxes are used as petite planters on this gate. **above:** The fountain nestles beside the wall among elephant's ears and petunias.

left: The sunny border brims with pentas, globe amaranth, spider flower, and colorful coleus. Votive candles, wired to bamboo plant stakes, twinkle under the moonflowers. **below:** Moonflowers are easy to grow from seed.

above, left: Inexpensive stepping-stones were purchased to extend the patio. **above, center:** Beth plants thyme, oregano, and creeping Jenny between the 18-inch stones. **above, right:** A light layer of mulch prevents splashed mud and presents a finished appearance. Mirrored windows reflect light into the courtyard, creating the illusion of more space.

hung a rusty metal trough on the wall above and let water drip into the tub through existing holes. They placed pots of creeping Jenny—known as a water-lover and land-lubber—in the fountain's top portion. Its cascading green foliage softened the metal's hard edge. Another plus to this courtyard fountain: The area's tight walls amplify its music.

Playful Touches, Design Tricks

Making a small space feel large requires a few tricks.

- Mirrors in old window frames reflect light into the garden. Hung on the shady side's wall, they add dimension and intrigue.
- Shallow terra-cotta bowls top the gate pillars with hot pink mandevilla and 'Blackie' sweet potato (*Ipomoea batata* 'Blackie') trailing downward. These pots elevate flower color and draw the eye beyond the confines of the walls.
- The blue picnic table and matching benches add accent color.

The Bottom Line

This garden is long on elbow grease and short on cost. With all expenses taken into account, Beth and Margaret spent less than $600 to create their garden—turning a sparse, neglected area into a lush, playful courtyard in a few summer months. ◆

This section of the courtyard border receives intense afternoon sun. The flower selections shown above face the heat head-on. Clockwise from bottom:

- white Star Series zinnias *(Zinnia angustifolia)*
- globe amaranth (*Gomphrena* sp.)
- spider flower *(Cleome hasslerana)*
- coleus
- pentas

Cooler quarters on this end of the garden allow these flowers to flourish. Clockwise from bottom:

- white impatiens
- coleus
- 'Illustris' elephant's ear (*Colocasia esculenta* 'Illustris')
- 'Aaron' caladium

PHOTOGRAPHS: VAN CHAPLIN

left: You can't beat 'Tangerine Beauty' crossvine for sheer impact. Vines planted at each of these brick columns filled in between them in just two years. **below, left:** Crossvine adorns an arched entryway that faces a quiet side street.

Bright Color Now

Want thousands of blooms for just a few bucks? Try 'Tangerine Beauty' crossvine.

Would you spend $120 for a living fence that's covered in spectacular blooms and practically takes care of itself? Dan Coffman did, and he's glad.

A few years ago, Dan bought a Dallas house that was in danger of being torn down. "People who looked at the place were mostly builders who wanted to replace it with a big, new house," he recalls. "But I lived alone and liked the idea of a small English cottage look with a closed garden that works like an outdoor room." So he bought the house and collaborated with Koller Home Design in Dallas to get the look he wanted.

The original front entry faced a busy street. Dan turned that into a porch and then added a new entrance on a quieter side street. To enclose the garden, he chose a black steel fence that runs between brick columns painted gray. Except at the front gate, the columns stand 20 feet apart. Dan needed a vine to quickly cover the fence and remain attractive year-round. 'Tangerine Beauty' crossvine (*Bignonia capreolata* 'Tangerine Beauty') was the perfect choice.

'Tangerine Beauty' is an improved selection of our native evergreen crossvine, which sports deep-orange flowers with yellow throats. Two years ago, Dan placed a 5-gallon plant costing about $15 at each of the eight columns. "Orange is one of my favorite colors, and I liked the contrast with the gray," he explains. "It's amazing how fast they have grown. For the color and coverage you get, they're very economical."

Dan credits the rapid growth to good soil preparation, plus the installation of irrigation and drainage systems. In truth, though, crossvine is very easy to grow. It likes sun or partial shade, has no serious pests, and needs little maintenance beyond the occasional pruning. This vine will climb wood, metal, or masonry. What more could you ask?

I didn't even know about Dan's crossvine until I happened to drive past his house last spring and was so astonished by the spectacle that I nearly totaled my car. So if you think you might be heading that way, be sure the driver wears blinders.

STEVE BENDER

'Tangerine Beauty' crossvine is part of our *Southern Living* Plant Collection from Monrovia. Call 1-888-752-6848 to find a participating nursery near you. ◆

'TANGERINE BEAUTY' CROSSVINE

At a Glance

Size: 15 to 30 feet
Light: sun or light shade (more flowers will grow in sun)
Soil: moist, well drained
Growth rate: fast
Pests: none serious
Prune: after it finishes blooming
Range: Upper, Middle, Lower, Coastal South

a natural
solution
for a slope

When Ken and Elaine Cole moved into their new home in Bethesda, Maryland, the backyard was a disaster. The patio consisted of an ugly concrete slab. There was no privacy from the neighbors. Water ran down a rear slope toward the house. The Coles wanted solutions. And they wanted them right then.

"We're the quintessential instant gratification people," admits Elaine. "We wanted the yard to look gorgeous immediately."

Elaine, an interior designer, thought the garden should function as an extension of the house. But there was no way that she and Ken could handle the job themselves. So they called on McHale Landscape Design of Upper Marlboro, Maryland, to fix the problem pronto. Today, they enjoy a quiet haven that's the focus of family activity.

The garden really begins in the Coles' family room, which looks out on the yard through large windows on three sides. So inviting is the sound of the splashing waterfall that Elaine keeps those windows open as often as possible. "When we're inside, we're still experiencing the outdoors," she explains. Exit through the kitchen door, and you're out on a flagstone patio that's surrounded by flowering shrubs, perennials, and ornamental grasses. The blend of flowers, plumes, foliage, and seedheads provides year-round interest.

A dry creekbed marks the transition between the more formal perennial garden and the naturalistic woodland area beyond. A perforated 6-inch pipe hidden beneath smooth river stones carries runoff from the slope away from the home's foundation.

Crossing a large stone that spans the creekbed, you come to the garden's central feature, a recirculating waterfall and fishpond. Thanks to some wise decisions by Kevin and Steve McHale, the scene appears quite natural.

First, they took advantage of the existing grade change and set the waterfall back into the slope. Second, they built the falls out of native stones of various shapes and sizes. Third, they covered the bottom of the pond liner with gravel, such as you might find beneath a real waterfall. Finally, they encouraged ground covers and perennials to fill in every available niche between the stones.

When you're looking back from the waterfall and adjacent terrace toward the house, you can tell how close the neighbors are. But now you can see a lot less of them than you would have before, due to a thick screen of newly planted shade trees and evergreens.

PHOTOGRAPHS: ALLEN ROKACH

far left: One way to make a waterfall look natural is by covering it with plants. Here, mazus and epimedium scramble over rocks, bringing life to a barren surface. **top:** Setting the waterfall into an existing slope helps it blend into the landscape. Lush foliage in the background creates an intimate atmosphere. **above:** This dry creekbed separates the naturalistic plantings from a more formal area near the house.

Elaine says she and Ken like to spend every season in the garden, "taking pictures, working, digging, sweeping, looking, fooling with it even on a cold day." So don't stand in the doorway when you see either of them with trowel in hand. They're headed to the garden, and they just can't wait.

STEVE BENDER

Big Show, Easy To Grow

Impatiens guarantee long-lasting success in your garden.

PHOTOGRAPH: JEAN ALLSOPP

To the beginning gardener, planting impatiens can be a great confidence builder. These popular flowers are easy yet effective in the landscape. That's why they're the number one selling bedding plant each year. Tiny, inexpensive transplants set out in spring and early summer will grow to be knee-high mounds of showy flowers by summer's end. In fact, because impatiens come in a rainbow of colors, choosing the right shade may be the hardest part of growing them.

Impatiens perform well in sweeps and borders, but they also make excellent container plants. Placed in pots, they can brighten an entrance, deck, or patio. Set out white impatiens around these high-traffic areas where they may be enjoyed during the day; at night, their white flowers will glow like little stars. These flowering annuals also mix well with foliage plants such as ivies and ferns. Oftentimes impatiens are used in hanging baskets, where they create mounds of color and cascade over the edges of the basket in brilliant waves.

Known as shade lovers, impatiens can take considerable sun when given enough water. Their stems are like liquid-filled vessels, and plants wilt when low on water, making it easy to tell when they need a drink. Once watered, though, they quickly stand up straight. The trick is to maintain even moisture by giving them a heavy soaking once or twice weekly. This will keep plants happy and stress free.

Impatiens are best suited for light shade, where they don't require too much water or care. They work well in woodland settings mixed with hostas and wildflowers, yet they're showy enough to use in formal gardens to fill in around clipped green shrubs. They have such a nice spreading shape that they can even be used as an annual ground cover. To make a dramatic show, plant blocks of a single color. Such mass plantings create a clean look. If you do mix colors, be sure to select shades that complement each other. Too many brightly colored flowers can make a garden or bed look cluttered or chaotic.

Although they are considered to be annuals, impatiens often reseed in the garden and return yearly. The offspring may have flowers in different colors than the parent

BY CHARLIE THIGPEN / PHOTOGRAPHY VAN CHAPLIN

above: This gazebo appears to rest on a cloud of white impatiens. **top, left:** Impatiens can brighten your garden with a rainbow of colors, including this salmon shade. **top, center:** 'Aruba' Pure Beauty Series New Guinea impatiens sport purple-pink flowers that look striking mixed with green hostas. **bottom, left:** Double impatiens fill a container with showy multipetaled blooms.

plants. If not for their beautiful blooms, impatiens would be considered weeds by some gardeners because they sprout up all over the garden.

A Choice of Types

New Guinea impatiens are starting to show up everywhere as their availability in nurseries and garden centers increases. This type has larger blooms than regular impatiens, and many selections have variegated or dark-colored foliage. They're striking enough to use as specimen plants or even to create a focal point. Most New Guinea impatiens are grown from cuttings, so they are usually a little more expensive. They are more sun tolerant than regular impatiens but can't withstand as much heat. Many times they'll shed all their blooms when summer temperatures reach the mid- to upper 90s.

Semidouble and double impatiens, blessed with showy flowers, are also gaining popularity. These plants have been around for years, but some of the older selections weren't very hardy. Today's plants, such as the Fiesta Series, are stronger and make a nice addition to any garden. Their silky petals cluster together to resemble tiny rose blooms.

When purchasing impatiens from a nursery or garden center, be sure to select transplants that look healthy. Plants should be short, stocky, and full. Set them out in loose, fertile soil. A sprinkle of slow-release fertilizer, such as 12-6-6, around the plants will give them a little boost. If your impatiens grow tall and leggy by midsummer, pinch them back by 4 or 5 inches. This will cause the plants to flush out and branch more for a fuller look. Then, with little care, impatiens will flower continuously until the first hard frost.

There you have it—if you want simple success in your garden or containers, look no further than these carefree bloomers. Impatiens just can't be beat. ◆

PHOTOGRAPHS: VAN CHAPLIN

A Path With a New Perspective

Perched in the rocking chairs on the front porch of their old family home in Marietta, Georgia, Will and Michelle Goodman can gaze out across their expansive domain. Okay, in reality, the distance from the front steps to the sidewalk is a modest 35 feet. But Will used a little trickery to make his front lawn look slightly larger.

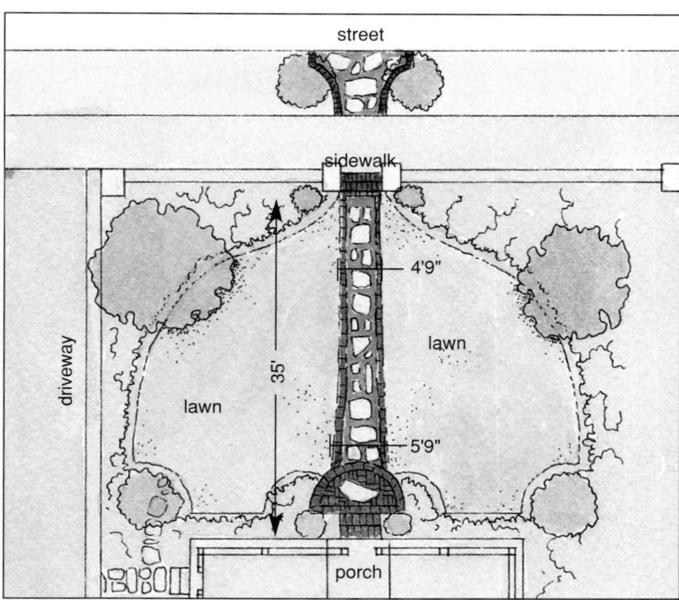

above: To make his humble front yard look larger, this homeowner created a path that plays tricks on the eyes. **far left:** The path to the front door is actually wider at the front stoop than it is at the sidewalk. This makes the path look longer and the lawn appear larger. **left:**The false perspective has the reverse effect when visitors look toward the house from the sidewalk. The home seems closer to the street and therefore more approachable.

"What I did was use a little false perspective on the path," says Will, a landscape architect. "It's slightly wider up by the house, so when you are looking toward the street, the path looks longer than it really is. I didn't do any math when I laid it out; I just pulled some string and decided what looked best. The path is about a foot wider at the end toward the house."

Think of standing in the middle of some train tracks in Kansas and watching the tracks disappear into the horizon. The rails appear to converge in the distance. Will re-created that optical illusion using the rowlock brick edging that borders his stone and grass path. By gradually narrowing the brick edging toward the street end, he made the path look longer. Because the path runs right through the middle of the front lawn, the yard looks larger. "You don't want to taper it in so much that it looks like somebody made a mistake," Will says. "You just want to pull the lines in and cheat a little bit."

Before he began the project, Will looked to the style of the home to help him come up with the design. "It's a really simple house built in 1923," he says. "It's very symmetrical, and you want to look at it from straight on versus from the side, where you can't appreciate its style. You always want to let the architecture dictate what's going on and to choose materials that are appropriate."

Will also noted how visitors usually approach the house. In their pedestrian-oriented neighborhood, guests typically arrive via the sidewalk. Those who do come by car usually park on the street out front. So a path that would lead visitors directly to the front door without having them walk halfway down the driveway made the most sense. To welcome passersby, Will removed the old concrete walkway that ran from the driveway to the front door, and he began a new path designed to deliver guests straight from the street to his porch.

The existing low brick retaining wall that runs parallel to the sidewalk acted as a barrier. So Will knocked out a 4-foot section of the wall to make room for a new set of brick steps. After removing a strip of grass leading from the steps to the front door, he carefully placed some large Cherokee stones that were salvaged from an old terrace in the backyard.

"Everyone has stepping-stone walks, but as a rule of thumb you don't want them leading to your front door," Will cautions. "Usually, it's just not quite formal enough." He added a touch of formality by introducing brick rowlock edging to the path. The stones were carefully set close enough to allow visitors to walk at a comfortable gait. He wanted to prevent them from having to hopscotch to the door, but he also wanted gaps wide enough to let thick sections of grass grow between the cracks. This allows the lawn to flow visually across the path so it isn't completely bisected. "Had it been a solid walk, it would have made a small yard seem smaller," Will says. "We sure didn't want that."

GLENN R. DINELLA

GARDENING
PLANTS AND DESIGN

A Family's Guide to Lawn Care

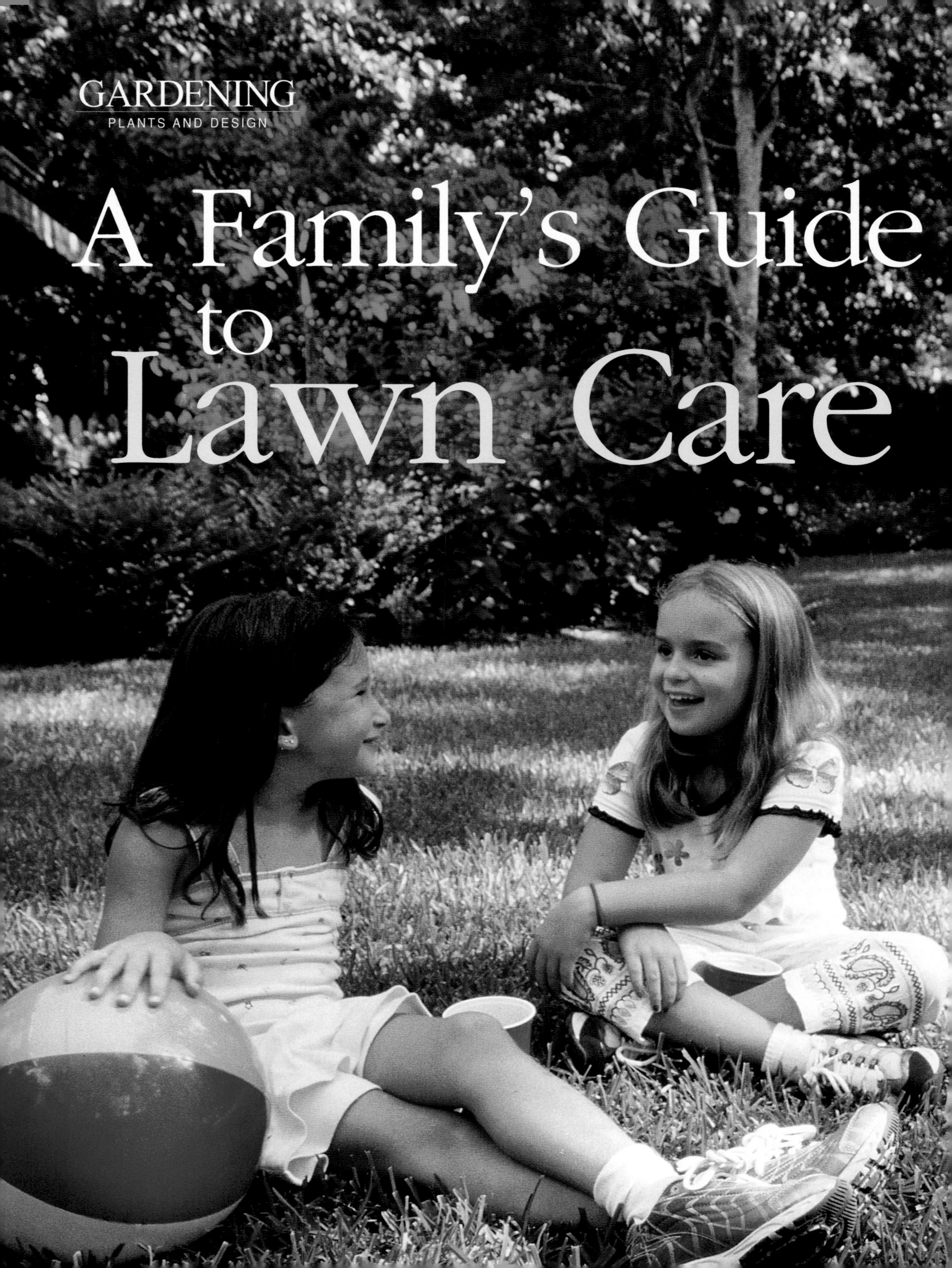

BY STEVE BENDER / PHOTOGRAPHY VAN CHAPLIN

Lawn care—let's be honest—is a male bastion. Research shows that turf density, power mower fumes, and testosterone are inextricably linked. All of which means that if your lawn doesn't meet community standards, there's probably a man to blame.

So put your foot down, ladies, in lieu of putting it somewhere else. Haul Bubba out from the recliner in front of his HDTV, and read him these very important questions.

Where in the state do we live? Most Florida grasses grow statewide, but reserve centipede for the Panhandle and carpet grass for wet soil.

Is our soil acid or alkaline? Bermuda, St. Augustine, and Zoysia don't mind either. But Bahia, carpet grass, and centipede need acid soil.

Do we live near the beach? If so, smile, and plant a salt-tolerant grass, such as Bermuda, St. Augustine, or Zoysia. A new type of lawn grass, seashore paspalum, also tolerates salt.

Is shade an issue? No grass prefers growing in shade. However, St. Augustine and the newer varieties of Zoysia will tolerate it.

Are nematodes present in the soil? These microscopic worms, which attack roots, ravage many lawn grasses. Irregular patches of yellowing or wilting grass with short, dark roots signal their presence. No chemical control is practical. Bahia and St. Augustine tolerate nematodes better than other grasses.

Does our grass get a lot of wear? Zoysia and Bermuda take the most wear, followed by Bahia and St. Augustine.

How much watering do we want to do? Zoysia, Bermuda, and Bahia need relatively little water. Carpet grass and centipede need more.

How much time are we willing to spend on lawn care? Zoysia and

A GUIDE TO FLORIDA GRASSES

Name	Area Adapted	Soil pH	Salt Tolerance	Shade Tolerance	Nematode Tolerance	Wear Tolerance	Drought Tolerance	Method of Establishment
Bahia	statewide	acid	poor	poor	very good	good	excellent	seed or sod
Bermuda	statewide	acid or alkaline	excellent	poor to fair	poor to fair	excellent	excellent	seed or sod
carpet grass	wet areas	acid	poor	poor	poor	poor	very poor	seed
centipede	Panhandle	acid	poor	poor	poor	poor	fair	seed or sod
St. Augustine	statewide	acid or alkaline	good	fair to good	fair to good	fair to good	good	sod
Zoysia	statewide	acid or alkaline	good	fair	poor	excellent	excellent	sod

ADAPTED FROM *THE FLORIDA LAWN HANDBOOK*

Bermuda need frequent mowing to look their best while Bahia, carpet grass, and centipede require far less attention. Bermuda and St. Augustine generally require regular feeding, but centipede, Bahia, and carpet grass do well with less frequent applications of fertilizer.

Having recorded all of Bubba's answers and analyzed the results, you now have a good idea of which grass you need. If it's not the type you currently have, kill the existing grass by spraying it with Roundup according to label directions. Then plant new grass, either by seeding or sodding. Seeding is cheaper but takes longer to produce a thick lawn, and not all grasses are available as seed. Sodding produces an instant lawn, but the initial cost can be expensive, depending on the grass type you choose.

The last three things you and Bubba need to discuss are watering, fertilizing, and mowing. So first tell him this—stop watering for 20 minutes every day. Light, frequent watering produces shallow roots and increases disease and insect problems. Instead, water deeply, applying ¾ to 1 inch of water each time (you can measure this by placing some empty glasses beneath the sprinklers). Don't water again until the grass looks dry (indicated by a bluish-gray cast or footprints that remain in the lawn). Water in early morning, not midday or night.

Don't go nuts with fertilizer either. You'll encourage disease and pest problems. Select a slow-release fertilizer formulated for your type of grass that contains nitrogen and potassium (most Florida soils have adequate phosphorus for growing turf). Apply at the rate specified on the bag. In North Florida, feed your lawn after the grass has completely greened up; in Central Florida, the best time to feed is in March; and in South Florida, apply the fertilizer as needed at any time. A supplemental feeding of nitrogen at the rate specified on the label in May or June will give Bubba's lawn the bright green color he craves.

Finally, don't scalp the lawn. Mowing too short increases insect, disease, and weed problems. Plus, you'll have to water more often. Mow Bahia at 3 to 4 inches; Bermuda at ½ to 1½ inches; carpet grass at 1 to 2 inches; centipede at 1 to 2 inches; St. Augustine at 2 to 4 inches; and Zoysia at 1 to 2 inches.

That's a lot of info to absorb, I know, but Bubba can handle it. After all, he did learn to work his HDTV.

The Florida Lawn Handbook, published by the University of Florida, is a good source of Florida lawn care information. Copies cost $19.95 plus tax and $4 shipping. To order call 1-800-226-1764. Be sure to mention the item number, SP45. ◆

Phlomis fruticosa

Phlomis russelliana

Two Plants, One Name

JERUSALEM SAGE
At a Glance

Size: 2 to 4 feet high and wide depending on species
Light: full sun
Soil: well drained
Pests: none serious
Prune: immediately after flowering
Propagation: seeds, cuttings
Range: all but Tropical South

Neither rain nor sleet nor bark of Rottweiler keeps tax assessors from making their appointed rounds. But obviously the chowderheads responsible for naming plants don't mind taking a little time off. How else can you explain two fine, under-appreciated perennials both being named Jerusalem sage?

The first Jerusalem sage *(Phlomis fruticosa)* grows 2 to 3 feet high and wide, featuring crinkled, gray-green leaves with soft, woolly undersides. In late spring and early summer, tiers of bright yellow flowers resembling candelabras appear up and down the stems. The show never fails to inspire two questions: "What the heck is that?" and "Where can I get some?"

Jerusalem sage number two *(P. russelliana)* looks a lot like the first one but is bigger in every way. Its soft yellow flower clusters are larger; its dull green leaves, 3 to 6 inches long, are about three times as large; and it grows 3 to 4 feet tall and wide.

Thanks to sprawling habits of growth, both sages make excellent filler plants for a mixed border. The grayish foliage of *P. fruticosa* is especially valuable, because you can use it between oranges, reds, and pinks to keep strong colors from clashing. Growing either plant is easy, easy. All they need are lots of sun and excellent drainage. Both tolerate drought well and are seldom bothered by pests.

Gardening is confusing enough without having two plants with the same name, so I have a simple solution. *P. fruticosa* is Jerusalem sage on odd-numbered days; *P. russelliana* is Jerusalem sage on even-numbered days. There, doesn't that make much more sense? STEVE BENDER

Beauty in the Bluegrass

Kentucky gives this garden character. Simple flowers give it style and grace.

IMAGINE KENTUCKY IN MAY—gentle hills of bluegrass, long undulating fences, and high-strung horses, restless in their paddocks. The season brings warm breezes carrying the fragrance of flowers, a reminder that spring's visit is brief. But for now, white hydrangeas, purple spiderworts, and orange daylilies brighten gardens, saluting the skies in unison before the hot days of summer arrive to quell their displays. Such is the scene at Kay Bullitt's garden, Oxmoor Farm, in Louisville.

BY GENE B. BUSSELL / PHOTOGRAPHY VAN CHAPLIN / STYLING CARI SOUTH

previous pages: (page 100) Through the vine-covered arbor, you can view the rock garden. (page 101, clockwise from top, left) 'Crimson Pygmy' barberry surrounds the birdbath. The edge of the terrace garden is brightened by yellow lilies. 'Annabelle' hydrangea has clouds of white blooms. Soft shadows pass through a classic gate.

This thoughtfully designed garden of simple flowers stages engaging displays of color throughout the year. But none can match the vibrant beauty that blooms here in spring. Whether you are a beginning gardener or an experienced one, consider this Kentucky treasure a gracious guide for the garden of your dreams.

Beginnings

Designed by pioneer landscape architect Marian Coffin in the early 1900s, this garden had a significant beginning. A native New Yorker, Coffin was one of the first female landscape architects in the country. When no established firms

Whether you are a beginning gardener or an experienced one, consider this Kentucky treasure a gracious guide for the garden of your dreams.

would hire her, she formed her own company, eventually attracting commissions from such prominent clients as Henry Francis du Pont. She is perhaps best known for her design of Winterthur, du Pont's Delaware garden.

Her work is still very evident at Oxmoor Farm, where her plan remains virtually intact, along with many of the original plantings. Coffin created a series of gardens and views that related to the entries of the house and the fields beyond. Structures and paths were softened by both formal and informal plantings of trees, shrubs, and perennials. Crabapples, hemlocks, and cornelian cherries defined the views, outlined the various gardens, and were accented by shrubs such as pearl bush, lilac, and Rose of Sharon. Perennials such as daylilies, iris, peonies, and yuccas provided dependable color and texture.

The Gardeners

Over the years, several gardeners have nurtured Oxmoor Farm, including Kay

top, far left: Kay Bullitt and Patrick Snider discuss the garden. **above, far left:** With their bold foliage, hostas define the border garden. **above:** Looking down the path in the border garden, you see white hydrangeas and multicolored annuals leading to a rose-covered arbor. **left:** A majestic green ash graces the other end of the border garden.

above, right: Beloved horses and hounds have a final resting place amid orange daylilies. **above, far right:** In the shade of a dogwood tree, white rocking chairs provide a cool spot to watch a sunset. **right:** Yellow, blue, and chartreuse conifers form the backbone of the rock garden.

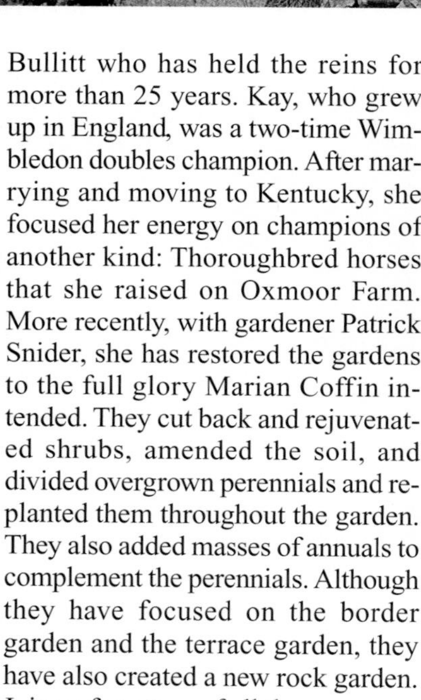

Bullitt who has held the reins for more than 25 years. Kay, who grew up in England, was a two-time Wimbledon doubles champion. After marrying and moving to Kentucky, she focused her energy on champions of another kind: Thoroughbred horses that she raised on Oxmoor Farm. More recently, with gardener Patrick Snider, she has restored the gardens to the full glory Marian Coffin intended. They cut back and rejuvenated shrubs, amended the soil, and divided overgrown perennials and replanted them throughout the garden. They also added masses of annuals to complement the perennials. Although they have focused on the border garden and the terrace garden, they have also created a new rock garden. Join us for a tour of all three.

The Border Garden

A majestic green ash anchors one end of the long path through the border garden. A simple arbor, graced with a climbing 'New Dawn' rose, serves as the entry. Easy-to-grow shrubs such as pearl bush, butterfly bush, and large groups of 'Annabelle' hydrangeas form the backdrop here. Perennials planted en masse scatter dependable color and texture throughout this garden. Daylilies, iris, spiderworts, and yuccas enjoy the area with full sun. Peonies, hardy begonias, and hostas thrive in partial sun.

Annuals bring the final touches to the garden, and Kay and Patrick are careful to select hardy ones that can take the heat of a Kentucky summer. Their favorites include 'Derby' melampodium, 'Purple Wave' and 'Pink Wave' petunias, 'Limelight' and 'Copper Queen' coleus, and several selections of impatiens. "The one thing I have learned from Kay," volunteers Patrick, "is to have lots of variety."

The Terrace Garden

Designed as a series of circles from the house, the terrace garden, too, is very simple. Brick paths form a figure eight crowned with the white gazebo at one end. A black reflecting pool in the center lawn reflects its crisp image. Kay likes to plant this area with annuals accented with a few perennials. Her choices of perennials include orange daylilies, blue-leaved hostas, and white astilbe. For annuals Kay prefers 'Climax' marigolds, Grape Cooler and Rose Cooler Series vincas, and white Madness Series petunias, which perfume spring evenings with their fragrances. Kay also includes Johnny-jump-ups, one of her old favorites.

top, left: Yellow and pink yarrow *(Achillea)* line the paths in the rock garden. **top, right:** Pin oaks form an allée on the entry drive to Oxmoor Farm. **above:** Spiky branches of barberry accent the rock garden.

The Rock Garden

Full of easy-to-maintain color, the rock garden is a careful addition to Coffin's original design. Stone-lined paths meander through a multitude of conifers and lead past a small water garden and birdbath. Forming the bones of the area, the conifers include 'Sunkist' arborvitae, hinoki false cypress, 'Fernspray Gold' cypress, and 'Wichita Blue' juniper. 'Crimson Pygmy' barberry, 'Bloodgood' Japanese maple, and nandina were included to complement the shades of green seen in the conifers.

The perennials echo the warm and cool colors found elsewhere in the garden, including the red of the building's brick walls and the various greens found in the conifers. Yellow, purple, and wine-colored columbines bloom early in the season, followed by pink, yellow, and white yarrow. 'August Moon,' 'Krossa Regal,' and variegated hostas are used for both foliage and flowers. 'Ruffled Apricot' daylily and 'The Fairy' rose also make bright additions. Patrick says the rose is a knockout that will bloom the entire summer.

All gardens grow and change through the seasons and, like friendships, they blossom into something beautiful with care and sharing. As spring moves forward and horses gallop in the bluegrass, the sun spotlights a landscape dotted with red cedars among outcrops of limestone. On the paths that lead from the gardens of Oxmoor Farm to the fences and fields beyond, the warm Kentucky breeze reminds us to savor the glory that is spring.

far left: In the rock garden, delicate pink petals of yarrow add color. **left:** At the end of the day, trees cast long shadows on the lawn. **below:** The gazebo is reflected in the dark, still pool of the terrace garden.

Crepe myrtle and watermelon both mean summertime in the South *(See pages 110–112.)*

June

Garden Checklist 108

Colorful Crepe Myrtles 110
these easy-to-grow trees keep blooming all summer long

Pool Your Resources 113
plants and stonework tie a landscape together

Tigers in the Garden 114
this spotted lily is known for its striking flowers

Walk This Way 115
a new pergola adds charm to the back of a house

Vertical Vegetables 116
creative ways to support your vegetables

No Longer in Morning 117
dwarf morning glory keeps its flowers open all day long

Playing With a Full Deck 118
a deck enlargement that makes room for the garden

Frogs and Flowers 120
flower arranging made easy

Good Looks, No Fuss 121
brick edging creates an elegant and easy-care yard

Essential Herbs 122
some little-known herbs for your garden

Hanging-Basket Liners 123
a great alternative to plastic pots

Garden Paradise 124
lush foliage and colorful flowers surround this home

garden checklist
JUNE

Editor's Notebook

PHOTOGRAPH: SYLVIA MARTIN

Every now and then, a garden needs an extra spot of color. And what better way to provide it than with a supremely tasteful gazing ball? This spherical garden ornament, so popular in Victorian times, is all the rage now too. It gets its name from its ability to capture the image of your garden on its shiny surface.

Gazing balls come in lots of different colors, from blue that evokes the color of the sky to green that matches the color of the money people make by convincing you to buy the dang things. Some are acrylic, some are stainless steel, but the prettiest ones are made of glass. I used to have a blue glass gazing ball until my son Brian, age 2 at the time, confused it with his basketball and dunked it on our deck.

If you fear a similar disaster, Liz Tedder of Newnan, Georgia, has the answer—a colorful and classic bowling ball. It's attractive, durable, and practically shatter-proof. And it scares the dickens out of those pesky gophers.

—STEVE BENDER

TIPS

- **Garden notes**—The summer solstice on June 21, which is also the longest day of the year, marks the beginning of the season. If you didn't start a garden journal this spring, there's still plenty of time. Keeping a small notebook of your observations throughout the seasons is a great idea for beginning gardeners.
- **Ground covers**—In the shade, ground covers can be a good alternative to lawns. Cast-iron plant, liriope, mondo grass, Asiatic jasmine, and ferns are good choices. Before planting, lightly till the area, being careful not to damage tree roots excessively. Water daily for the first two weeks, then taper waterings to every other day and eventually to every third day. Immediately after planting, broadcast 6 pounds of 15-5-15 fertilizer per 1,000 square feet. Wash the fertilizer off the foliage. Fertilize again in six to eight weeks.
- **Mulch**—Conserve moisture in soil with at least 2 to 3 inches of shredded pine bark or pine straw.
- **Nurture plants**—Young trees and shrubs should have deep, thorough waterings at regular intervals. The next few months will be crucial to new root establishment. Fertilizing shrubs and trees during their first year isn't necessary, but water-soluble fertilizer may be applied after vigorous growth begins.
- **Planting flowers**—Replace your spring plants that are past their prime with ones more tolerant of hot summers. Sun-loving annuals include moss rose, salvia, pentas, and narrow-leaf zinnia. Perennials such as lantana, butterfly bush, verbena, and coneflower will provide color for sunny areas year after year. In the shade, try impatiens, caladium, Brazilian plume (Jacobinia), and ginger.
- **Vegetables**—Harvest squash, okra, beans, and cucumbers regularly to ensure a constant supply of tender vegetables. Pick every other day, either in the early morning or in the late afternoon.
- **Water conservation**—Use your irrigation system early in the day to reduce water loss through evaporation. Infrequent, deep watering is better than frequent, shallow watering as it promotes deeper root growth. Soaker hoses can be an efficient way to water newly planted trees and shrubs. Hide the hose by using 2 inches of pine straw or pine bark mulch. The mulch will also help reduce water loss.

PLANT

- **Drought-tolerant annuals**—There is time to set out transplants of narrow-leaf zinnia, globe amaranth, moss rose, celosia, and marigold. These easy annuals will provide dependable, carefree color and need minimal watering.
- **Hibiscus**—The Chinese (tender) types and the modern mallow hybrids such as 'Moy Grande,' 'Lady Baltimore,' and the Disco Belle Series offer nonstop, easy-care color. Because hibiscus are sensitive to frost, gardeners often place them in large containers that can be moved during winter.

Daylilies

Add or transplant new ones to your garden while they are in bloom. That way you can choose the colors, sizes, and flower forms you prefer. Thousands of selections are available, and new selections are added annually. Reliable favorites include 'Mary Todd,' 'Hyperion,' 'Stella de Oro,' 'Ida's Magic,' and 'Happy Returns.'

■ **Moonflowers**—Sow seeds of moonflowers to brighten your summer nights with sweet-scented, white beacons of light. Flowers open in the early evening and are great to watch unfold. This annual vine will need a trellis or an arbor to climb. Nick the seed, and soak it in warm water overnight to soften the seed coat before planting.

■ **Summer tubers and bulbs**—Add cannas, dahlias, gladioli, blackberry lilies, montbretias, and caladiums to your garden for bold foliage and bright flowers.

■ **Sunflowers**—These annuals are drought tolerant, sun loving, and easy to grow from seed. The cheerful flowers will brighten your garden until fall. When the seedheads dry out, they'll even provide food for the birds. A very large selection is available, both in size and color. Try selections such as 'Mammoth,' 'Sunbeam,' 'Italian White,' and 'Sonja.'

PRUNE

■ **Trim**—Many annuals and perennials need to be reshaped now to encourage a new surge of flowering. Carefully prune rose stems down to just above the first leaf with five leaflets to divert energy from seedpod development into new blooms. Shorten leggy or lopsided growth on shrubs and perennials. Cut back overly ambitious perennials to keep them compact.

CONTROL

■ **Poison ivy**—This pesky vine can be spot-sprayed. Carefully use Roundup or Brush-B-Gon herbicides as directed on the label. Only spray when the wind is not blowing to avoid herbicide drift, which injures desirable plants nearby. To kill large vines growing up trees, cut the vines at their bases. The part of the vine above the cut will die. Spray the new growth each time it resprouts.

FERTILIZE

■ **Applying iron to the lawn**—If your lawn is growing well but the color looks a little pale, use iron to green it up. Use either liquid sources of iron or ferrous sulfate. If you opt for the liquid, follow the directions on the bottle. If you go with ferrous sulfate, mix 2 ounces in 3 to 5 gallons of water and apply over 1,000 square feet. Both can be purchased at home garden centers.

■ **Maintenance**—Plantings of moss rose, hybrid purslane, and sedum should be aerated, fertilized, and watered to encourage growth and blooming. Aerating allows water and fertilizer to penetrate the soil.

Enhance Summer Color

Use heat-loving annuals such as zinnias, with their variety of heights and colors. The smallest are the Zinnia angustifolia hybrids such as the Pinwheel Series with bright, compact blooms of yellow, pink, or white. Medium zinnias such as the 'Cut and Come Again Mix' in shades of red, pink, yellow, lavender, and purple and large types such as the State Fair Series add height to the back of the flowerbed. Zinnias combine well with society garlic, which has evergreen tufts of long slender leaves and spheres of small light purple flowers that will bloom throughout the season.

June notes:

Tip of the Month

Pipe cleaners, with their fuzzy, soft surfaces, make the best fasteners for securing plants and flowers to supports. They are easy to bend and won't bruise the tender stalks and stems.

CHARLOTTE BRYANT
GREENSBURG, KENTUCKY

Colorful C

Summertime wouldn't be complete without a slice of watermelon and the brilliant blooms of this Southern classic.

Crepe Myrtles

We Southerners share certain memories—the smell of a freshly mowed lawn, the high-pitched cry of cicadas on sweltering days, the juicy taste of sweet watermelon, and the vision of huge crepe myrtles bent low by the weight of their blooms.

Although native to China, crepe myrtles have set deep roots in our Southern soil, becoming a part of both our landscape and our traditions. This time of year they dress up historic cities such as New Orleans, Savannah, and Charleston, South Carolina. They also grace many of our own private gardens, a sign of their enduring popularity.

And why not? These easy-to-grow trees possess many outstanding features. Sinewy and strong, crepe myrtles have gray, tan, or cinnamon-hued branches that bear glorious clouds of colorful, long-lasting blooms starting in June. In the fall, they dependably produce radiant foliage in reds, oranges, and yellows. Winter reveals their exfoliating bark, which makes their naturally sculpted trunks look like living works of art.

Crepe myrtles boast year-round appeal, but in the heat of summer they show their true colors, from red and pink to lavender, purple, and white. Widely available, they can be found at most any nursery or garden center, and this is a great time to purchase them because you can see exactly what color you're getting. Just remember, if you plant them now, give them lots of water to help them adjust to the garden and promote new root growth.

They Keep on Blooming

Unlike spring's cherry trees, with delicate flowers that may last only a week or two, crepe myrtles can bloom all summer. Light tip pruning or snipping off old blooms will encourage more flowers (see "Pruning Tips" on page 112). Although tip pruning may be recommended, heavy cutbacks (sometimes called crepe murder) in late winter or early spring are never a good idea. Many people who don't know better cut back trees in February or March, leaving only 4- or 5-foot trunks sticking up out of the ground. This ruins the natural shape of the trees. It

left: Crepe myrtles sprinkle their paper-like blooms onto this sidewalk. These old trees also provide shade from the hot summer sun.

BY CHARLIE THIGPEN / PHOTOGRAPHY VAN CHAPLIN

above: Watermelon red is a popular color of crepe myrtle. They also come in pink, purple, lavender, and white.

also causes multiple shoots to sprout from the cut-back point. Trees then grow so thick that air circulation is reduced, making the plants more susceptible to aphids, sooty mold, and powdery mildew. The numerous branches also create too heavy a load, which can cause them to split or crack during heavy rains or high winds.

Know a crepe myrtle's mature height before you plant it. If you don't want it to be too big, look for a low-growing selection (see chart at right). Crepe myrtles range in height from 2 feet to 30 feet. Trees such as 'Natchez' or 'Tuscarora' reach 25 to 30 feet in height. 'Sioux' and 'Regal Red' are medium-size selections that will grow only 12 to 15 feet tall. These medium trees are perfect for a small courtyard or patio. Breeders also market dwarf selections. Some of those, such as 'Chickasaw' and 'Pokomoke,' have been around for a while, and many new dwarf selections have been introduced in recent years. A number of trees grow less than 3 feet tall.

Crepe myrtles have many landscape uses. They can be planted together to make a large hedge or screen, or a single tree can act as a specimen to create a distinctive focal point. Some of the smaller growing selections even look great in large containers.

These trees do need a sunny site to grow full and bloom heavily. Left in the shade, they become leggy and produce few flowers. Crepe myrtles also may suffer from cold damage in cooler climates, so if you live in the Upper South, be sure to plant cold-hardy selections such as 'Acoma,' 'Centennial Spirit,' or 'Hopi.'

If you've already planted a crepe myrtle that's overgrowing its boundary, you might want to move it. These trees may be transplanted easily, and only a small root ball is needed for success. It's best to move them in late fall or winter, when they're leafless and dormant.

When you need a small tree and have a sunny spot, make a point to try a crepe myrtle. This classic plant will beat the heat and make your summer garden more colorful and memorable. ◆

CREPE MYRTLES— IN THREE SIZES

Large

- 'Centennial Spirit'—20 feet tall, dark red flowers
- 'Muskogee'—20 feet tall, lavender flowers
- 'Natchez'—30 feet tall, white flowers
- 'Tuscarora'—23 feet tall, dark coral flowers

Medium

- 'Acoma'—10 to 14 feet tall, white flowers
- 'Sioux'—15 feet tall, bright pink flowers
- 'Yuma'—15 feet tall, lavender flowers
- 'Regal Red'—12 feet tall, deep red flowers

Small

- 'Centennial'—3 feet tall, bright purple flowers
- 'Chickasaw'—3 feet tall, pink flowers
- 'Pixie White'—24 inches tall, white flowers
- 'Worlds Fair'—24 inches tall, deep red flowers

PRUNING TIPS

Once crepe myrtles have bloomed and shed their flowers, they will set seed. The small round seedpods or capsules usually weigh the limbs down, making them sag. Using a sharp pair of clippers or hedge trimmers, cut off the seedpods. New shoots with buds will quickly appear, and you will get a second bloom.

Sometimes people are hesitant to remove seedpods because they think the round capsules are flowerbuds. This is not so. The seedpods are larger than the flowerbuds and extremely hard.

If temperatures stay warm into the fall and you continue to remove spent flowers, you may even get a third or fourth bloom out of your crepe myrtles.

WHY IT WORKS

This design succeeds because:

- The pool fits in with the surrounding garden.
- Graceful curves give a natural look.
- Flagstone paving is richer looking and less reflective than concrete.
- The pool's dark color appears natural.
- Plantings add color, contrast, and privacy.
- The waterfall provides soothing sounds.

Pool Your Resources

Plants, stonework, and a natural look tie this landscape together.

Ask real estate agents about adding a pool, and they'll all tell you the same thing: Put it in because you want it, but don't expect to recoup your money. Well, here's a pool that's the landscaping equivalent of buying a blue-chip stock at $1 a share.

Put simply, it's one of the prettiest pools I've ever seen. Planned by garden and interior designer Charles W. Freeman of St. Louis, it's a superb example of how integrating a pool into a landscape can supply beauty and recreation, as well as many happy returns.

Too often, homeowners plop a pool into any unoccupied portion of the yard that's large enough to hold it, giving no thought as to how it will impact its surroundings. But from the onset, Charles thought of this pool as the center of a garden. The owner wanted a naturalistic, informal look that would harmonize with a nearby cottage garden. So Charles gave the pool graceful curves instead of straight lines, and he added the gentle splash of a shallow waterfall. He used flagstone for the pool terrace, rather than blinding white concrete, and stacked native stone boulders by the steps. Then he wrapped the entire pool area with lush plantings of trees, shrubs, perennials, and ground covers to tie it to the garden.

Thanks to the imaginative combinations of colors, shapes, and textures, the plantings have impact from near and far. The burgundy leaves of 'Crimson Queen' Japanese maples contrast with the blue-greens and yellow-greens of hostas, ferns, and leucothoe. Ferns rise beside the cascading, soft mounds of maples. Bold hosta leaves, juxtaposed with foliage of ferns and maples, clamor for attention. On a still day, water mirrors the images of all.

Notice the dark color of the pool. The robin's-egg blue you often see would have looked artificial. To avoid that, the sides and bottom of the wet gunite shell were painted a blue-gray to make the water seem deeper and more natural. The stonework also merits scrutiny. Charles decided to use Oklahoma flagstone, which blends bluish-gray stones with rusty-brown ones to enhance the natural look. Extending the flagstone for several inches over the water makes the pool seem like a grotto.

The result? A beautiful, peaceful, private place to enjoy a quiet morning, a sunny afternoon, or the end of the day. This pool is one investment that has rewarded its owner handsomely. STEVE BENDER

PHOTOGRAPHS: ALLEN ROKACH

top: This pool is integrated into the garden. **above:** The burgundy leaves of Japanese maples seem to float like clouds among the blues and greens of hostas and ferns.

TIGER LILY
At a Glance

Size: 3 to 6 feet tall
Light: sun to partial shade
Soil: garden soil, well drained, lots of organic matter
Moisture: Water sparingly.
Pests: none serious
Propagation: Plant bulbs in fall or early spring; plant bulbils a few weeks after flowering.
Range: all zones
Bloom: roughly May through June in Lower South, June through August in Middle South, July through September or later in Upper South

Tigers in the Garden

This spotted lily is still burning bright.

You can't miss these distinctive felines. Flashy curls of orange petals dappled with dark spots, a long sweep of stamens, and a 3- to 6-foot-tall stem make these lilies an outstanding addition to any planting. It's no wonder that gardeners have adored these striking flowers for the last 200 years.

Tiger lilies (*Lilium lancifolium*, formerly *L. tigrinum*) are a traditional cottage-garden favorite. Despite their fierce name, tiger lilies are surprisingly easy to grow throughout the South. They're much less fussy about soils and moisture and having their roots shaded than many of the Oriental and Asiatic lilies, so they're a perfect first lily for beginners. They're also super for a child's garden, because they're gaudy and nontoxic—and have an undeniably great name.

For the quickest results, plant tiger lily bulbs either in fall or early spring, in a sunny site with good drainage. With prepared garden soil containing plenty of organic matter, they won't need any extra fertilizer. Plant the bulbs 6 to 8 inches deep, and space them about 8 inches apart. You can also start tiger lilies by planting the tiny bulbils that form during blooming season. These look like fat purple seeds tucked in where the leaves join the stalk. Collect some of the bulbils a few weeks after flowering, and plant them 1 to 2 inches deep to increase your own tribe of tigers. Or share the spares with friends. Tiger lilies take several years to reach maturity if grown from bulbils, but the price is definitely right.

With up to 12 vivid flowers adorning each stalk, dramatic tiger lilies are among the long-blooming delights of the summer garden. If you haven't grown them for a while, perhaps it's time to get some back into your flowerbeds. LIZ DRUITT

THE TRUTH ABOUT TIGERS

- Easy-to-grow tiger lilies are highly resistant to mosaic virus, but they can still carry it. Tigers should be planted far enough away from other lilies (beds on opposite sides of the house, for example) so that aphids can't spread any infection from one to the other.
- Tiger-spotted lilies are now commercially available in several different colors. While these are in the Asiatic lily group and not quite the same as the true tiger, they have a similar effect. Try one of the white, yellow, red, pink, or salmon selections. There's even a new, more compact Asiatic lily selection called 'Tiger Babies,' with large salmon-peach flowers and a chocolate-pink reverse. These tiger-type lilies are a little more demanding than the true tiger, but all have endearing dark freckles.

PHOTOGRAPH: ALLEN ROKACH

PHOTOGRAPHS: VAN CHAPLIN

Walk This Way

A new pergola adds style and a welcoming air to this beachside home.

When guests arrive at the oceanfront home of Joshua and Betty Darden, they often report being drawn to the back of the home as if by some unseen force. Many believe it's the call of the ocean waves or the caressing sea breezes. Or it might have something to do with the moon phases and tidal cycles. But more than likely, it's the enchanting new pergola.

Bill Pinkham of Smithfield Gardens in Suffolk, Virginia, suggested this structure to lead guests down the path from the street-side parking court to the beachside deck. Besides drawing visitors to the opposite side of the house, the pergola also adds depth and character to the facade of this Virginia Beach home.

Built To Last

Bill worked with another member of the Smithfield Gardens staff, architect Anne Urbi, to design the pergola, which consists of two parallel rows of six columns each, with open rafters overhead. The pergola is fastened with galvanized nails and stainless steel screws that resist corrosion in the salty air. Although treated pine and white cedar are less expensive choices for outdoor structures, the Dardens decided on redwood because it will resist twisting and splitting. After applying an oil-based primer to the wood, they added a white stain to match the trim on the house.

Bill also included a stone path beneath the arbor and a low concrete retaining wall parallel to the structure. Before the wall was built, the small slope falling away from the house was too steep for a level path. The existing topsoil was essentially sand, so Bill backfilled behind the wall with a mix of one-third compost, one-third sand, and one-third topsoil.

Resilient Plants

Horticulturist Linda Pinkham, Bill's wife, stepped in to add durable plantings that soften the structure. Even with improved soil, tough plants, and regular watering and fertilizing, beach plantings need longer to get established. The Pinkhams chose 'Becky' Shasta daisies (*Chrysanthemum* x *superbum* 'Becky') to place along one side of the path, while rose campions (*Lychnis coronaria* 'Alba') fill out the other side with silvery foliage and white blooms. 'Preziosa' hydrangeas (*Hydrangea serrata* 'Preziosa') thrive in the niche between the pergola and the house, where they are protected from strong winds, salt spray, and ruthless sun.

top: The Dardens' pergola is an open invitation that brings guests from street side to beachside. **above:** Gardener Rita Rawls prunes the Shasta daisies and white rose campions to open up the path.

A variety of hardy climbers was planted by the pergola's posts to twine their way skyward. Trumpet honeysuckle *(Lonicera sempervirens),* hybrid trumpet creeper (*Campsis tagliabuana* 'Madame Galen'), and sweet autumn clematis *(Clematis terniflora)* are beginning to temper the hard lines of the pergola. The clematis also adds colorful, fragrant blooms from spring until fall and provides shade for the people and plants below.

Thanks to Bill and Linda's shrewd choices of materials and plants, the project is a big success. Although it seemed that all the forces of nature were working against them in the beginning, the pergola and the plantings are now right at home.

GLENN R. DINELLA

Vertical Vegetables

Many vegetables are like trapeze artists; they can twist and turn high above the ground. These daredevil plants put on an aerial show while dangling from a mere piece of twine. Vegetables, in fact, are actually healthier when they are airborne. Grown above the ground, they are less susceptible to soil-borne diseases.

Gardeners with a limited amount of space may want to take advantage of this trait and train their vegetables to grow on trellises or through cages. Some vegetables, such as pole beans and cucumbers, climb naturally, while others, such as tomatoes or eggplants, may have to be coaxed to make the upward push. Plants growing vertically take up much less room, freeing up space for other plantings and increasing your garden's productivity per square foot.

Trellises or plant supports don't have to be expensive. Bamboo is a good example—it's often free. People who have bamboo growing in their yards will probably be glad to let you harvest a little, because it is often considered a weed. Bamboo stakes usually last a couple of growing seasons before they become too brittle.

Build little tepees of bamboo for beans and peas, tying the pieces together with sisal twine. The twine is heavy enough to hold plants yet decomposes naturally over time. Use it in the garden for the growing season, and then roll it up and dispose of it in the compost bin.

Metal rebar (available at home-center stores) works well when building trellises or plant supports. Rebar is strong, supports heavy plants, and is easy to drive into the ground with a hammer. It's also durable and can be used for years.

These supports and trellises are great tools for gardeners. They require a little work to set up, but in the long run they make gardening more efficient by keeping your tastiest prizes up off the ground so that snails, slugs, sowbugs, and ground beetles can't damage them. In addition, harvesting mature vegetables is much easier.

CHARLIE THIGPEN

WILLING PERFORMERS

- beans
- peas
- cucumbers
- tomatoes
- Malabar spinach

top: This trellis adds a design element to the vegetable garden. Fashioned from twine and bamboo, it makes an attractive and functional support for cucumber vines. **above:** To hold these white eggplants off the ground, we used a single bamboo stake for each plant. **above, right:** Keep vegetables standing tall with tepees made of bamboo and twine.

PHOTOGRAPHS: JEAN ALLSOPP

No Longer in Morning

Everything people know about morning glory goes pretty much like this—it's an annual vine with showy flowers that open at dawn and close by noon. But when it comes to this old-fashioned type of morning glory, everything that everyone knows is wrong.

Most often seen in older or historic gardens, dwarf morning glory *(Convolvulus tricolor)* forms a sprawling mound. It isn't a vine, and it doesn't climb. This lesser-known plant makes an excellent filler between annuals and perennials. And here is the best part of all—unlike the vining morning glory, the dwarf one keeps its flowers open all day long.

The mature plant is only about a foot tall, so dwarf morning glory is great for massing at the front of the border. You can also use it in hanging baskets and window boxes. It thrives in hot weather and will be happy to bloom all summer as long as it's watered moderately during dry spells.

To speed germination, start this annual from seeds that have been soaked in water for 24 hours. Then, after your last frost date in spring, sow them ⅛ inch deep in the garden. For earlier flowers, start seeds indoors five to six weeks before your last frost date. If soil is reasonably fertile, you won't need to feed dwarf morning glory very often. Just apply a water-soluble 20-20-20 fertilizer two to three times during the course of the growing season.

A number of catalogs carry seeds for this easygoing annual. Flower colors include magenta red, deep blue, pink, and white. Left to themselves, plants will reseed, but the colors of the flowers may not be true.

Now you know the rest of the story on beautiful morning glories. They're not just for morning anymore. ◆

DWARF
MORNING GLORY
At a Glance

Size: 1 foot high, 2 feet wide
Light: full sun
Soil: loose, well drained
Pests: none serious
Uses: bedding plants, window boxes, and hanging baskets
Range: throughout the South

By midsummer, the Williamses' deck is a haven enveloped by colorful flowers and foliage.

Playing With a Full Deck

People enlarge their decks for many reasons, but this homeowner just needed room to grow.

Even before she moved into her new house in Acworth, Georgia, Barbara Williams knew the existing 20- x 10-foot builder deck was going to be too cramped. Although her first instinct was to expand it immediately, she took time to plan and build it right. "The first summer we were here I walked around in the backyard a lot and studied the way the sun moved across the back of the house," Barbara says. "Then I came up with the design of the decks." Now, a new two-level structure gives her 1,100 square feet of planting space.

At the height of summer, Barbara's deck bursts at the seams with containers that billow over with creative combinations of annuals, perennials, shrubs, and even small trees such as Japanese maples *(Acer palmatum)* and Harry Lauder's walking stick (*Corylus avellana* 'Contorta'). In some areas, guests have to walk single file to move between the bountiful pots, which seem to multiply just as quickly as her beautiful plants do.

Barbara clearly believes that more is more, but she never plants more than she can maintain. Although some friends and family have accused her of overdoing it, she has an answer for that. "I say the front yard is for landscaping. I keep everything neat and trimmed out there, but the backyard is my space."

Tricks of the Trade

Barbara recommends a method she calls the hidden pot technique. If she has a plant she knows will fade before summer's end, she sometimes leaves it in its plastic nursery pot and places it in the center of a large container surrounded by showy plants that cover the plastic pot. When the center plant is past its peak, she can easily lift it out and replace it with a fresh one without disturbing the surrounding plants.

Barbara's experience has taught her a few other things as well. "I

PHOTOGRAPHS: ALLEN ROKACH

above, center: Pot feet prevent containers from resting directly on the deck. This helps with drainage and prevents unsightly stains and damage to the wood. **above:** To get the best selection, Barbara Williams knows the delivery days when all the local garden centers receive shipments. She often shops for plants as they are being unloaded by the wholesale growers.

far left: Because they receive wind from all sides, these hanging baskets lined with moss dry out quickly.
left: This pairing of variegated aucuba and red caladiums is stunning.
below: Barbara's lush border garden is composed of plants that outgrew their pots or had to be transferred at the end of the season to prevent them from freezing. When the border fills up, she gives plants to friends.

learned the hard way that you should water the lower deck first," she says. "Because it drips all over you if you do the upper deck first and then come down below." Barbara and Wendell recently solved the dripping problem by installing Dry-B-Lo, a system of aluminum channels and gutters underneath the upper deck to keep the lower one clean and dry.

Water, Soil, and Fertilizer

Barbara diligently checks her plants every morning during warmer months to see if they need water. She uses water-saving crystals in the porous terra-cotta pots and hanging baskets, which have a tendency to dry out on her raised deck where wind hits them from all sides.

She gives her plants a good start with a quality growing mix containing sphagnum peat moss, vermiculite, perlite, and processed pine bark. "Some people make the mistake of using plain potting soil," she says, "and then plants just drown or dry out." Barbara also adds Osmocote slow-release fertilizer to the pots and occasionally uses a liquid fertilizer for an extra boost. At planting time, she often applies a liquid fertilizer at half the recommended rate to give plants a jump-start.

Color Coordinating

"I group things into little collections," Barbara says, "keeping the purples together in one area and the oranges and yellows in another space. I concentrated yellows in the corner by the French doors because they match my home's yellow interior. It's a subtle way of bringing the inside out."

She doesn't adhere strictly to any color theories, preferring to think of them as general guidelines. "You can read and read and read what the experts say, but there comes a time when you just need to try something for yourself," she says. "Sometimes I just put leftovers together, and those turn out to be the best combinations.

"I don't like things too perfect," she continues. "I like the way the rosemary goes where it wants and the Harry Lauder's walking stick is twisted and doing its own thing." Referring to a colorful pot of purple fountain grass surrounded by zinnias and variegated ivy, she says, "I envisioned something different when I planted this, but plants have minds of their own." GLENN R. DINELLA

DECK-O-RATING WITH CONTAINERS

Here are a few tips for successful container gardening on a deck or patio.

- Place pot feet under your containers to prevent stains and water damage.
- Group terra-cotta pots in one area and gray concrete pots in another.
- Pay attention to the light exposure on different areas of your deck. Group sun-loving plants in bright spots and shade lovers in darker niches.
- Cut watering time by installing a drip irrigation system in your container garden. Add a timer, and you'll only need to check periodically to make sure the system is functioning properly.
- Move a plant in full bloom into the limelight where you can enjoy it.
- Buy plant stands with casters or a hand truck to help you move heavy pots and save your back.
- Use large shrubs or vines in containers to soften a railing, create privacy, or mask a view.

left: Supported by a needle-holder frog, these hydrangeas celebrate the best of summer color. **below:** Colorful caladium foliage makes a playful arrangement with this frog. **bottom:** Hosta leaves and blooms come together for a cool summer centerpiece.

Frogs and Flowers

Don't let flower arranging intimidate you—make it simple with this sturdy device.

The summer garden produces a wealth of marvelous materials for casual arrangements. The idea of cutting a few stems of this and a few snips of that is fun and relaxing. And placing flowers in a vase in an easy-going design sounds like an effortless task. But once indoors, those inviting buds and blooms take on another life, refusing to stand in the container where you place them. Frustration is almost guaranteed.

However, flower arrangers have a secret. Their fabulous compositions—whether simple or complex—don't just happen. Certain devices make these endeavors doable; one of these is a prince of an invention known as a frog.

Placed in a vase, a frog's job is to hold flowers and foliage exactly where you want them. Depending on the stem size and arrangement style, there are a number of these implements from which to choose. One type has small needles or pins held within a container or on a heavy metal base. Another version has a sturdy metal cage that may incorporate a needle holder as well. A third type sports holes which can harbor single or multiple stems.

That said, be sure to select the correct frog for your arrangement. Small flowers and those with thin stems require only a tiny needle holder. Thick stems, tall branches, and top-heavy blooms need more support: A large metal-caged frog will work for these jobs.

Another secret: Attach the frog to the vase with a piece of florist clay or sticky-um. Place a small wad of clay on the frog's underside, press it firmly into the vessel, and then fill with water.

See and Be Seen

Frogs have been used since the 16th century, when the Japanese developed their ikebana arrangement style. As time passed, frogs turned into decorative elements shaped like lily pads, blossoms, or literally, frogs. Such items have become popular collectibles found in antiques shops and flea markets.

Large, intricate arrangements call for utilitarian mechanics that are usually hidden within the vase. But in simple everyday collections, a frog in a clear container adds appeal. Our arrangements demonstrate several simple ways to use these devices.

The hydrangea arrangement is an example of true simplicity. A needle-holder frog was used along with a narrow-necked container. The top of the vessel helps support the heavy blooms, while the needle holder provides direction for flower placement. This arrangement, assembled without a lot of fuss, illustrates the impact of displaying one type of flower in a mass.

Flower arranging needn't be serious, as shown in our collection of caladium leaves. Fashioned after an antique device, this new frog adds whimsical fun to an array of colorful and frilly foliage.

A wide, low vase is a good choice for an assortment of hosta leaves and flowers. The shape of the container allows the leaves to drape gracefully over the sides, as if they were still in the garden. The tall, lightweight frog keeps the stems in place and helps the blooms stand straight and tall.

Enjoy your garden twice as much by bringing natural beauty indoors. Flower arranging is quick and easy when you have an assortment of frogs to count on. ELLEN RUOFF RILEY

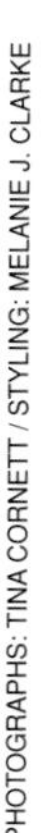
PHOTOGRAPHS: TINA CORNETT / STYLING: MELANIE J. CLARKE

PHOTOGRAPHS: VAN CHAPLIN

Good Looks, No Fuss

A small lawn is edged in brick, adding elegant form to this easy-care yard.

When you want a private backyard that looks great year-round with minimal maintenance, who are you going to call? If you live in Dallas, an excellent suggestion would be landscape architect Naud Burnett.

This particular garden borders a busy street and nearby neighbors. So Naud decided to enclose the yard with a handsome wooden fence. But because local ordinances limited how tall the fence could be, he planted tree-form 'Savannah' hollies in front of it. This effectively doubled the fence's height.

A striking elliptical lawn in the yard's center provides open recreational space. It keeps the small yard from feeling claustrophobic and takes only a few minutes to mow. To reduce maintenance time even more, Naud edged the lawn in brick. This makes it easy to give the lawn a clean, crisp edge with the mower instead of having to use a nylon-string trimmer or hand clippers.

Plantings of evergreen trees, ground covers, and shrubs around the perimeter of the yard supply attractive foliage and strong form throughout the year. Sweeps of impatiens along the brick edging add months of brightly colored flowers. Impatiens are the perfect annuals for the time-pressed homeowner because they need little upkeep besides watering.

STEVE BENDER

top: An oval lawn gives this small, fenced yard a surprisingly spacious feeling. **above, right:** Brick edging emphasizes the lawn's form while simplifying maintenance. **above:** Embraced by trees, shrubs, and ground covers, this outdoor dining area—nestled into a corner of the yard—seems peaceful and secluded.

Essential Herbs

Packs of curly parsley, sweet basil, and chives are necessities in every cook's garden. But there are other herbs that are culinary essentials—ones you may not be familiar with. "Try something different," says Calera McHenry, owner of CalMac Nursery in Cullman, Alabama. "Otherwise, you'll never know what's out there," she says. Here are some suggestions to broaden your horizons.

■ Add lemon basil to your garden. Its crisp citrus flavor is great in marinades and salad dressings. Lemon basil also makes a tasty addition to baked goods. Another herb that's a bit out of the ordinary is cinnamon basil. "It's a flavorful complement to baked apples and makes a wonderful tea," Calera says. All basils have the same requirements—full sun and well-drained soil.

■ Chives are basic, even for self-proclaimed nongardeners. Grow garlic chives for diversity. The flavor is strong, and a little goes a long way. But it's a delight to use in place of plain chives. Both types flourish in good sun and well-drained soil.

■ Curly parsley is pretty in the garden and on the plate, but the flat-leaf Italian selection offers superior taste. For unexpected flavor, plant Par-cel, a parsley cousin. "It gives that good fresh-celery flavor, but it's a cutting green—one you continually cut and use," Calera says. Try some in chicken salad. Parsley and its relatives like shade from afternoon sun in hot summer months.

When you purchase herbs, try a few new selections along with all of your old standbys. Your garden and meals will certainly benefit from diversity.

■ Thyme offers more options than days in the week. For true, strong flavor, plant tiny-leaved French thyme. Lemon thyme has slightly larger leaves and contains a healthy dose of citrusy oil. Use it in marinades for extraordinary zest. Look for caraway, lime, and lavender thymes for interesting taste. They may not all suit your palate, but they're fun to try.

Plant different flavors, and explore fresh ways to use them. You'll find new favorites that will become indispensable in your garden. ◆

Hanging-Basket Liners

Move beyond plain plastic pots. Combine wire baskets with lining materials for a natural look.

Sheet Moss

This type of moss, which ages from green to rich brown, works well in baskets and allows you to plant between the wires with small transplants, covering the basket with colorful flowers. Because sheet moss dries out quickly, baskets will require frequent watering as plants mature.

Purchase moss in sheets, not small crumbles. If you are layering it in a wire basket, you may have to overlap pieces to prevent soil from washing through weak spots.

Put a thick piece on the basket bottom, with the edges coming up the sides slightly. Add some potting mix to cover the moss. Gently push a transplant's root ball through the wires, and rest it on the soil. Repeat this process around the basket, with the roots of the plants barely touching each other. Gently work the moss around the transplants' stems and up the sides a few inches. Fill with more soil, and place another ring of flowers around the basket.

Continue this process until the basket is completely filled. Plant the top with more flowers, and water thoroughly. Look for the places where water seeps through the moss and allows soil to escape. Tuck more sheet moss around the holes, and then water again.

Coco-fiber

A natural by-product of the coconut industry, this durable liner is porous and drains well; in addition, it prevents soil from escaping. Coco-fiber is a very tough material that will last for several growing seasons. It will dry out more slowly than other materials, so water less often.

You can probably find preformed coco-fiber liners to fit specific basket sizes. Measure your basket across the top in inches, and purchase that size liner. Drop it into the wire basket form, fill with potting soil, and plant the top. If the liner doesn't fit, slit it down one side, and mold it to conform to the sides, cutting off excess.

Sphagnum Moss

The shaggy texture of this moss makes a beautiful lining. There are several ways to purchase sphagnum—you may find it packed loosely in a bag or in a dehydrated preformed basket liner. The secret to success with sphagnum is to moisten it thoroughly before using. Put loose moss in a bucket, and wet it well. Squeeze out any excess water, and place the moss in a 1-inch-thick layer inside basket.

The preformed liners may be purchased in measured sizes. Moisten the liner, and arrange it inside the basket for a snug fit. Wet it again, and you're ready to plant. ◆

garden paradise

Plants and pups live in beautiful harmony in Marion and Charlie Shaw's yard.

In Marion Shaw's garden, the dogs seem happy—and so do the flowers. In fact, if her plants had tails, they'd be wagging. This fine gardener gives her annuals, perennials, trees, and shrubs everything they need, and it shows. Lush foliage and colorful flowers surround the house. Even when the dog days of late summer arrive and most plants elsewhere have fizzled, this Rome, Georgia, garden stays in full bloom.

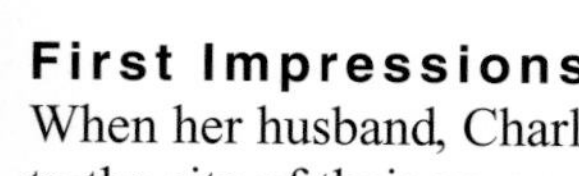

First Impressions

When her husband, Charlie, first brought her to the site of their prospective home, Marion refused to get out of the car. There was absolutely no way she would move into that ugly house. But it stood on top of a mountain, so he insisted that she take a look at the view. After Charlie agreed to update the house, Marion decided the view was pretty nice, so it was time to garden. In fact, she started landscaping before they even closed on the home.

Working Her Magic

On this hilltop, Marion has tended the soil and planted nonstop for 16 years. The hundreds of plants that thrive in her care rejoice in this well-maintained garden. The once-barren sloping lot has been transformed. If the view was nice when the house was purchased, it is absolutely breathtaking now. Standing on the back deck, you can see for miles. After admiring the distant sights, you can look anywhere in the yard and see glorious color-filled beds.

On the day before we photographed, 3 inches of rain fell on the garden, but most of the flowers were still standing tall when we arrived. The lilies had all been securely staked to bamboo and twigs so they could withstand the downpour. Marion's yard always seems to be well taken care of. As she walks among the plants, she's constantly picking up sticks, pulling unwanted weeds, or deadheading spent blooms.

BY CHARLIE THIGPEN
PHOTOGRAPHY
VAN CHAPLIN AND
SYLVIA MARTIN

A colorful arrangement picked from the garden rests in front of Marion's billowy lace cap hydrangeas. **left:** Marion has a heart of gold. Just ask her three dogs and three cats; all of the animals were once strays.

Marion has done most of the work herself, but she required a little help building a stone wall on the side of the house. Most of the rocks that form the wall, which measures 75 feet long and about 3 feet high, were dug from or picked up around the yard. When the wall was finished, it was backfilled with topsoil that was mixed with cow manure. Then annuals and perennials, which flourish from spring through fall, were planted.

She says the garden looks a little rough in the winter. She doesn't cut back any of the dead foliage on her perennials so she will know where they are located. Then each year as a special Valentine's Day gift, Charlie gives her a truckload of cow manure, which she spreads around all the dormant perennials. Only then does she cut them back.

This Garden's a Zoo

Marion gladly takes in stray animals and nurtures them with lots of love. Her dogs, thankful to have found this wonderful caregiver, follow her through the garden wagging their tails. The only creatures this animal lover is not very fond of are poisonous reptiles. If she sees a copperhead sunning on a rock in her yard, she dashes to the house to grab a shotgun. Her dogs have been bitten over the years, so she disposes of venomous snakes to protect her pups.

Her many plants attract lots of other wildlife, too. Bees buzz as they work the flowers. Hummingbirds create a blur as they insert their pointy bills into the tubular and funnel-shaped blooms and then disappear in the blink of an eye. Songbirds sing cheerily, and brightly colored goldfinches wait in line for a shot at the 23 feeders around the home. Marion even cooks cornbread for the bluebirds. They won't eat the birdseed, she declares, but they certainly do like her cornbread.

Marion feeds deer in the back corner of her property. She says that they won't eat hostas by the house if they have bellies full of corn—and so far it's worked. A few exotic birds have also been spotted in the yard. One time, a large male peacock suddenly appeared and roosted at night in a tree near the house. She never knew where it came from, but she swears that it loved pepperoni pizza. And recently a pair of Eurasian doves showed up at a feeder.

A True Plant Lover

In addition to collecting a host of animals, Marion also enjoys amassing plants. She

left: Cuttings in trays line one side of the house. Marion propagates many of her favorite plants and passes them on to friends. **right:** Perennials fill the long border on the side of the house. Its colorful combinations change throughout the seasons. **below:** Plants blanket a hillside in the backyard, with black-eyed Susans and daisies dominating the slope in the summer. **below, far right:** Marion likes 'Becky' daisies because they bloom later and don't fall over. She says that if you remove spent flowers the daisies will bloom throughout the summer.

Over the years Marion's beloved plants have joined together like a colorful quilt. No bare soil in her yard is empty for long.

considers herself to be a true plant collector and has a keen eye for design. The long flower border on the side of the house flows with bright, well-planned colors. It changes seasonally, and while there may be lulls, there are never any downtimes. Marion is always experimenting and trying new plants. Point to any specimen in the garden, ask her what it is, and she'll reel off the Latin name, where she got it, and how she takes care of it. She buys plants and seeds from both mail-order catalogs and local nurseries, and she even searches the *Farmers and Consumers Market Bulletin* for any interesting finds. Many of the plants she cherishes most came from the gardens of her mother and grandmother. In fact, the large boxwoods around the house were rooted by her grandmother 58 years ago.

A Green Thumb

Marion claims to have a magic spot on the side of her house where all her cuttings seem to root. It's the perfect microclimate, and aluminum pans and trays of all shapes and sizes are lined up there side by side and neatly labeled. When these plants root out, she gives them to friends or sets them out in the garden. Marion also regularly donates some to a plant sale that raises money for a local museum.

Ask her if she has a favorite flower, and she'll tell you it depends on the time of year. Each season, she insists, brings a new favorite, but Marion does have a special place in her heart for Oriental lilies and hydrangeas. She prefers the lace caps over the mophead hydrangeas, but she plants them both.

Over the years Marion's beloved plants have joined together like a colorful quilt. No bare soil in her yard is empty for long. She quickly fills it with a small flower or a scattering of seeds, and there is little doubt that new plantings will prosper with the help of this caring gardener.

Flowers and garden gadgets decorate a Georgia toolshed (See pages 138–141.)

July

Garden Checklist 130

Flowers From the Farm 132
a family grows and sells vibrant blooms on their South Alabama farm

Trumpets for Summer 135
Phillipine lilies thrive in the heat

Shady Retreat 136
an inviting bench provides a cool refuge

Garden on Campus 137
explore a beautiful garden on the Clemson University campus

Garden in the Pines 138
a Monroe, Georgia garden of simple uses and colorful flowers

garden checklist
JULY

Editor's Notebook

You've heard of kudzu, "The Vine That Ate the South." How about lantana, "The Plant That Ate a Town"? You haven't? Then welcome to Bath, the oldest city in North Carolina and a favorite haunt of the pirate Blackbeard. The folks in Bath decided that the sign outside the visitors center needed some dressing up. So they went to the garden center, bought some lantanas, and then planted them at the foot of the sign. Lantana is great—it blooms from spring to frost, attracts clouds of butterflies, and laughs at summer drought. But some selections grow nearly flat, some grow 3 feet high, and some grow as big as a VW Beetle. Parking six of those cars around your town sign doesn't do much for tourism. So Special Forces equipped with hedge shears were quickly dispatched from Fort Bragg. The town was saved. Now the troops have a new mission: find the grave of Blackbeard. My guess is that it's near the visitors center, under a bed of lantana. —STEVE BENDER

Summer Color

Gardeners should plant flowers that are tolerant of summer heat and storms. Melampodium, narrow-leaf zinnia *(Zinnia angustifolia),* globe amaranth *(Gomphrena globosa),* angelonia, cleome, and portulaca are good annuals for sunny areas. Sun-loving perennials include pentas, scarlet sage *(Salvia splendens),* lantana, butterfly bush (*Buddleia* sp.), daylily, verbena, and black-eyed Susan *(Rudbeckia hirta).*

TIPS

- **Basil**—To keep plants producing leaves, cut stems by one-third, and place the cuttings in a vase in your kitchen window. The basil will actually root in the vase.
- **Cut flowers**—Cut stems early in the morning and at an angle to ensure long vase life. Immediately place flowers in a bucket of tepid water. Good cut flowers include zinnias, rudbeckias, sunflowers, crinums, dahlias, and Mexican sunflowers *(Tithonia rotundifolia).*
- **Lawnmowers**—Raise the height of your mower for the summer. Cutting your grass too short can stress your lawn. Elevate blades to a height of 2 to 2½ inches for St. Augustine, 1½ to 2 inches for centipede, 2 inches for Bermuda, and 2 inches for Zoysia.
- **Sunny days**—To minimize your exposure to sun, work in the garden during mornings and evenings, when the sun is at a lower angle and the temperature is cooler. Avoid gardening between 10 a.m. and 4 p.m. Don't forget to wear sunscreen and a hat.
- **Trees**—Long periods without rain can stress your trees. Water and provide more mulch to keep roots cool and conserve moisture.
- **Water**—Remember to irrigate early in the morning or later in the afternoon to conserve water.

PLANT

- **Crepe myrtles**—Now, while crepe myrtles are blooming, is the best time of year to pick your favorite. Choose one that will have the color and mature size and shape that will fit your needs. If you want a large crepe myrtle (20 to 30 feet tall), use 'Natchez,' 'Muskogee,' or 'Tuscarora.' For a medium crepe myrtle (10 to 15 feet tall), choose 'Regal Red,' 'Yuma,' or 'Acoma.' Small crepe myrtles (2 to 3 feet tall) include 'Centennial,' 'Pixie White,' and 'Chickasaw.'

Perennial Color

Purple coneflowers *(Echinacea purpurea)* bloom throughout the summer and are great additions to your border. They prefer full sun, good drainage, and soil that has some organic matter in it. When planting them this time of year, place them at the same depth as they were in the container, and water them well until they're established. Coneflowers are drought-tolerant, happy perennials you will grow to cherish. Their flowers attract butterflies and bees, and after they have finished blooming in the fall, their seedheads will be eaten by birds.

- **For hummingbirds—**Provide more nectar for these birds by planting "nature's feeders." Trumpet honeysuckle *(Lonicera sempervirens),* trumpet vine *(Campsis radicans),* and cardinal flower *(Lobelia cardinalis)* are flowers hummingbirds love to visit.
- **Turf-free areas—**In the shade where grass won't grow, mulch or plant ground covers for interest. Mulch with wood chips, bark, or pine straw laid 4 to 6 inches deep. Avoid piling mulch directly against tree trunks; this can lead to rot or insect invasion. For ground covers, choose low-maintenance plants such as liriope, mondo grass, Asiatic jasmine, English ivy, or periwinkle.

CONTROL

- **Centipede lawns—**If your yard has received a lot of rain this summer, be sure to check your centipede lawn for damage from spittlebugs—small dark brown-to-black insects with two bright orange stripes across their backs. A few spittlebugs do little damage and require no spraying. But large populations can cause yellow or red streaks down the grass blades, which eventually turn completely brown. Apply a granular lawn-insect control only if there is significant damage. Be sure to follow all label directions and precautions carefully.
- **St. Augustine lawns—**Sharpen your lawn mower blade if you notice ragged cuts on grass. Cutting your yard with a dull blade can stress the lawn and give it a brown cast. If straw-colored patches show up in sunny areas, look for chinch bugs. Adults are about 1/5 inch long and are black with white wing patches on their backs. Immature chinch bugs are red with white bands across their backs. If you find 20 to 25 chinch bugs per square foot, apply a granular lawn-insect control such as Orthene. Follow all label directions and precautions carefully.

FERTILIZE

- **Annuals—**Cut back your leggy annuals now so that they will look full in the fall. Although it can be a little hard to do, think of it as tough love. Impatiens, begonias, and 'Lady in Red' and 'Coral Nymph' salvias can be trimmed by one-third. The plants will grow back faster if you leave some green foliage. Water and then add a slow-release, granular fertilizer such as Osmocote or Scott's All-Purpose Plant Food.

Perennials

Plant fall-blooming ones such as Brazilian sage *(Salvia guaranitica),* with deep blue-purple spikes, and Mexican bush sage *(S. leucantha),* with its gray-and-silver stems and rose-purple flower spikes. Create a fall border by placing tall salvias near the back of the planting and shorter perennials in contrasting yellow or gold, such as Copper Canyon daisy *(Tagetes lemmonii)* or Mexican mint marigold *(T. lucida),* in the front. Set out 1- or 5-gallon container plants now so they will have plenty of time to establish themselves for a brilliant fall display.

July notes:

Tip of the Month

Fill a yellow dishpan halfway with water, and set it in the garden. Aphids are attracted to yellow, so they will land in the water and drown. You'll have fewer insects on your plants.

ANNA VICTORIA REICH
ALBUQUERQUE, NEW MEXICO

flowers from the farm

On your way to the Gulf Coast this summer, stop by the Peadens' roadside stand, and pick up a colorful bouquet of zinnias.

BY CHARLIE THIGPEN
PHOTOGRAPHY JEAN ALLSOPP

Waist-high rows of multicolored zinnias shine in the hot summer sun. A family sweats in the field, harvesting the vibrant blooms. They clip the long-stemmed flowers and drop them into galvanized buckets filled with water. Riding in a red wagon, the buckets slosh their way to a small roadside flower shop. Here, the family grooms and divides the zinnias. After the blooms are tucked into tin cans or mason jars, the arrangements are ready for display in the Peadens' small store, Southern Petals.

About five years ago, Gary and Sherry Peaden started growing flowers on their 16-acre farm to harvest and sell. They thought the colorful crop might help generate a little added income for their large family. Sherry was surprised by the immediate success. At first they sold to a local florist, and then they began selling to the public. Gary quickly built a small shed in which the flowers could be stored and sold. Nowadays, the shed's window-unit air conditioner hums constantly in the summer, keeping the small space chilled and the flowers fresh.

Moving to the Country

Sherry and Gary used to live in Pensacola, Florida, but they saw that their kids were growing up too fast in the city. Looking for a simpler life, they bought the old farm and moved their family to the country. Now, you would be tempted to call the Peadens' six children John Boy, Mary Ellen, Ben, Erin, Jim Bob, and Elizabeth. They are like a modern-day version of *The Waltons*. Hardworking, good-natured, and polite, they help with the many tasks around the farm.

The shop is open throughout the year, but fresh flowers are available only during the warm months. At the height of the season, the family picks about 3,000 flowers a week. In addition to zinnias, the Peadens grow watermelons, cantaloupes, tomatoes, peas, beans, and okra. Much of the produce is canned or frozen for the

top: Laura Peaden holds a bucket of freshly cut zinnias. **above:** Southern Petals sits beside a grove of pecan trees alongside U.S. 98 near Elberta, Alabama. There is no cashier to run the store, only an honor box to take your money.

family, but they sell some of it fresh from an old farm wagon set up next to the flower shop. They also keep bees and sell honey. In his spare time, Gary even builds rustic birdhouses and feeders that are popular with shoppers when flowers aren't available. In the winter months, they make wreaths of grapevine gathered from around the property. Sherry decorates them with dried flowers and displays them in the shop.

All this keeps the Peadens busy, so there is no one to mind the store. An honor box is the only cashier, and customers just drop their cash or checks into a slot when they make a purchase. So far everyone has been honest, and nothing has been stolen. It surely doesn't hurt that Gary works for the local sheriff's department.

top: Working on the farm is a family affair. (Back row, from left to right) Robert, Sherry, Gary, and Laura; (front row, from left to right) Chris, Sarah, Matt, and Anna Claire **above:** The family grows and harvests thousands of zinnias for the shop each year.

Making Arrangements

While the whole family helps with chores, Sherry is the heart and soul of the operation. She loves being surrounded by flowers and enjoys wading through the blooms in the early morning. Each year, she purchases all the seeds and plans the garden. Sherry likes flowers that are easy to direct seed into the field, but they must hold up after they've been cut.

The Peadens set up shop each spring with bachelor's buttons, larkspurs, daisies, and daffodils, which they plant in the fall. As the spring bloomers play out from the heat, they are replaced by summer crops. The warm-season flowers include celosias, cosmos, globe amaranths, sunflowers, strawflowers, and zinnias. Customers love them all, but zinnias are the Peadens' biggest draw. People love the vibrant colors and how well they hold up in arrangements. The California Giants Strain grows tall, making it perfect for big arrangements. The Lilliput Series has smaller blooms, about the size of a half-dollar, which look nice in a can or jar.

Some customers leave their containers to be filled at the flower shop. The Peadens paint the silver cans bright colors. Once the cans or jars are filled with flowers, the Peadens tie raffia around the containers and attach a small card displaying the shop's name. These rustic arrangements go for \$5 to \$25.

Those who don't want a can or jar with their flowers can purchase a large bunch of blooms in a florist sleeve for \$5. Sherry also takes special orders from people who call saying they need 300 or 400 flowers for a wedding or a party.

Working the Fields

Sherry may be the heart of the flower farm, but Gary is the workhorse. Driving an old 1953 Ford Jubilee tractor, he plows across the dusty fields. To put out the sacks of flower seed, he uses an Earthway seeder, bought at the co-op, to evenly distribute the tiny flower seeds. Weeds and grasses are typically the biggest problems. They grow fast and spread quickly in the warm soil, competing with small seedlings. Gary carefully sprays Roundup around the rows with a handheld sprayer until all the flowers are tall enough to fend for themselves. The drip irrigation system works so well that he wouldn't mind if it didn't rain all summer long. The zinnias mature quickly and can be harvested within about six weeks of planting.

Each morning as the sun rises, Sherry and the girls move down the long, straight rows, clipping the flowers like mechanical harvesters. Their hands move in high gear as they stoop over the rainbow of blooms. Occasionally, they stand upright to wipe their foreheads or fan away bothersome gnats. They want to get the flowers out of the sun and into the shop quickly to keep them fresh.

Tending the farm is hard work, but it's also very rewarding. On this piece of land, the Peadens have witnessed the miracle of seeing tiny seeds transform lifeless rows of dirt into sweeps of beautiful flowers.

Southern Petals is 2 miles east of Elberta, Alabama, on U.S. 98. For more information call (251) 986-5190. ◆

Trumpets for Summer

The middle of July in the South can be a challenging time for gardeners, so it's nice to have some plants that don't mind the long, hot days. One such flower is Philippine lily, a variety of *Lilium formosanum.* This old Southern favorite has been rediscovered by gardeners interested in plants with ease of maintenance and spectacular flowers. The blooms are a welcome sight during July and August, when few other plants are at their peak.

A Faraway Treasure

Originally found on the island of Taiwan (formerly known as Formosa), this lily occurs in several types. Philippine lilies are more at home in warmer climates but will be hardy anywhere in the South. The flowers resemble those of a downward-hanging Easter lily but have a slightly longer trumpet shape. They are white with maroon shading along the outer base. One of the flower's most attractive features is its wonderful ability to rebloom later in the season—a time when almost every other lily has finished its show.

In the Garden

If someone were to invent the ideal plant for a cottage garden, Philippine lily would definitely be it. The blooms look most appealing when springing forth behind masses of foliage and flowering plants, such as blue cape plumbago, cockscomb, gomphrena, balsam, or coleus. Ornamental plants such as maiden grass (*Miscanthus sinensis* 'Gracillimus') or fountain grass *(Pennisetum setaceum)* provide effective textural contrast with the large clusters of 8-inch trumpet-shaped lilies, which are gracefully arranged on 3- to 7-inch leafy stems.

Greg Grant, a horticulturist at the Mercer Arboretum & Botanic Gardens in Humble, Texas, has been growing and admiring Philippine lilies for many years. One August day while he was a student at Texas A&M University, Greg spotted what appeared to be thousands of tall Easter lilies blooming in the woods. He turned the car around and drove back. There was a little white house nestled among the pines; the surrounding yard, the woods, and even the roadside were covered with hundreds—if not thousands—of giant white Philippine lilies. It seemed to be a scene from heaven. "I decided right then and there that I wouldn't stop trying until I had re-created that magical scene for myself," Greg recalls. "I have been growing them successfully ever since but still haven't achieved the magnificent vision I first experienced."

BILL WELCH

PHILIPPINE LILY
At a Glance

Height: 5 to 7 feet tall
Light: partial shade to full sun
Soil: well-drained, organic, slightly acid soil
Color: white with maroon shading
Propagation: Plant container-grown lilies, or grow from seed.
Range: all South
Bloom: late summer; July and August

PHOTOGRAPHS: VAN CHAPLIN

DESIGN: JEREMY SMEARMAN, PLANTERS NURSERY, ATLANTA

Shady Retreat

Various shades of green surround an inviting bench.

A cool refuge from the summer sun was a big priority for these homeowners. Their backyard swimming pool is a favorite seasonal stop for grandchildren, and a wooded area just beyond the diving board provides a shady haven. Several design tips were employed to make this simple little garden a comfortable and tranquil addition to the landscape.

Define the Space

The lawn shape was outlined with soft curves as a gentle counterpoint to the angular lines of the concrete that surrounds the pool. Brick edging keeps the area neat and manicured. This tiny oasis is cooling and makes a soft grassy carpet for bare feet. The back of the garden is defined with the existing mature trees and shrubs. This green backdrop pulls your attention toward the front of the garden.

Supply a Focal Point

Set back under the canopy of trees, the teak bench anchors the garden and provides an attractive and practical resting place out of the sun. Broad stepping-stones make access to the bench convenient, and their natural look nicely complements the wooded setting. A secondary point of interest is a multitrunk Japanese maple, which is placed to the left of the bench between the existing trees and the concrete pool surround.

Fill In the Gaps

Plants were selected to give the garden a cool appearance. Green is the primary hue, with bold textures emphasized rather than fussy colors. Assorted hostas provide broad leaves with varying green shades, while Southern shield fern grows behind for a soft backdrop. Creeping jenny wanders between the stepping-stones and crawls over the brick edging. A clump of chartreuse Japanese sweet flag along the edge adds a long, pointed leaf for contrasting shape.

Blue mophead hydrangeas to the right of the bench add a refreshing hue to the garden and provide bulk and height. Without this shrub, the garden might have appeared too flat and symmetrical. Pale pink astilbe brings color close to the bench, and a smattering of white impatiens will bloom throughout the summer.

The key elements of this garden's charm are simple design, an obvious focal point, and excellent plant choices. Use these tips, and you can't miss. ◆

PHOTOGRAPHS: GARY CLARK

This fantastic structure, titled *Spittin' Image,* was woven by North Carolina artist Patrick Dougherty. Trees are planted within the dead limbs.

Garden on Campus

Beautiful blooms and a lush tapestry await at the South Carolina Botanical Garden.

If you're traveling I-85 this summer, take a break to stop by the South Carolina Botanical Garden and Fran Hanson Discovery Center, on the Clemson University campus. Exploring the beauty of the garden is the perfect roadside diversion, and the center is a trove of information about the surrounding area.

A furry guide, Calhoun the Raccoon, is on hand to chatter about the nearby areas. Kids are bound to love this talking critter.

The Fran Hanson Discovery Center occupies The Wren House, a former *Southern Living* Showcase home. Architect Keith Summerour and garden designer Ryan Gainey collaborated on the design of the house and surrounding gardens, which opened in June 1998. In May 2001, the structure found a new purpose as a learning center, educating visitors on historical, cultural, and natural attractions.

New selections of annual and perennial flowers undergo trials at the garden.

The center is a major part of several buildings connected by pathways and a lush garden filled with roses, perennials, ground covers, and other plantings laid out by Ryan.

Next door sits The Betsy Campbell Carriage House Coffee & Gift Shop, which carries light snacks, specialty coffees, garden gifts, and regional artwork. Downhill from the Carriage House is the Bob Campbell Geology Museum, which showcases a collection of minerals and fossils, many of which were discovered in the area.

"One of the most popular exhibits is the fluorescent-mineral room," says Dave Cicimurri, museum curator of collections. "There are about 70 minerals sitting on four shelves in an 18- x 6-foot room." You can hear the oohs and aahs rise up from visitors when the black lights are turned on, causing the minerals to glow in eerie, neon-bright colors. Cool.

There are more pretty colors out in the botanical garden, which stretches over 295 acres. Among the many highlights are the Woodland Wildflower Garden/Belser Nature Trail, the Class of 1939 Caboose Garden (complete with a bright red Southern Railway Company caboose), and the Lark Wildflower Meadow.

Strategically placed throughout the garden are several incredible sculptures made from natural materials, including tree limbs, old vines, and other garden prunings. One of the most impressive is *Spittin' Image,* created by North Carolina artist Patrick Dougherty. A circular wall connects three domed towers, about 25 feet high, much like an ancient castle. Small trees planted inside will gradually overtake the structure and claim the small rise it now commands. Go ahead; wander around inside. There's never an age limit on having fun in a garden.

MARK G. STITH

The South Carolina Botanical Garden is located on Perimeter Road, near the intersection of U.S. 76, on the Clemson University campus. It's open from dawn to dusk. For more information, call (864) 656-3405, or visit www.clemson.edu/scbg. The Fran Hanson Discovery Center is open 9 a.m.-5 p.m. Monday-Saturday and 1-5 p.m. Sunday. Admission is free. ◆

garden in the pines

Returning to their roots, this Georgia family embraces their land and their heritage.

As the wind passes through the needles of pine trees, it creates a quiet song of summer, lulling us to peaceful thoughts. It makes us pause and look at clouds, stuffed like pillows, floating gently across the sky. Among the pinewoods of Monroe, Georgia, lies the garden of Dexter and Kelley Adams. It is a garden of simple uses and colorful flowers. It is also a refuge where their sons, Sam and Tyler, can hide and play among the tomatoes, blueberries, and sunflowers of summer. It is a place for imaginations to grow and run wild.

Paths run from the garden, through the pinewoods, to places for exploration and play. They meander through a meadow of black-eyed Susans and lead to a tree house with

top, left: Dexter uses a 4-pound masonry hammer to cut bricks and stones that shape the distinctive paths. **top, right:** Kelley grows a variety of flowers to cut for arrangements. **above:** Sam hugs Kate, the family's Jack Russell terrier, while Tyler holds a bowl of fresh-picked blueberries.

BY GENE B. BUSSELL / PHOTOGRAPHY RALPH ANDERSON

top, left: A tin roof, a rusted spring, and a spiraling piece of metal make this birdhouse seem right at home in the garden. **above, left:** An old tractor seat, mounted on a galvanized pipe, can be moved around the garden to serve as a chair or a place to set tools while working. **above, right:** Gadgets gathered from nearby fields and from relatives decorate the toolshed.

burlap windows. They then continue through the woods and around a creekbed that a beaver has dammed to make its own pond. They lead to the homes, gardens, and fields of relatives: Grandma Evelyn, Uncle Tony, and cousins beyond. The Adamses' garden remembers family and their ties to this land.

It Was Meant To Be

Both Dexter and Kelley grew up around gardeners. Dexter's family has lived in Monroe for generations. His father, Grady, was an avid gardener. Dexter remembers his father always "sweating and digging. He gravitated to the outdoors because he couldn't fix a washing machine," Dexter says.

Grady grew over a hundred selections of daylilies. Dexter recalls his fascination when opening boxes of mail-order bare-root plants destined for the family's small orchards. They grew figs, blueberries, peaches, and tomatoes. Such ties to land and gardening imparted more than just memories to Dexter; they later inspired him to become a landscape architect.

Kelley, who grew up in Little Rock, has similar memories. She says her father did a lot of gardening and began with daylilies. Her mother, an artist, now runs her own perennial nursery. Kelley, who is an elementary school art teacher, is also an artist. After finishing college at Sewanee in Tennessee, she made a trip to Athens, Georgia, to visit a friend. There she met Dexter at the Bluebird Café. He confesses that he asked her about a newspaper just so he could talk to her; they've been together ever since. Although they first lived in Athens, Kelley says, "We moved to Monroe after Sam was born, because we needed to be around family."

To Grow and To Eat

A circular stone wall surrounds the kitchen garden. Terraced along a slight slope, it is, in effect, a large raised bed that supplements meals with tomatoes, squash, eggplants, beans, and peppers. Kelley says, "You can buy corn on the cob from the grocery store, but you just cannot buy homegrown tomatoes." She cooks all summer long with herbs planted in the openings around the vegetables and flowers. She regularly uses thyme, rosemary, oregano, tarragon, and basil, the king of herbs, which she reserves almost exclusively for pesto sauces.

Dinners are memorable summer events at either Kelley's table or at Grandma Evelyn's next door. Slices of fresh tomato, green beans, fried okra, and yellow squash—peppered and cooked in butter and onions—are served with fried chicken. The cornbread has to be strategically placed because, as Dexter admits, "We fight over the corner pieces." And for those who might still have room, there is also blueberry pie and ice cream. Colorful bouquets of fresh flowers cut from the garden—bright sunflowers, daylilies, zinnias, black-eyed Susans, and cosmos—grace the family's summer table.

More Than a Toolshed

Generations of Adamses have lived in Monroe. Most worked the land at some time, but now the numbers are fewer. In the fields that surround his home, Dexter has come across various parts of tools and machines from times past. He has collected them and created a thoughtful display on the sides of his rustic toolshed. Saw blades, chrome hubcaps, chains, locks, picks, wrenches, license plates, springs, pulleys, pitchforks, and hooks—each has its own place. The tailgate from his father's Studebaker serves as the centerpiece. Each find has intrinsic worth, but as a group, the tools are perhaps more beautiful because they represent and honor those who used them.

The Path to Inspiration

Dexter can always be found tinkering with different things. Several years ago, Dexter went through what he likes to describe as his "birdhouse period." That's when he began making a series of birdhouses from old wood, rusted tin, and whatever else he found that was weathered, including antique farm implements. Fifteen birdhouses later, the air is filled with the vibration of flight and the joyous sound of birdsong.

His latest fascination with stone and pattern, paired with a love of history, has inspired him to create mosaic paths in the spirit of South American landscape architect Roberto Burle Marx. So now, using a 4-pound masonry hammer, Dexter taps, cuts, and sets brick and stone on sand. His pathways, made of scrap brick, granite cobble, and river stone, are merged with the native ferns and mosses.

As the light fades along the edges of the pinewoods, the calming sounds of a summer evening begin to rise. Frogs from the beaver pond fill the air with a constant "mmmmmrrrrkk, mmmmmrrrrkk," and a whippoorwill calls out to see who else is in the woods. As comforting as these sounds can be, it is the blue cast of early night that brings the most assuring sounds. Around the edges of the garden, the happy laughter of Sam and Tyler echoes in the air as they chase the luminous lanterns of fireflies. ◆

top and above: Dexter created this intricate path to the toolshed, which uses old plow points for door pulls. **above, center:** Kelley likes to fill a simple bucket with flowers cut from the garden. **above, far right:** One of Dexter's birdhouses looks ready to fly off to find a resident. **right:** The kitchen garden's mainstays are tomatoes, squash, peppers, and eggplants, with sunflowers, zinnias, and marigolds for color. Herbs such as basil, rosemary, oregano, thyme, mint, and chives fill the small openings among the vegetables and flowers.

Sunflowers are great take-home flowers *(See pages 158–161.)*

August

Garden Checklist 144

Night Whites & Candlelight 146
a few bright little ideas to add magic
to summer evenings

Hummingbirds Love Firebush 149
this long-blooming favorite is easy to grow

Making History 150
a garden full of old treasures

Coleus Makes a Splash 152
make a bold statement by adding this plant to the mix

Easy Potpourri 153
dry pretty petals of your favorite flowers

Personal Paradise 154
a landscape evolves into a tropical oasis

Symphony of Sunflowers 158
these blooms thrive as the temperature rises

Editor's Notebook

It is with the greatest pleasure and excitement that I announce the first (and only) Steve Bender Black Spot Contest. This thrill-packed competition is open to those whose lack of attention to proper gardening methods has resulted in the spotting, yellowing, dropping, and gross uglification of at least 75% of their rose foliage. Now many of you are probably asking, "How can I, a mere amateur, hope to achieve this lofty level of fungal infection?" Easy. First, keep the foliage as wet as possible, using sprinklers to water at night. Second, refuse to apply a proper fungicide, such as Funginex, Immunox, or Daconil. Finally, fail to plant black spot-resistant roses, such as 'Bonica,' 'Carefree Beauty,' 'Dr. W. van Fleet,' 'Flower Carpet,' 'Mrs. B. R. Cant,' 'Old Blush,' and yellow Dream Series. Well, time's a-wasting. Get out there, and abuse those roses. First person to attain total defoliation will win a year's supply of powdery mildew and a pair of dull pruners.

—STEVE BENDER

Vegetables

The garden is going full speed, and it's important to harvest regularly to ensure an ongoing supply of tender vegetables. Use sharp clippers when harvesting to avoid tearing stems. Gather tomatoes, peppers, eggplants, cucumbers, and squash early in the morning on the day you plan to eat them. If you have extras, they will make welcome gifts for your neighbors—just go easy on the zucchini.

TIPS

- **Amaryllis—**If you want to force your potted amaryllis to bloom for the holidays, now is the time to get your old bulb in shape for the season. Stop watering, and place the plant in a dry location. After the leaves turn yellow, remove the dead foliage from the bulb, and remove the bulb from the pot. Store the bulb in a paper sack in a cool, dry, dark place for about two months. Then pot the bulb so the top one-third of it is above the soil. Water and place in a cool, lighted spot. Your amaryllis should begin to bloom in six to eight weeks.
- **Basil—**Keep blooms trimmed and foliage harvested to increase production of new leaves.
- **Bougainvillea—**Train wayward stems of bougainvillea to guide them onto a trellis or fence. Use dark green twine or twist ties to hold the new growth in place. Tie loosely as not to choke the stems.
- **Mulch—**Shaded annual beds of caladiums, begonias, and impatiens will benefit from an extra layer of pine straw mulch. The mulch will help conserve moisture and keep roots cool.
- **Seeds—**Get a head start, and plan your fall garden now. Review your mail-order seed catalogs, and select flower and vegetable seeds for fall planting.

PLANT

- **Fall perennials—**Excellent perennials for seasonal color include Mexican bush sage *(Salvia leucantha),* pineapple sage *(S. elegans),* Brazilian sage *(S. guaranitica),* Philippine violet *(Barleria cristata),* swamp sunflower *(Helianthus angustifolius),* cigar plant *(Cuphea ignea),* firespike *(Odontonema strictum),* chrysanthemum, goldenrod, Mexican mint marigold *(Tagetes lucida),* and 'Autumn Joy' sedum. Plant in full sun and well-drained soil. If you keep them watered till roots are well established, these plants will be able to withstand a winter freeze and return next spring.
- **Iris—**Divide and transplant your bearded iris (*Iris* x *germanica*) and Japanese roof iris *(I. tectorum)* this month. Cut back the top two-thirds of the leaves into a fan shape. Lift, divide, and remove any dirt from around the rhizome. Discard any dead portions of the rhizome. Reset in a well-drained, sunny location so the top one-third of the rhizome is above the surrounding soil level. Water well to help establish new roots.
- **Small flowering trees—**Two good choices for summer bloom in the Texas are chaste tree (*Vitex* sp.) and desert willow *(Chilopsis linearis).* Chaste tree provides masses of bluish-purple flower spikes. Desert willow has orchid-like tubular flowers ranging from purple to lavender and white. Both of these plants cast

a light shade, so annuals and perennials can grow beneath them.

■ **Water gardens**—Pots of calla lilies, cannas, sedges, and cattails make handsome additions to Southern pond landscapes. Place decorative rocks or heavy gravel on top of pots to keep soil in place and also to discourage fish from damaging plants. Stimulate plant growth by inserting fertilizer spikes into the potting mix. Inspect and clean filters to maintain water quality.

PRUNE

■ **Crepe myrtles**—Encourage a second flush of blooms this time of year by removing spent flowers and seedheads. A light application of all-purpose fertilizer, watered in thoroughly, will also help stimulate new blooms and additional growth.

■ **Fall-blooming perennials**—In early August, it is still okay to groom and shape perennials such as salvias, asters, and mums. Just lightly pinch back any loose or unkempt growth with your fingers. This will maintain the plant's compact growing habit and it will also help the plants produce more blooms for a great fall show.

■ **Roses**—Now is a good time to prune hybrid tea roses back by one-third to help promote new growth and increase fall blossoms. Feed with either a granular rose food, such as 7-11-9, or composted manure.

FERTILIZE

■ **Citrus**—In the Tropical South, make another application of citrus fertilizer to your plants this month. Measure the distance around the trunk 6 inches above ground level. Use ¼ pound of citrus fertilizer (such as Vigoro Citrus Food 10-4-10) for each inch of this distance. Apply the fertilizer under the spread of the branches and slightly beyond.

■ **Preparing lawns for winter**—If your grass is not as thick as you would like, you can make one last application of fertilizer in August or September. Select a fertilizer that's high in potassium and low in nitrogen, such as 5-0-15 or 5-0-20. Apply 10 pounds per 1,000 square feet of lawn.

■ **Young trees and shrubs**—If you want the most growth, now is the best time of year to make another application of fertilizer. Choose one that is low in nitrogen (the first number in the formula) and high in potassium (the second number) and with a rate of potash (the third number) that is equal to or greater than the rate of potassium. Apply this at a rate of two teaspoons per foot of plant height (or width, whichever number is larger). Keep in mind that small shrubs less than a foot tall should receive no more than a teaspoon. Apply the fertilizer on the mulch surface underneath the spread of branches and slightly beyond.

Hot-Weather Color

Plant red yucca *(Hesperaloe parviflora)* and yellow bells *(Tecoma stans)* now. Red yuccas (shown at right) have 5- to 7-foot-tall spikes of long-lasting, soft coral blooms that attract hummingbirds.. Yellow bells tolerate heat and resist insects and diseases. The stunning bright yellow blooms occur from early summer till frost. They thrive in containers or in sunny, well-drained beds. Cut faded flowers to prolong bloom and prune to remove dead, bushy growth.

August notes:

Tip of the Month

Here's a way to keep grass from growing into your flowerbed without laying down a wooden or brick border. Just work up the soil a couple of inches deep along the edge, and stir in a little dry cement mix. Then when you water the garden, the dirt edge will harden, and grass will not grow through it.

CONNIE HONEYCUTT
ROCKY MOUNT, NORTH CAROLINA

GARDENING
PLANTS AND DESIGN

night whites & candlelight

Add a little bit of magic to your summer evenings with these easy garden ideas.

Nighttime is prime time for summer garden enjoyment. In the cooler air, simple tasks such as clipping and trimming become pleasant undertakings. It is also a terrific time to relax, entertain, and enjoy the efforts of your labors. Maximize the impact of the night garden with white blooms and light-reflecting foliage. Masses of snowy blossoms clustered snugly together shine and sparkle in evening light, whether it is from an incandescent source, candles, or the full moon.

Great Flowers, Fabulous Foliage

This pristine palette contains numerous floral options. Choose your plants according to daylight conditions—either sun or shade. The correct plant choices ensure a stellar evening show. In shady beds and hanging baskets, masses of white impatiens produce a dynamic display. During daylight the blooms appear cool and collected, but after sundown they glisten and glow like a shower of stars.

White caladiums are an excellent choice for showy foliage. The selections 'Candidum' and 'White Christmas' fare beautifully in shade, while 'Aaron' holds its own in a sunny location. Plant these tropical tubers in a large group, or use them as a tall element behind other pearly bloomers.

For a spot that's sunny by day, my favorite flowers are white petunias. Their trumpet-like blooms not only reflect light but

Caladium leaves bring bright, reflective foliage to an impatiens border. Candles in faceted cylinders illuminate the area and provide a safe way to keep the flames contained.

BY ELLEN RUOFF RILEY / PHOTOGRAPHY RALPH ANDERSON

also perfume the air with spicy, intoxicating fragrance. Petunias are perfect in containers, where they are somewhat immune to hungry slugs and are easy to pinch back and groom. In a flowerbed, consider planting the appropriately named White Star Series zinnias *(Zinnia angustifolia).*

Ignite a Spark

Truth be told, we're all romantics at heart, and candlelight is a favorite source of illumination. Turn an ordinary evening into a lingering occasion with a single scented pillar on a table or a garden full of luminarias and tea lights. Remember these safety rules regardless of the number of flickering flames: Never leave candles unattended, and always confine the flame within a glass container if it's close to flowers, foliage, or anything else that may be flammable.

Light a candle just for yourself, or go all out for company. Try these ideas to bring lively sparkle to your garden.

- Place floating candles in a birdbath or fishpond.
- Suspend jewel-studded jars from tree limbs.
- Use tall canning jars with petite pillars along a pathway or tucked along the edge of a flowerbed.

TREE LIGHTS

Whether you safely suspend them from a branch or an arbor, these easy-to-make candleholders add sparkle to the evening. Collect jars in assorted sizes and shapes for an imaginative display.

Step 1: Cut a piece of tie wire (available at home-center stores) at least 3 feet long. With needle-nose pliers, make a spiral at one end.

Step 2: Hold the spiral in place on the jar while winding the wire around the container's neck. Secure the hanger by twisting it around the spiral.

Step 3: Using a hot-melt glue gun or epoxy, attach clear glass jewels to the outside of each jar.

Step 4: Cut wire hanger to the desired length, and make a loop at the end. When hanging multiple jars, vary the wire lengths for interest.

GROWING CANDLELIGHT

An 8-inch clay pot provides plenty of room for flowers and a slender pillar candle. Use it as a centerpiece or with multiple pots on a plant stand.

Step 1: Fill the vessel with moist potting soil. Place a clear cylinder vase in the pot's center, twisting it slightly to secure.

Step 2: Surround the vase with white impatiens and variegated vinca vine trailing over the edge. Fill around the plants' root balls with additional moist potting soil.

Step 3: Feed the impatiens once a week with a blossom-boosting fertilizer such as 15-30-15. When the flowers are in full bloom, place a pillar candle in the vase, and enjoy the glow.

Hummingbirds Love Firebush

Want to make hummingbirds see red? Plant a firebush in your garden. Also called scarlet bush, it is not only among the easiest of plants to grow, but it also stays in bloom throughout the growing season with clusters of tubular red buds and flowers. Because the Southern growing season overlaps the spring and fall migration times of the ruby-throated hummingbird, and red is by far their favorite color, these blossoms will summon them to your garden.

Firebush *(Hamelia patens)* can be found at most nurseries and garden centers across the South, partly because it's so well adapted to our growing conditions. It's drought tolerant but doesn't mind regular water or even occasional wet feet. It is perfectly happy in alkaline soils but also fine in acid ones. Full sun will keep it happy and blooming, but so will a fair amount of shade. Firebush makes a great, fast-flowering annual shrub for borders or containers in the Middle and Upper South. It's a South Florida native, though, so it does equally well with the intense heat of a south-facing wall. It can even be used as an evergreen perennial shrub for hedges in the Tropical South, where it will reach up to 12 feet high.

Maintenance for firebush couldn't be easier. Water well while it's getting established, and then once a week if there's no rain for a while. Put mulch over the roots in the fall—firebush freezes down but usually comes back quickly in the Lower and Coastal South. Lightly shear the plant a couple of times during the growing season to promote the heaviest flowering.

In addition to attracting hummingbirds, vivid, long-blooming firebush serves as both larval food and nectar plant for butterflies. And other birds will relish its fruit. But it's those zooming crowds of hummers, particularly during fall migration when firebush has reached its full potential of size and bloom, that make this plant so popular.

LIZ DRUITT

PHOTOGRAPHS: SYLVIA MARTIN

above: Colorful firebush will easily reach 4 or 5 feet high and wide during a growing season. **below:** The tubular red flowers are perfectly designed for a hummingbird's slender beak.

FIREBUSH

At a Glance

Size: 9 to 10 feet tall, possibly more
Soil: any well drained
Water: while getting established, or during periods of drought
Fertilizer: minimal
Sun: full sun to light shade
Bloom season: heaviest from early summer until frost
Range: Lower, Coastal, and Tropical South as a perennial; Middle and Upper South as an annual
Comments: Occasional light shearing will keep firebush in bloom.

Making History

Your garden doesn't have to be old to have a sense of the past.

For Calder Loth, history is not just a bunch of dates and drawings tucked away in musty old books in some dark corner of a library. He lives it every day. As an architectural historian for Virginia's Department of Historic Resources, he spends most days delving into antiquity in one way or another. But Calder doesn't just study architectural treasures in a distant, academic way. He has brought them to life in his own backyard.

When Calder moved into his home in Richmond's Fan District in 1976, the backyard was quite different. Originally, he planted only a modest 24- x 36-foot space outside of his back door. Even then he designed an unusual finishing touch—a small, five-sided, Gothic-style garden shed based on an engraving from a book of architectural designs owned by Thomas Jefferson. Calder fashioned

above: Now just one small part of the yard, this area was originally the entire garden. **right:** This Gothic shed was inspired by a book on Britain's Kew Gardens. The shed has a chair just in case Calder ever finds time to rest.

BY GLENN R. DINELLA
PHOTOGRAPHY VAN CHAPLIN

the walls from stock lattice panels that allow for cross ventilation. For the roof, he used standing-seam copper that has acquired a soft patina, and the floor is laid in sand-swept brick. Its old-fashioned appearance suits his interests and garden style. He placed the shed in the corner of the small garden at the juncture of two paths. The entrance faces both paths, beckoning visitors to step into its cool shade. Draped in Virginia creeper, the high-style shed is eye-catching from any viewpoint.

above: Using a mirror in the doorway gives the appearance that Calder's garden goes on forever. In reality, it abuts a neighbor's brick garage. **inset:** The folly is based on this image of a primitive Doric temple in an 18th-century architectural treatise.

Collecting Ideas

In his travels, Calder looks for concepts he can adapt to his own garden. Bric-a-brac paths are an example. "I stole the idea for the paving from the Prince of Wales, who has a walk like this at his Highgrove estate," he says. In addition to architectural ideas, Calder also collects plants as he tours old homes and gardens. He prefers locally grown pass-along plants for their proven ability to thrive in Richmond's climate, which can be brutally hot in summer and bitterly cold in winter. "It seems like Richmond is at the junction of about 20 climate zones," he says jokingly. But many plants do prosper in the garden, including spiderwort, four o'clocks, hostas, hydrangeas, phlox, fennel, bearded iris, ferns, and Kentucky curly mint.

Smoke and Mirrors

After establishing his small garden, Calder decided he wanted a little more space, so he leased an additional 48- x 72-foot plot adjoining his backyard. "The soil is so good back there because the owners planted a vegetable garden every year from the early sixties up until I began leasing it seven or eight years ago," he says.

Although the added land gave him much-needed breathing room, Calder resorted to trickery to make his garden seem even larger. Borrowing from another book in his collection, he designed a garden folly for the back of the property. A folly is defined by Webster as "an extravagant picturesque building erected to suit a fanciful taste," and his certainly fits that description. But Calder used unconventional materials to make the project more practical. Recycled telephone poles form the columns, and rope is attached around the poles for moldings. Terra-cotta pots placed in the upper beam area (entablature) represent metopes, the often decorative areas on a frieze.

It's impossible to tell from a distance, but the structure backs up to a brick garage and is essentially two-dimensional; there is scarcely room to stash a broom behind it. A full-length mirror mounted behind the gate completes the three-dimensional effect. "I wanted it to look like the garden goes on and on," Calder says. The result is very convincing. At one of his garden parties, a guest caught a glimpse of herself in the mirror and remarked, "Oh, my, that lady back there is wearing the same dress I am." That's when Calder knew his work was a success.

Coleus Makes a Splash

above: Mix coleus with impatiens and ferns for a showy summer garden. **below:** In this container, the reddish-orange leaves of coleus contrast with chartreuse potato vine.

COLEUS FOR SUN AND PARTIAL SHADE

For sunny sites—'Alabama Sunset,' 'Burgundy Sun,' or 'Plum Parfait'

For shade—'Freckles,' 'Rustic Orange,' 'Cranberry Salad,' 'Red Ruffles,' or 'Wizard Mix'

For plants guaranteed to grab attention, try coleus. Just a few added to a landscape or container can make a bold statement. Many gardeners use cool pastel colors in summer gardens, while others choose bold foliage.

Increasingly popular, coleus takes sun or shade depending on the selection. It grows little in spring's cool temperatures, but once summer's heat sets in, it shoots up, rapidly becoming bushy.

If you start with transplants, water them frequently (two or three times weekly) until they are established; then reduce waterings to once a week. Large-leaved selections will droop in extremely hot or dry weather, but they'll recover quickly if you don't let them get totally dry. Coleus do not need much fertilizer, will grow in poor soils, and have few pest problems.

These plants can grow from 6 inches to 3 feet in height. Taller-growing selections may need to be pinched back occasionally to maintain a full shape. Yes, coleus do bloom, but that is not what makes them special. In fact, any flowers that appear will need to be clipped off to encourage new growth. It's the different leaf shapes and exotic colors that make these plants a treasure in the garden. The foliage can range from lime green to burgundy red, and some selections sport variegated and multicolored leaves.

Shade-loving coleus can brighten wooded areas where flowering plants won't grow. They also combine well with ferns and other fine-textured foliage. Mix sun-loving coleus with flowers in a sunny border or in containers. Place brightly colored coleus beside light-colored blooms for contrast.

So, when you're searching for color, don't forget about coleus. When many other annuals and perennials quit blooming in the summer, the bright, showy leaves of coleus can pull your garden through the lean times. ◆

Easy Potpourri

It's a breeze to dry pretty petals of your favorite flowers.

DRIED BOUQUETS

Follow these tips to create arrangements with your dried flowers.

- Cut flowers at their peak, and immediately place the stems in warm water.
- For fast results use silica gel, which is available from florist and craft stores. Using this method will absorb moisture from the flowers and result in brighter colors.
- Before arranging dried flowers, insert their wires into hollow celosia stems which serve as a realistic substitute for the original.
- Some good candidates for drying include peony, rose, bittersweet, zinnias, lilies, Queen Anne's lace, and philadelphus.

Sensuous flowers. Bright bursts of stimulating color. Fragrance to be teased out of aromatic leaves. The garden is an intoxicating place, so much so that if nongardeners knew the pleasure it gives, they'd probably want it outlawed to prevent addiction. Fortunately, it's too late. We're already hooked on the multidimensional wonders springing from our earth.

You can spot true garden addicts by the way they touch plants. They can't go through a garden without stroking, patting, grooming, and plucking. The result is a constant supply of fragrant, pretty blooms and herbs, some of them too irresistible to leave outside. Even if they're wilted, plants are still attractive in color or scent. Here's a delightfully easy way to make this daily harvest do double duty.

Find a handsome colander, and set it on the counter by your kitchen door. Every time you come in from the garden, drop your bounty of new petals into its airy bowl, and stir your fingers through the drying flowers that were dropped in on previous days.

The combination of aeration from the openwork of the colander and the frequent stirring by hand helps the potpourri to dry. Your reward is an ever-changing blend of colors and scents, a delightfully mixed-up diary of the season's blooms, and a dose of wonderful aromatic oils that will perfume your hands for hours.

Once the colander is full and the mix is dry, you can place dainty bowls of this effortless potpourri on tables or in guestrooms to give others pleasure, too. If well dried, it lasts quite a long time, and the unique scent can be revived occasionally by a slight warming in the oven or microwave, or with the addition of a few fresh blossoms. But you may find that your potpourri is never finished and never fully dried, because you can't stop adding more flowers. If so, then you've just found another enjoyable aspect of your garden addiction. ◆

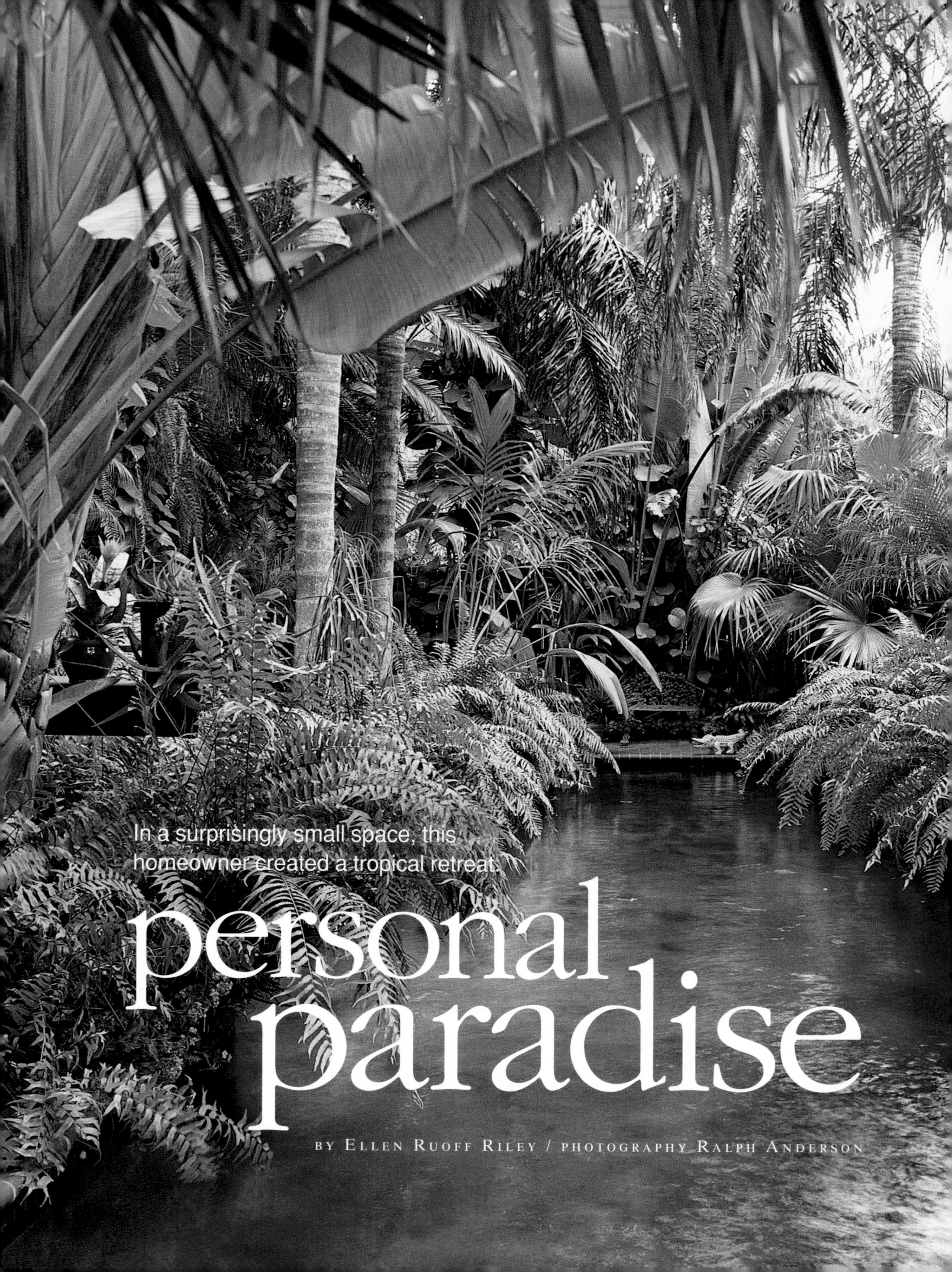

In a surprisingly small space, this homeowner created a tropical retreat.

personal paradise

BY ELLEN RUOFF RILEY / PHOTOGRAPHY RALPH ANDERSON

On a quiet street in Coconut Grove, Florida, modest homes reside comfortably on groomed lawns, with an occasional palm punctuating the landscape. In one lovely spot, however, a tropical oasis oozes over the curb, with effusive greenery supporting outbursts of shrieking pink bougainvillea and flamboyant firecracker plant.

By day, Deborah Balter teaches aviation language skills. After hours of highly skilled work, she shifts gears, becoming an artist, designer, and adventurer. This equatorial Eden is her canvas, drawing board, and urban rain forest. It is an enigmatic garden—tranquil and spirited, serious and animated, intimate and sociable.

The appearance of grand scale and large proportions is an illusion, a part of Deborah's mystical approach to design. Her garden, which feels so big, is squeezed into a petite 67 x 140 feet. Every inch of that space is deliberately planned and planted to instigate curiosity and wonder. "The garden is my palette—it fulfills my need to create. The colors, textures, plants, and placement are all part of my creative process," she says.

above: Deborah Balter fills her garden with plants that are carefully chosen to bring color and texture to the landscape. **left:** The lap pool reflects Deborah's principles of artistic design—the palms' magnificent trunks draw the eye upward for depth, the ferns convey serenity and softness, and the pool's hand-painted finish produces the illusion of a lagoon.

An unyielding spirit of adventure feeds Deborah's artistic appetite, while her travels from the tropics to the Orient fuel her garden's design. "A tropical climate signifies easy living, beauty, and lushness," she says. The framework of the garden is established with palms—some native and some exotic. "I've always been enchanted with palms. They hold an enormous amount of romance," she says. In addition, the towering trees are used to generate depth by going up—a design trick for small spaces.

The garden is a study in shades of green. "It is a refuge from my business," Deborah says. The verdant palette gives her the freedom to add color in carefully chosen places, to focus attention, and to draw an unexpected smile.

Elevated walkways connect one garden vista to the next, with a surprise always just around the corner. "The decks take you on a journey through the garden. I designed them so you can view this controlled tropical jungle without disturbing it or any hidden animals. They're also low maintenance," she says.

From the deck outside the back door, you take the walkway around the garden. The lap pool spans the narrow lot from one side to the other. A cool, serene lagoon appears to stretch lazily for miles, another vision of Deborah's artful eye. The effect is not difficult to create—a textured paint finish and massive ferns in poolside beds combine for the idyllic illusion. The palm-frond canopy overhead diffuses the hot Florida sun and creates

top, left: From the front entrance, the garden appears to be a tropical rain forest. **top:** Even the colorful furniture becomes a design element enfolded in the peaceful green landscape. **above, left:** The garden is tropical in nature, spiced with reminders of Deborah's travels to the Orient. **above, right:** Carefully planning the details of her small garden, Deborah takes advantage of every inch of space.

a dancing shimmer on the water.

Next stop is a hike to the top of a mountain. While the garden was under construction, Deborah had a plan for the coral-based soil being dug to make a spot for the pool. "While I was at work one day, the construction crew took away all the soil they had excavated for the pool's foundation. I had plans for all of that—I made them bring it back for my mountain," she recalls. Allegedly one of the highest natural points in Dade County, her "mountain" is an elevated patio tucked craftily into the lot's corner. "The mountain was made from the fill when the pool was dug, so it is earth and therefore natural," Deborah teases. It serves as a private retreat in a nest of vines and branches, from which dangle orchids and bromeliads. Deborah introduces color carefully, using both flowers and furniture to draw the eye.

The pool house is next on the pathway, with a hot tub occupying the lower space and a screened sleeping porch above. Its dual-level design reflects her passion for flight. "The Jacuzzi house is for relaxation, indulgence, and thought," she says. "I designed the second level so I could be among the palm fronds but not have to scale the trunks to get there. It gets me above ground level."

After winding around the opposite end of the pool, the tour is complete. Within this small space, every inch is accounted for—with perfect plant choices, extraordinary design principles, and a large dose of magic.

If gardening has a measure of attitude, Deborah's endeavors are a marvelous model. She refers to her screened porch as a rain room—a place to sit and enjoy the soul-soothing sounds of a tropical shower. Perhaps the sign painted over this door says it all: "An hour in the garden puts life's problems in perspective." Grounded in tranquility, this garden is Deborah's paradise.

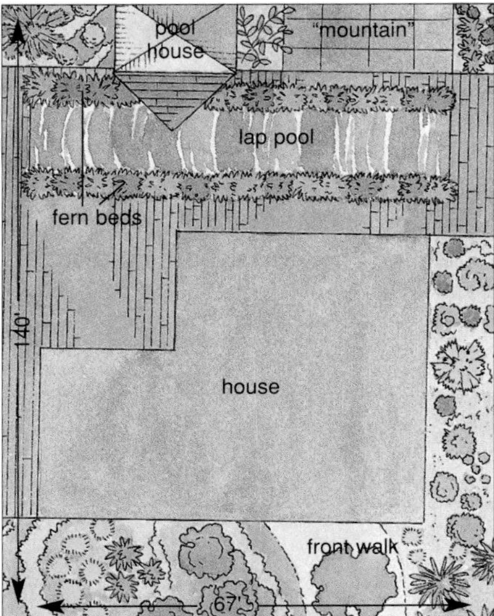

above, right: A guardian of the garden, this docile dragon is one of Deborah's creations. **right:** Deborah weaves subtle surprises and humor into the garden. Notice the iridescent purple reptile sneaking from the edge of a fabulous potted orchid. **below, left:** The pool house is focused on relaxation. A hot tub on the lower level allows visitors to look out over the landscape while relaxing, and the sleeping porch above holds the promise of an excellent nap. The color of the facade blends seamlessly with trees. **below, right:** The reclusive "mountain" garden is the high point of Deborah's plan.

symphony
OF SUNFLOWERS

As temperatures rise throughout the day, sunflowers open wide—a radiant overture to the summer sun.

Sunflowers epitomize everything that is summer—jubilant and hospitable. In the garden they get sassy with the ruthless heat; indoors they radiate with a resounding chorus of charm and nonchalance. Either way, a collection of these simple blooms celebrates the season like no other.

BY ELLEN RUOFF RILEY
PHOTOGRAPHY VAN CHAPLIN

Sunflowers are essential everyday flowers, and there's still time to plant seeds for an Indian summer display. "Here, we plant sunflowers through the end of July," says Mark Priest, owner of Coyoté Farms in West Fork, Arkansas. August offers the opportunity for starting a late-season garden in the Lower South. Choose selections with fast bloom times—the number of days it takes a seed to germinate, grow, and flower. "This time of year, sunflowers that would normally mature in 60 days may take 70 due to shorter day length," he says. A few of Mark's favorites are 'Sunbright,' 'Moonbright,' and 'Sunbeam.' Each plant produces a large, strong-stemmed blossom. " 'Autumn Beauty' is a smaller, multibranching type that is wonderful for fall color," he adds.

Avoid battling seed-eating critters by starting sunflowers on a sunny windowsill in small paper cups filled with damp potting soil. When the first sets of leaves unfurl, gently remove the bottoms from the cups, and plant the seedlings in the garden, wrappers and all.

Sneeze Protection

If your plans include cutting blooms to enjoy indoors, be aware that some sunflowers shed pollen. " 'Sunbeam,' 'Sunbright,' and 'Moonbright' are pollenless selections that will not drop staining yellow dust or cause an allergic sneezing frenzy," Mark says.

left: As Mark and Kilia Priest's son, Eli, knows, sunflowers put a smile on a boy's face during a summer day. **below:** Whether you purchase them or cut them from your own garden, sunflowers are the ultimate, affordable take-home flowers.

SUITABLE FOR CUTTING

Here's a list of more sunflowers that cut like a charm.

- **Bright Bandolier**—a mix of yellow and warm mahogany-edged selections
- **'Sunrich Lemon'**—a pollenless selection with lemon-yellow petals and black centers
- **'Valentine'**—Each stem produces sprays of small blooms, averaging 4 to 6 inches across.
- **'Floristan'**—Bicolored flowers appear on branched stems, each bloom's petals ranging from creamy yellow to deep maroon.

Others, including many of the multibranching selections, cut beautifully but may drop some pollen. Prevent furniture damage by protecting the area under the flowers.

Mark offers some tips for long-lasting cut flowers: "Gather blooms early in the day, just as the buds are opening. Make a diagonal slice on the stem, and place it immediately in water. Remove all foliage except for the top two leaves under the blossom." Changing the vase water every few days also increases the cut flower's life span.

Some types of flowers are solo performers—a single blossom is more than enough. Sunflowers, however, aren't that way. Individually, each one is bright and pretty, but collectively, they stage a symphony of feel-good, uncomplicated happiness.

Mexican bush sage *(See pages 178–183.)*

September

Garden Checklist 164

The Season's Best Perennials 166
great-looking blooms that come back
year after year

A Courtyard with Old-world Charm 169
a Texas garden with a Mediterranean air

Compact Kitchen Garden 170
a flavor-filled garden by the back door

An Azalea for Fall 171
this Southern classic will soon herald autumn

Tropical Ladies 172
orchids that even a novice can grow

Doctor Dirt 174
a Delta gardener creates a fantastic cottage garden

Glorious Fall Garden 178
a Lowcountry landscape filled with a tapestry of color

garden checklist
SEPTEMBER

Editor's Notebook

PHOTOGRAPH: JEAN ALLSOPP

There are two reasons why grocery stores stock certain selections of fruits and vegetables, and great taste is not necessarily one of them. Most grocers decide a particular fruit or vegetable's fate based on how pretty it is and whether it can be launched into orbit without bruising. So the best tasting produce isn't always the best looking. My 'Golden Russet' heirloom apple is a good example. The tree grows quickly, flowers abundantly, and produces tons of sweet, juicy apples—which are far superior, in my humble opinion, to the store-bought 'Red Delicious' kind that look and taste like wax. Of course, my tree's yellowish-green apples are covered with golden-brown splotches, and if you don't spray them with fungicides (I don't), they get spots. But I don't care. Good taste is better than good looks...something my wife reminds me whenever I stand in front of the mirror.

—STEVE BENDER

TIPS

■ **Autumn equinox**—September 23 marks the end of summer and the beginning of fall. Cooler weather makes it much more enjoyable to be outside. Now's the time for grooming fall borders, planting spring borders, sowing the fall vegetable garden, digging holes for bulbs, and planting trees and shrubs. But, most importantly, just be sure to get outside and enjoy your garden.

■ **Basil**—Keep harvesting, as this herb will produce new leaves until the cool nights of fall slow it down. To extend your supply, take cuttings about 2 inches long, and place them in jars on a sunny kitchen windowsill. The cuttings will root quickly and continue to grow. Add a little liquid fertilizer to the water to promote the growth of foliage.

■ **Moisture**—Water slowly, deeply, and infrequently to promote deep rooting and prevent excess runoff. Add mulches where needed, and control weeds because they compete for water and nutrients.

■ **Seeds**—Collect and dry annual flowering seedheads, such as zinnias, marigolds, cosmos, and Mexican sunflowers *(Tithonia rotundifolia).* Store seeds in a cool, dry place, and sow late next spring for your cutting garden.

PLANT

■ **Fall greens**—Sow the seeds of turnips, mustard greens, collards, and spinach now in the Middle South and Lower South. If you want to get a jump on fall growth, set out container-grown plants, which work just as well.

■ **Fall perennials**—It's not too late to add these autumn bloomers to your garden. They're flowering now at garden centers. Mexican bush sage *(Salvia leucantha)* is a must-have with its velvety, purple-and-white flower spikes. Philippine violet *(Barleria cristata)* will be loaded with lavender flowers. Cigar plant *(Cuphea ignea)* lights up the landscape with tiny, oblong, orange-and-yellow flowers.

■ **Garden mums**—These can be found in every shape, color, and size at nurseries now. For additional color, place them in fall beds, in containers, or in arrangements. Be sure to keep mums well watered. If adding them to your fall border, provide ample mulch to protect roots as they become established. For something different from tight pincushion mums, look for loosely growing old-fashioned types such as 'Hillside Pink Sheffield' and 'Single Apricot Korean.'

■ **Roses**—Fresh plants begin arriving in garden centers this month in the Lower and Coastal South. Plant them in full sun and well-drained soil. Water daily for the first two weeks and then every other day until they're established and the weather cools. Eventually you will be able to reduce watering to only twice a week. Fertilize monthly with rose food.

Wildflower Seeds

Prepare soil by tilling the top few inches. Choose a seed mix adapted to your area. Mixes may contain native wildflowers such as bluebonnets, Drummond phlox, Indian paintbrushes, blanket flower (*Gaillardia* sp.), coreopsis, and purple coneflowers as well as introduced types such as larkspur, cornflower, poppies, and ox-eye daisies. After scattering the seeds evenly, firm or roll the soil with a hand roller. Drifts of wildflowers are a nice transition between lawns and the natural landscape.

Fragrance

Enjoy the sweet scent of ginger lilies *(Hedychium coronarium)* till frost. In the Lower and Coastal South, you can still add them to your border. Provide good drainage, and don't plant too deeply. Mulch well to protect plants as they become established. In the Middle and Upper South, you can enjoy these plants in terra-cotta pots. Before the first frost, move ginger lilies inside to a sunny location to extend their bloom. Around November, cut back the foliage, and allow the plant to rest. Leave the plant in the pot, keeping soil slightly dry. Or remove it from the pot, and store the tubers in a warm, dry location.

■ **Spring-flowering perennials—**Louisiana iris, daylilies, purple coneflowers, yarrow (*Achillea* sp.), ox-eye daisies, and phlox can be divided and planted now for spring bloom. Begin by mixing 4 to 6 inches of organic material into the top 8 to 10 inches of soil. Add 3 to 5 pounds of balanced fertilizer per 100 square feet of bed. Set each division or new plant at the same depth that it was growing. Arrange in drifts or elongated masses of at least five to seven plants.

PRUNE

■ **Cutting back perennials—**Prune or top fall-flowering perennials such as Mexican mint marigold *(Tagetes lucida)*, Copper Canyon daisy *(T. lemmonii)*, aromatic asters *(Aster oblongifolius)*, and Mexican bush sage *(Salvia leucantha)*. This will produce more compact plants that will not require staking.

CONTROL

■ **Citrus care—**In the Coastal and Tropical South, it is important to ensure that plants receive enough water. Uneven moisture causes fruit splitting and drop. Water when the top few inches of soil are dry. Citrus trees need moist soil but never standing water. Prop up limbs that have heavy fruit loads to avoid breakage. Mites can become a problem in drier weather. They will cause curled leaves, which yellow and then drop from the tree. To control mites, spray plants with an insecticidal soap, coating the entire leaf, especially the undersides.

FERTILIZE

■ **Cool-season lawns—**Now is a great time to establish grasses such as fescue, perennial ryegrass, and bluegrass. If you are sowing seed for a new lawn, use a lower nitrogen, higher phosphorus fertilizer such as a 18-24-10. If you have an established lawn, go with a higher nitrogen formula such as 31-2-4.

■ **Early-fall lawn care—**There is still time to apply fertilizer to all lawns except centipede, which will need to wait until spring. Use a 16-4-8 mix, and apply at the rate recommended on the bag for your type of grass. Water your lawn whenever it begins to show signs of wilt. Long, infrequent watering is better than short, frequent watering. Look for gobs of white foam on the stems and leaves of centipede (a sign of spittlebug problems) and random brown patches in St. Augustine (a symptom of chinch bugs). For either of these problems, apply a granular lawn insect control according to label directions.

September notes:

Tip of the Month

I keep an old cutting board handy outside and use it for cutting the stems of fresh flowers to the desired length. This is much easier than trying to hold the flowers and cut the stems in my hands.

CHARLOTTE BRYANT
GREENSBURG, KENTUCKY

the season's best perennials

BY STEVE BENDER / PHOTOGRAPHY VAN CHAPLIN

'Honorine Jobert' Japanese anemone, 'Harrington's Pink' New England aster, and 'Lavender Bright Eyes' butterfly bush provide splendid fall flowers at the home of André and Claire Viette in Fishersville, Virginia.

GARDENING

PLANTS AND DESIGN

Perennials are beautiful, affordable, come back every year, and they're blooming their heads off right now.

The hot month of August is a bit like a Sunday sermon—sometimes it seems to go on forever. But just when you think you'll spend eternity shuttered inside an air-conditioned room, September turns down the thermostat. It's fall outside, the days are cooler, and the flowers are simply killer. Asters, mums, sedums, and fall sunflowers. For these and many other perennials, now is their time to shine.

So why aren't you planting? Maybe you're not sure what a perennial is (it's a nonwoody plant that comes back every year, provided you don't subject it to polka music). Or perhaps you're worried that September is too late to start. Worry not. Garden centers know that instant color sells and are awash in blooming potted perennials. Give them sun, good soil, and enough water to get established, and they'll bloom for weeks this autumn and many autumns thereafter. Here are a few of my favorites.

Love Your Mum

Many of us grew up thinking mums were *the* autumn perennials. We bedded them out, enjoyed their color for a few weeks in fall, then felt ripped off when they didn't bloom again in spring like pansies. So we dismissed them as too much trouble. In the process, however, we forgot about the *good* garden mums—the abundant, mounding, durable types that bloom for decades with minimal care. I especially like daisy-type mums in the peachy-apricot-orange range. So I covet the peach-orange blooms of 'Pumpkin Harvest' and the apricot-pinks of old 'Sheffield Pink.' But I also tout the new My Favorite Mum Series, particularly 'Autumn Red.' Without the slightest pruning, it forms a solid mound 18 inches tall and 36 inches wide and bears thousands of showy red blossoms with yellow centers. It's a champ.

NEW ENGLAND ASTER

Size: 2 to 6 feet tall
Light: full sun
Soil: varies but fertile is best
Pests: none serious
Divide: late winter or early spring
Range: Upper, Middle, Lower, and Coastal South
Recommended selections: 'Harrington's Pink' (shown above), 'Alma Potschke,' 'Hella Lacy,' 'September Ruby,' 'Purple Dome'

GARDEN MUM

Size: 20 to 30 inches tall
Light: full sun
Soil: moist, fertile, and well drained
Pests: aphids
Divide: late winter or early spring
Range: throughout the South
Recommended selections: 'Pumpkin Harvest' (shown above), 'Sheffield Pink,' 'Venus,' and 'Autumn Red' (part of the My Favorite Mum Series)

Master the Aster

New England asters sound as if they would melt in our Southern summers. Not so. In fact, they're tough, dependable, and trouble free. Their blossoms resemble daisy mums in form, but asters usually grow loose and tall (good for the back

'AUTUMN JOY' SEDUM

Size: 18 to 24 inches tall
Light: full sun
Soil: well drained
Pests: none serious
Divide: Don't divide; instead, root cuttings in summer.
Range: Upper, Middle, Lower, and Coastal South

of the border) and offer the blue and purple colors mums lack. Favorites include 'Harrington's Pink,' 'Hella Lacy' (purple), 'September Ruby' (red), 'Alma Potschke' (salmon-rose), and 'Purple Dome.'

Sedum Is Believing

It's hard to imagine another plant that gives you as much show for as little work as 'Autumn Joy' sedum. This hardy succulent tolerates heat and drought and has no serious pests. All it wants is sun and good drainage. Broccoli-shaped clusters of pale pink flowers sit atop gray-green foliage in late summer. In fall, flowers change to rose, brick red, and finally copper-bronze. Butterflies love them. Use sedum in mixed borders, masses, rock gardens, and planters.

Anemone Is No Enemy

Say "uh-NEM-oh-nee." Now you understand the clever subtitle and also how to pronounce this fall jewel's name. Japanese anemone, a hybrid of several species, offers handsome, maple-like foliage. Every autumn, long, upright wands rise from the leaves, bearing silky blooms with green eyes surrounded by yellow or orange stamens. They make excellent cut flowers. Anemones like moist, fertile, well-drained soil and light afternoon shade. 'Honorine Jobert' (single white blooms) is my top pick, but I also recommend 'September Charm' (single rose-pink), 'Bressingham Glow' (semidouble raspberry-pink), and 'Queen Charlotte' (semidouble pink).

Obedience Is Mandatory

Know how the obedient plant *(Physostegia virginiana)* got its name? If you point an individual flower in one direction, it remains there. That's all that's obedient about the plant, though. Give it rich, moist soil, and it spreads aggressively. Still, its 10-inch spikes of pink or white blossoms make good cut flowers and add long-lasting color to the fall border. If it spreads too much, dig up what you don't want, and share it with someone you like—or even someone you don't.

JAPANESE ANEMONE

Size: 2 to 4 feet tall
Light: morning and midday sun, afternoon shade
Soil: moist, fertile, well drained
Pests: none serious
Divide: late winter or early spring
Range: Upper, Middle, and Lower South
Recommended selections: 'Honorine Jobert' (shown above), 'Bressingham Glow,' 'Queen Charlotte,' and 'September Charm'

OBEDIENT PLANT

Size: 2 to 4 feet tall
Light: full to partial sun
Soil: varies
Pests: none serious
Divide: late winter or early spring
Range: Upper, Middle, Lower, and Coastal South
Recommended selections: 'Vivid' (shown above), 'Summer Snow' (white)

Here Come the Sunflowers

Most of you have planted those giant annual sunflowers with heads as big as Luciano Pavarotti's. But you've probably missed out on perennial sunflowers. Their blooms may not be as huge, but one plant can produce hundreds, and the show goes on for weeks. Swamp sunflower *(Helianthus angustifolius)* and willowleaf sunflower *(H. salicifolius)* look similar, though the first one blooms later and has wider leaves. They're both tall (definitely for the back of the border) and feature multitudes of 3-inch yellow daisies with brown centers. They spread quickly in moist, fertile soil, so they'll always be with you—unless you like polka music. ◆

PERENNIAL SUNFLOWERS

Size: 4 to 8 feet tall
Light: full sun
Soil: moist, fertile (tolerant of wet)
Pests: none serious
Divide: late winter or early spring
Range: throughout the South
Nice to know: spread rapidly underground in moist soil

PHOTOGRAPHS: VAN CHAPLIN

A Courtyard With Old-world Charm

Stylish design and attention to detail give this Texas garden a Mediterranean air.

top, left: Terraces, sitting walls, and level changes divide this garden into intimate spaces. **top, right:** Saving a large pecan tree meant surrounding its base with a deck. **above:** Limestone pavers are detailed with granite diamonds and edged in brick.

Sydney and J. L. Huffines had a vision for their backyard in Highland Park, Texas. "We wanted it to feel like a small Italian garden," Sydney says, "something we could treat as an outdoor living room for dining and entertaining." They also needed privacy from a nearby busy street and shade from the Texas sun. To achieve all this, they called Dallas landscape architect Harold Leidner.

Protecting a Tree

Among the first problems to be addressed was a large pecan tree that, unfortunately, was located just a few feet from the main glass doors that opened to the back. Removing the tree wasn't an option. "It provided the only real shade," says Sydney. "And in Texas, *all* trees are important," she says. To accommodate the tree, Harold surrounded it with a wooden deck edged with brick. The deck allows the roots to breathe and obtain water and keeps the soil above them from becoming compacted. Moreover, the opening around the trunk can be easily enlarged as the tree grows. The deck also permits easy access to the doors from either side of the tree.

Adding Privacy

The backyard slopes gently away from the house. Harold took advantage of this to create a series of levels that include the back steps, deck, patio, and raised planters. "Different elevations always add to the interest," notes Sydney. Impatiens and caladiums lend summer color to the planters that rest against a rear stucco wall. Magnolias, crepe myrtles, and hollies growing in the planters rise above the wall for additional privacy.

An ornate patio, consisting of limestone pavers on a concrete base, gives the garden a Mediterranean look. Detailed with black granite diamonds and edged in handmade brick, the pavers are set on the diagonal. To complete the picture, Harold added an elegant fountain against the rear wall in line with the glass doors.

When the weather is nice, chances are you'll find J. L. and Sydney in the garden. Music from hidden speakers and splashing water from the fountain mask the sounds of traffic. Night lighting showcases the sculptural forms of the trees. Yes, the garden is still in Texas. But for the moment they can close their eyes and imagine themselves in *Italia*. STEVE BENDER

Small but flavor-filled, this cozy little plot of herbs sits conveniently outside the kitchen door, where the bouquet garni is but a step and a snip away.

Compact Kitchen Garden

Sometimes little things bring the greatest pleasure—their rewards outweigh the efforts required. When a garden overflows with flavor and fragrance, the appeal zooms off the charts. That's the case with this little plot of herbs, located in a sunny spot right outside the kitchen door of a Birmingham home.

Working in collaboration, garden designers Norman Kent Johnson and Mary Zahl did a lot of the initial work, getting the soil and drainage right so planting would be easy and growth would be ensured. "The garden, enclosed on three sides, was defined by the house and retaining wall," says Norman. "The fourth side is a paved terrace. At the time of construction, a catch basin was installed in the center of the garden for surface drainage, but the real problem was the clay soil."

The existing clay had to be dug out and replaced with loam mixed with sand and organic matter—a gardener's ideal. "A doughnut of PVC pipe was installed in the garden to drain the improved soil," Norman explains. "The pipe drains into the catch basin."

They concealed the catch basin by placing four bricks at the corners to hold up a 24-inch-square paving stone. An urn stands on top of that. Today thyme planted in the soil between adjacent pavers has crept over the edge of the basin so no one knows it is there.

A grid of 2-inch-thick bluestone pavers serves as a walkway, with space between stones allowing for planting. Some areas are left uncovered to provide space for larger plants to grow. A key to the design's success is that the stones sit above the finished grade, so surface water courses between them, leaving feet and foliage high and dry.

A ½-inch blanket of gravel was put down atop the soil, and then plants were set through it. Gravel helps the area to dry quickly after a rain and reflects light back onto lamb's ears, sage, and other plants prone to rot. Carefully chosen for its color and shape, the dark gravel doesn't create a blinding glare in the direct sun, and because it's not round, it doesn't roll underfoot.

No garden lives without change, especially not an herb garden. Here, lettuce thrives in the bright light of fall's cooler days. Violas bloom in winter and early spring until they're replaced by basil. Sometimes the owner grows tomatoes on tepees. When the oregano or lemon balm gets out of hand, it is beaten back with trowel and glove. A known thug, mint is kept in a pot to contain its aggression. Fig trees, along with the cool silver of lavender in a concrete pot, lend their own special charm to complete this small but hardworking city garden.

An Azalea for Fall

If there's one plant that declares spring has arrived, it's the azalea. But it may soon herald autumn, too.

Imagine if you could capture the fleeting spring production of one of the South's most talented troupers—the azalea—and then stage a command performance again amid the gilded backdrop of late summer and early fall. Gardeners already familiar with Encore azaleas know this scenario is possible. This relatively new group of azaleas was developed in the 1980s by crossing traditional spring-blooming plants with a rare Taiwanese summer-blooming azalea, *Rhododendron oldhamii*. The offspring boast blooms in springtime and then an encore in late summer and fall. Although Encore azaleas don't offer a profusion of flowers like the common spring bloomers, they make up for it with a much longer blooming period.

"What's amazing is the duration of the total flowering period," says Jim Berry, general manager of Plant Development Services, Inc. (PDSI), in Loxley, Alabama. "We've had reports of nine months of flowering in the Coastal South," he says. PDSI owns the patent to propagate Encore azaleas, and they've been working overtime to keep up with the demand.

What's the Story?

The history of the Encore azalea started when avid azalea lover Robert Lee of Independence, Louisiana, began experimenting in his own garden. "Azaleas are easy to grow, and they're really colorful. I was just fascinated with them," Robert says. He began cross-pollinating different types and comparing notes with other azalea fanatics. Robert soon made an agreement with PDSI and Flowerwood Nursery to develop and market the best of the best. After a 15-year hybridization and selection process, Encore azaleas became commercially available in 1997.

The Autumn Series is composed of 13 selections, including 'Autumn Royalty,' 'Autumn Amethyst,' 'Autumn Rouge,' and 'Autumn Cheer,' which are fuchsia or bright pink. 'Autumn Twist' sports large white blossoms with purple stripes. Look for the release of deep red 'Autumn Sangria' in 2003 and a pure white one to be named in 2004. 'Autumn Embers,' 'Autumn Monarch,' and 'Autumn Bravo' mix well with vibrant fall tones. Encores vary in size and habit—some are compact and shrubby; others are more loosely branched and upright.

Although the horticulturists at PDSI are working to develop more cold-hardy selections, there is some debate as to how far north they should be planted. If you garden in the Middle or Upper South, experiment with a few Encores in an area protected from cold winter winds. Selections that are a bit more cold hardy include 'Autumn Cheer,' 'Autumn Rouge,' and 'Autumn Royalty.' If you can grow them successfully through a couple of winters, then invest in a few more.

'Autumn Rouge' Encore azaleas bring color to this front entrance during spring, summer, and fall. Here, they pair well with 'Natchez' crepe myrtles.

PHOTOGRAPH: ALLEN ROKACH

Caring for Your Encores

Midspring and early fall are the best times to plant. Because Encores are sensitive to cold, they do better if the roots are well established before winter arrives. Plant them high, with the top of the root balls showing 1 to 2 inches above ground. Amend clay soil with organic matter such as sphagnum peat moss or compost. Add a 4-inch layer of mulch, such as pine straw, to hold moisture in the soil and provide a warm winter blanket.

Water your new azaleas periodically for the first year and during dry spells thereafter. Because they bloom frequently, they need two annual feedings with an azalea fertilizer. Feed them after your last frost in spring and again in August before their fall flush. When your Encore azaleas get leggy, prune them immediately after spring flowering, and they will have time to set buds for a second show in the fall.

Now if the researchers at PDSI could just develop a fall-blooming dogwood to accompany Encore azaleas, they could retire comfortably.

GLENN R. DINELLA

Tropical Ladies

Exotic colors, patterns, and forms beloved by orchid enthusiasts combine with an agreeable nature to make these plants good for even beginning growers.

PHOTOGRAPHS: VAN CHAPLIN / STYLING: BARB GLASER AND ELISSA STEEVES

above: Although tropical lady-slippers need bright, indirect light in order to thrive, it's okay to display them in the middle of a room for a short time while you enjoy the flowers. **above, left:** A bloom's fantastic form consists of an upright sepal and a pouch or "slipper" that distinguishes these flowers. The petals can be striped, dotted, and even lined with "eyelashes."

Lady-slipper orchids are living proof of nature's imagination. Their blossoms are as colorful as they are fantastical in their form. At times they seem to be as much animal as plant, with thick fleshy petals, a pouch with visible veins of color, and outstretched arms. They do not stop with a wash of color. They employ dots, stripes, and gradations of hue that make them seem to be flowers not just of another continent, but of another world.

Related to the lady-slipper orchids that grow naturally in the temperate forests of the South, these cold-sensitive cousins hail from the forest floor of tropical Asia. They will not enjoy life in our gardens, but they will survive and prosper in our homes.

If you have grown butterfly orchids *(Phalaenopsis* sp.), you will most likely succeed with tropical lady-slippers *(Paphiopedilum* sp.). They need similar conditions. Full sun is not necessary with most types; morning or late afternoon light is sufficient.

Unlike other orchids that are found growing in the treetops, tropical lady-slippers are at home in a layer of rich decaying leaves that rarely dries out. Consequently, they shouldn't dry out in a pot either. You can expect plants to rebloom annually beginning anytime from fall to spring with flowers lasting from several weeks to several months, depending upon the type.

There are several groups within the tropical lady-slippers, and these divisions are a guide to their cultural requirements as well as their appearance. But don't be put off by the complexity. Like all living things, they are forgiving within a reasonable range of conditions.

left: Here both single-flowered (far left) and multiflora types are displayed in the same art pottery bowl.

LADY-SLIPPER GROWING MEDIUM

5 parts medium grade Douglas fir bark
3 parts coarse sphagnum peat moss
2 parts coarse perlite
1 part ¼-inch charcoal
½ teaspoon dolomitic lime per 5-inch pot

above: The hard-leaved types, called bulldogs for their full, rounded flowers, prefer cool temperatures at night and do well on sunny windowsills.

You'll find plants with both mottled- and solid-green leaves. For most, the mottled-leaved types are more agreeable to life on the windowsill. Those with green leaves need slightly cooler conditions at night (50 to 55 degrees) and don't quite flower as freely. Some catalogs and books refer to these as "hard-leaved." These may be better for experienced orchid growers and those living in colder areas. Mottled-leaved types (or "soft-leaved") like slightly warmer temperatures at night (60 to 65 degrees). About a 10-degree increase in the daytime is good, similar to the temperature variation in most homes.

Tropical lady-slippers are also divided by flowering habits. Some bear one bloom per stem, while others, called multifloras, have multiple blooms. While more blooms may sound good, these plants require higher light. They are the favorite of orchid grower Ed Gilliland in Orlando. "Multifloras are easier to grow if you have the right light—a Southern exposure or all day light." If you live in a more temperate area, the solitary blooming, mottled-leaved types may be easier to grow.

An easy type for the beginner to grow is Maudiae, a hybrid with many color variations and named selections. It has mottled foliage and ability to bloom in low light at moderate temperatures. Flowers last 6 to 10 weeks. LINDA ASKEY

left: The Maudiae hybrids boast spectacular colorations in both flowers and foliage. They are also some of the easiest to grow in the home.

WHAT LADIES WANT

Growers agree that periodically repotting your plants is essential to success. "Don't let them stay in the same pot too long," says Gene Crocker, vice president of Carter and Holmes Orchids in Newberry, South Carolina. "Repot preferably every six months; definitely, once per year." Use a fresh mix containing Douglas fir bark, sphagnum peat moss, and perlite (see recipe above). When repotting, take care not to break or cut existing roots. The strength of the plant depends on the roots.

"Tropical lady-slippers are happier in plastic pots because they like moisture around the roots," says Gene. "And don't overpot; use the smallest pot practical." Water regularly to maintain the moisture around the roots. Feed monthly with water-soluble fertilizer (20-20-20 or 20-30-20). Make sure the pot has a drainage hole.

While you can order rare and expensive plants, you may also find affordable ones in both local nurseries and specialty stores. Expect to pay $15 to $35 for a flowering plant. Select specimens that are just beginning to flower. That way, you'll get the longest bloom for your buck.

Doctor Dirt

Sitting in front of vivid cockscombs, Doctor Dirt shows off a pair of mustard seedlings encased in mud and ready for planting.

Leon Goldsberry came home to the Delta, and it captured him heart and soil.

Leon Goldsberry doesn't mind if you call him "dirt." Just be polite and put "Doctor" in front of it.

"Doctor Dirt" is the self-appointed title of this Pied Piper of flowers in the Mississippi Delta. His garden, located in the little town of Edwards, near Vicksburg, is as unpretentious as the man. Don't expect to see teak-handled shovels or copper weather vanes here. Look instead for scarlet cockscombs, outstretched banana trees, lemon yellow sunflowers, and spiny hardy orange—all time-tested plants of Leon's childhood. Virtually exploding with flowers, his yard preaches a special gospel—that husbanding plants is the best way to connect with our past, participate in our present, and proclaim to the world who we are.

Doctor Dirt (a name he took from one of the many radio gardening shows he listens to every Saturday morning) wakes these days in the same house in which he grew up, built by his great-grandfather in 1895. Yet he spent most of his adult life outside the South. After studying sociology at Rust College in Holly Springs, Mississippi, he moved to Toronto and became a childcare worker. His Canadian sojourn lasted 30 years, until 1995, when he returned to care for his mother, Millie. "I always promised that when she got older, I'd come home and spend time with her," he recalls. "I planted a lot of these flowers for her." After Millie passed away in 1998 at age 79, Leon named his yard, "Millie's Gardens."

His is a classic swept-yard cottage garden emblematic of parts of the rural South. No lawn, no mulch, no regimentation. Paths and patches of bare earth separate garden beds teeming with raucous assemblies of annuals, perennials, bulbs, shrubs, fruit, and even agronomic crops, such as cotton.

Some folks dismiss his garden as a jungle, but Doctor Dirt takes such criticism in stride. "I don't want everybody's yard

BY STEVE BENDER
PHOTOGRAPHY VAN CHAPLIN

Dr. Dirt
WELCOME

Far left: Flamingos, cotton, swamp sunflowers, and banana trees welcome you to Doctor Dirt's office.
Left: Leon loves to share plants.
Below: Leon's mother's old punch glasses

looking like my yard, because I don't look like everybody else. No two paintings are alike, and gardens shouldn't be either," he declares. "Suburbia is so artificial—everything's in rows. But I like to be an individual. Society ladies will say, 'Ooh, you can't mix those colors.' And I'll say, 'Says who?' "

> Society ladies will say, "Ooh, you can't mix those colors." And I'll say, "Says who?"
>
> *Leon Goldsberry*

Making your way in this garden is like turning the pages of a family album. "Every plant in my yard reminds me of my past," he says. "The flowering quince is 93 years old. My great-grandparents put that in. My purple dahlia is from Mom's time. So is 'Paul's Scarlet Climber' rose given to us by a garden club between 1929 and 1932. Even the native stuff, like devil's walking stick, I remember getting from the woods with my uncle, stepdad, and granddad."

One native plant, swamp sunflower *(Helianthus angustifolius)*, forms yellow blooms in fall. In the region's rich soil, it grows 14 feet tall. "I remember the sunflowers from when I was 6 or 7 years old," he says. "The rain would bend them over, and I'd try to jump up to touch them. I used to take them as bouquets to my teacher."

A central tenet of Doctor Dirt's philosophy is that gardens should start out by the street and say welcome. "The garden is how I meet people," he explains. "It starts a conversation." Voice any interest, and you are invited in to wander the paths and inspect dozens upon dozens of old Southern pass-along plants, including reseeding orange cosmos, candlestick plant *(Cassia alata)*, turk's turban *(Malvaviscus arboreus drummondii)*, and a gorgeous purple-and-white angel's trumpet (*Datura metel* 'Cornucopaea').

Seedlings abound. Should you want any to take home, Doctor Dirt has a novel packaging technique. He squeezes a ball of Delta mud around the plant's roots. The mud dries on the outside, but stays moist on the inside. When you plant your prize in its new home, it never suspects it's been moved.

Leon now works as a landscape gardener, supervising various plantings around town. Money is tight, but that hasn't curbed his artistic expression. Millie's old punch glasses sparkle like Christmas lights on the branches of the hardy orange *(Poncirus trifoliata)*. His decorations prove that when it comes to creativity, imagination is the most valuable currency.

Doctor Dirt's influence is growing. Seeds and plants shared from his garden are popping up all over town. Folks in Edwards are rediscovering the joys of a garden, which, to Leon's way of thinking, is a journey home.

"In the beginning, God put us in a garden," he observes. "That is where we all come from." ◆

glorious fall GARDEN

BY GENE B. BUSSELL / PHOTOGRAPHY JEAN ALLSOPP

In this Lowcountry garden, shared plants are woven into a tapestry of color.

As you swing open the old iron gate into the garden of Frances and Milton Parker, it creaks reassuringly, welcoming you to their home as if you were opening the screen door to a friendly porch. Now is the perfect time to visit their quiet Beaufort, South Carolina, garden. The clear, blue skies of late summer and the cooler weather of early fall breathe life into the plants. Blooms that faded in the heat of August re-emerge in exuberant colors, creating a grand fanfare to welcome autumn. Though blossoms mark the occasion, what really makes the Parkers' garden special is the multitude of plants given to them by family and friends.

It Began in the Garden

Frances's earliest memories revolve around gardening. Even as a little girl, she loved flowers. One day while her father was away during World War II, she and her mother were outside in the yard. Frances said, "Momma, let's pray for Daddy June." (They called her father June, short for Junior.) While her mother closed her eyes to pray, Frances picked all the daffodils. She laughs mischievously at this story even now.

Frances grew up in McClellanville, South Carolina, a small fishing and farming village between Charleston and Georgetown. "We lived out in the country on the farm," she remembers. "My father would bring home wonderful things from the woods: wild ginger, pinxterbloom azaleas, common sweetshrubs, and fringe trees. We would take these and plant them in huge masses in the yard." Frances's birthday and her sister Katharine's both came in early spring, and their parents would always take them to a nursery to buy azaleas and camellias as presents.

Her mother, a nurse at a hospital in Georgetown, was known as "The Flower Lady" because she always carried flowers from her garden to patients. She also shared with neighbors—gladly handing out iris, daffodils, white flowering quince, and deutzia. Frances says, "I have always considered myself a good plant propagator, but my

"My soul requires that I garden; it's just necessary."

Frances Parker

top: A clipped boxwood hedge defines one side of the front garden. On the other side of the path, a perennial border spreads beneath loosely clipped sasanqua camellias and mock oranges.
above: A group of pots welcomes visitors to the garden at the beginning of the front path. The planters contain (clockwise from top) golden club moss (*Selaginella kraussiana* 'Aurea'); chartreuse grassy-leaved sweet flag (*Acorus gramineus* 'Pusillus Minimus Aureus'); and angel's tears *(Lindernia grandiflora)*. **above, right:** The colors of yellow thryallis *(Galphimia glauca)*, orange impatiens, and a chartreuse coleus enhance one another.

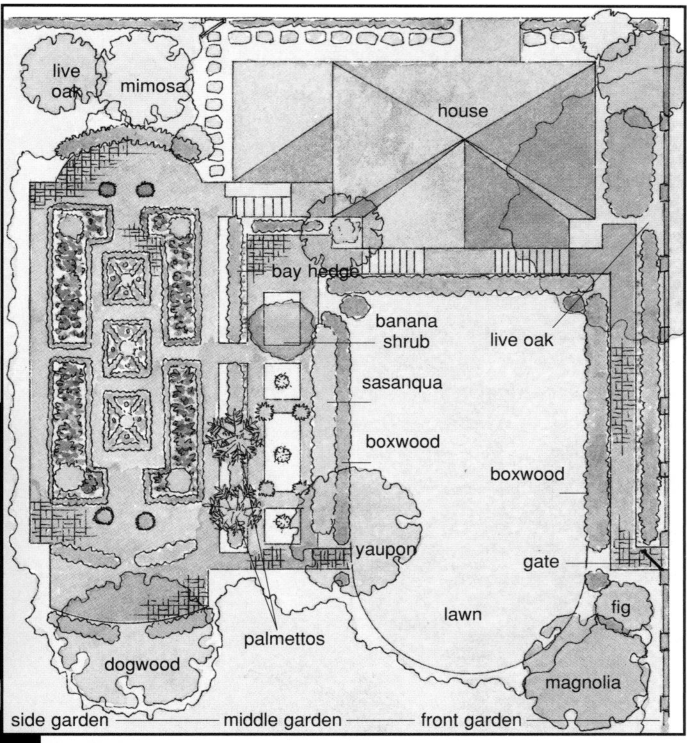

mother could root anything—at any time of the year. She would break off branches of blooming azaleas and spirea and stick them in the ground to root." Frances recalls that at the memorial service for her mother, the church was filled with flowers—flowers that came from neighbors' gardens, flowers that her mother had once shared with them. Reflecting on all this, Frances declares, "My soul requires that I garden; it's just necessary."

A Garden of Treasures

Plants shared by family and friends define the Parkers' garden. It's divided into three separate areas: front, middle, and side. Each boasts its own character, and each has diverse colors and textures to take advantage of the ever-changing light.

When Frances and Milton began their garden more than 25 years ago, very few plants occupied the space. An ancient bay hedge, a large multitrunked yaupon, a dogwood, and a few palmetto trees were all that stood in the yard. Keeping those plants in mind, the couple first created an oval lawn in the front to make the space seem deeper. They added paths and hedges to divide the garden, planning the three areas around the plants to be saved. Next, they gathered plants from both sides of their families—mock oranges, spireas, roses, iris, phlox, quince, and ginger lilies—and wove them into three garden rooms.

Along the Path

While the garden really begins outside the pierced brick walls, it's first defined along the brick path that leads through the front. A trimmed hedge of 'Wintergreen' boxwood (*Buxus microphylla koreana* 'Wintergreen') lines one edge of the path. The manicured boxwood balances the large, loosely clipped 'Yuletide' sasanqua

above: Palmetto trees, clipped boxwood, sasanqua camellias, and bay hedges anchor the middle garden.
above, center: The coarse texture of 'Golden Sword' yucca (*Yucca filamentosa* 'Golden Sword') contrasts with the fine texture of Asian star jasmine *(Trachelospermum asiaticum)* beds. **above, right:** An ancient banana shrub *(Michelia figo)* draped in Spanish moss serves as the centerpiece of the middle garden.

camellias (*Camellia sasanqua* 'Yuletide') and mock oranges on the other side. Yellow, orange, red, and green foliage and flowers find a home braided between and underneath the large shrubs.

Framed by Hedges

The middle garden lies between another clipped sasanqua hedge and a culinary bay *(Laurus nobilis)* hedge. This garden is primarily one of texture. Central to this area are large beds of trimmed Asian star jasmine, trained onto rebar frames. A bit whimsical in character, they are topped with blue ceramic pottery and look as if they could have emerged from a Dr. Seuss book. 'Golden Sword' yucca accents the corners of the center bed, while yellow-striped 'Bengal Tiger' cannas, 'Black Magic' elephant's ears, and orange butterfly gingers provide bold color and texture along the outside edges of the beds. "Foliage and texture are the things most exciting to me," Frances says. "I am not into blooms so much anymore—at least not primarily. I want everything to be a tapestry of color and texture."

On the Side

Of all the areas, the enclosed side garden holds the most surprise. "It's the secret garden, a retreat," Frances allows. As you enter through the bay hedge, a red China rose that belonged to Milton's grandmother waves out to greet you. A sundial serves as the central focus of this garden, and abundant colorful flowers radiate from it. Clipped boxwoods, serissa hedges, and brick paths establish the borders. Trimmed, variegated Asian star jasmine topiaries accent the center axis of the garden. Cherished roses such as 'Old Blush,' 'Louis Philippe,' and 'Maggie' grow among boxwoods on the outside edge.

A wild assortment of colorful coleus, salvias, torenias, phlox, impatiens, and gomphrena complements the rose blooms. A 'Neon' eggplant, mixed into the border, stands out in this secret garden of flowers. Frances says, "I often use herbs, such as bronze fennel and purple basil, and vegetables, such as cherry tomatoes, peppers, and eggplants, for additional color and texture."

The side garden has changed over the years. The path used to be lawn, and the borders were defined by mondo grass. "Gardens evolve," Frances says. "Nothing is static in the garden."

above: Sheared-boxwood parterres, trimmed variegated Asian star jasmine (*Trachelospermum asiaticum* 'Variegata'), camellia standards, and brick paths form the bones of the side garden.
above, right: Flowerpots grace the back steps to the house.
right: Cherry-colored coleus complements the peach-colored impatiens.

To Name a Few

With the many flowers in her garden, it is no wonder there are surprises to be found between the bricks and borders. Often Frances will select and name these finds for family and friends, to honor them. She says, "It makes them feel very special to have a plant named after them." Her keen eye noticed a salvia seedling just in time for her to rescue it before the lawnmower could chop it down. She named it after her grandson Anthony. Salvia 'Anthony Parker' is a cross between 'Midnight' Mexican bush sage (*Salvia leucantha* 'Midnight') and pineapple sage *(S. elegans)*. It is clearly one of her favorites and is now available on the retail market. Coleus 'Christopher Fermin,' one of her latest seedlings, is named for her other grandson.

Frances doesn't always leave things to chance; she also develops plants for her garden. She recently named a fragrant pink rose seedling for her daughter Aletha and another rose for her granddaughter Emmy.

Why Garden?

Frances has spent her life experimenting with the plants that grow in the Lowcountry of South Carolina. She says, "I began designing gardens, but then could not find anyone who was growing good plants for the Lowcountry. I then started a nursery propagating the grandmother plants from my garden and used them in my designs. "I feel very strongly that we need to use native plants and the plants of our grandparents. A lot of the things in my gardens were shared with me. Sharing plants is part of gardening," she explains. "All the plants that are passed along from other people are special. When I walk through my garden, it's as if I were visiting with family and friends."

above, left: purple 'Neon' eggplant and 'Buddy' gomphrena **top:** Mexican bush sage *(Salvia leucantha)* stretches out to enjoy the autumn air. **above:** Frances shows grandson Anthony Parker Fermin how to take a cutting of a coleus. **above, right:** Grandson Christopher Fermin holds a potted coleus seedling that Frances named after him.

Maple leaves and apples shine under a Japanese Maple tree *(See pages 188–190.)*

October

Garden Checklist 186

Magical Japanese Maples 188
these trees brighten the fall landscape with vibrant orange, red, and yellow foliage

Simple Seasonal Arrangements 191
autumn offers a wide pallet of colors for decorating

Plant a Pot of Gold 192
a container filled with daffodil bulbs in the fall will produce a vibrant arrangement come springtime

This Walk Works 193
the art of guiding guests to the front door

Splendor of the Grasses 194
these easy-to-grow choices make an impact in the landscape

Pumpkin Alley 198
a Kentucky neighborhood creates a splendid Halloween display

Editor's Notebook

October is a great month for the vibrant color of maples. Check out our feature story on pages 188–190 where Charlie Thigpen waxes poetic about Japanese maple. And now I have nice things to say about another one, 'October Glory' red maple (*Acer rubrum* 'October Glory'). I love fall in general and fall color in specific. And there is no better, more dependable tree for mesmerizing fall foliage in the South than 'October Glory.' Each autumn, the leaves of this easy-to-grow shade tree (up to 60 feet tall) turn a brilliant, clear scarlet. When backlit by the sun, they seem to blaze. In the Upper and Middle South, 'October Glory' is aptly named, for that's when the show occurs. In the Lower South, where fall comes later, it really should be called 'November Glory.' I just love the fall.

—STEVE BENDER

Color Beds

In the Lower and Coastal South, begin planting cool-weather annuals now for bright color throughout the fall and winter. Dianthus, alyssum, lobelia, snapdragons, calendula, pansies, and flowering kale or cabbage are good choices. In Central and South Florida, petunias (pictured at right), marigolds, zinnias, ageratum, salvia, dusty miller, and verbena perform well.

TIPS

- **Dahlias—**In the Upper and Middle South, now is the time to lift and divide dahlia tubers. Make sure you do this before the first frost. Cut stalks to about 1 inch above the tuber, shake off any loose soil, and let the clump dry. Store in a cool, dry place that does not freeze. In the Lower and Coastal South, tubers can stay in the ground. Be sure to mulch them well to overwinter.
- **Dried flowers—**Remember to collect some of the season's last annuals for drying. Zinnias, globe amaranth, Mexican bush sage *(Salvia leucantha)*, goldenrod, and cockscomb all dry well. Cut flowers in midmorning, after the dew has dried. Then tie in bundles and hang upside down in a warm, dry place with good air circulation.
- **Harvest—**Cut gourds now, and allow them to dry in a cool, well-ventilated area such as a garage, attic, or garden shed. Gather stems of oakleaf and mophead hydrangeas, and tie them in bundles. Hang these upside down to use later in floral arrangements. Gomphrenas and celosias are easily dried. Artemisia flowers and ornamental grasses, such as miscanthus, pennisetum, and pampas grass, make wonderful additions to dried bouquets.
- **Mulch—**As leaves begin to fall, they create an ample supply of organic mulch for plant beds. Decomposing leaves enrich the soil, nourishing your plants. The extra layer of leaves keeps roots cool, retains moisture, and slows weed growth.
- **Water efficiently—**This is one of the driest months, so it is important to ensure plants get adequate moisture. Water early in the day to reduce evaporation. If you have a sprinkler system, adjust it too. Infrequent, deep watering

Instant Color

Set out large, ready-to-bloom chrysanthemums (pictured below), Mexican bush sage, Mexican mint marigold, Copper Canyon daisy *(Tagetes lemmonii)*, and 'Indigo Spires' salvia. Arrange them in masses of three or more with taller plants in the back of the border, or place them in large pots. Set out zinnias, marigolds, petunias, cosmos, and celosias in containers that are 6 inches or larger to provide color until it's time for cool-weather pansies, alyssum, calendulas, and ornamental cabbages and kales.

is better than frequent, shallow watering. Soaker hoses are efficient for giving moisture to newly planted trees and shrubs, and you can install them yourself at a relatively low cost. The supplies you need can be purchased at garden or home-improvement centers.

PLANT

■ **Containerized roses—**Plant now in the Middle, Lower, and Coastal South so they can establish themselves by winter. Remove spent flowers and weak growth when planting, and then water well and fertilize lightly.

■ **Cool-season grasses—**Annual and perennial ryegrass seeds may be planted now for winter cover. They are also excellent choices for new lawns and areas in the landscape that may be subject to erosion. Prepare the area by tilling or raking the soil surface, and apply seeds as evenly as possible. Ryegrass seeds can also be applied over established Bermuda grass and other permanent lawn grasses. Perennial ryegrass can be permanent in this area, as can tall fescue, which is particularly useful in partially shaded areas where other grasses often fail.

■ **Holiday amaryllis—** Pot bulbs at least six weeks in advance. After flowering, amaryllis can be set out in the garden in the Lower, Coastal, and Tropical South where they should be perennial.

■ **Seeds—**In the Lower and Coastal South, sow seeds of collards, radishes, lettuce, mustard, and turnips for a garden of winter greens. Prepare your bed by lightly raking the soil. Sprinkle the seeds on top of the loose soil, and then water gently.

■ **Spring-flowering bulbs—**Plant daffodils, anemones, ranunculus, and Dutch iris now in the Lower and Coastal South for glorious early-spring blooms. Tulips and hyacinths will need to be chilled before they are planted. Place in the refrigerator for six to eight weeks after they are purchased; then plant.

■ **Trees and shrubs—**Fall is an excellent time to plant trees and shrubs. The cooler days of autumn allow roots to develop and help condition plants for the upcoming spring growing season. Be sure to water well after planting, and spread mulch such as pine straw or pine bark. Adding trees and shrubs during the fall will make gardening easier next spring.

■ **Vegetables—**Set out transplants of cool-weather vegetables such as cabbage, collards, and broccoli; sow seeds of carrots, beets, radishes, turnips, and English peas. Keep the soil around the transplants or seeds moist until the plants are well-rooted and growing. After that, reduce watering, checking the garden every two to three days to make sure the soil has not become too dry. Fertilize lightly at least once a month with a liquid fertilizer such as 16-16-16, or use a granular product such as Osmocote.

Pumpkins

Whether you are harvesting your own pumpkins or purchasing from a roadside stand, carving a jack-o'-lantern is a great project to introduce kids to the bounty of the autumn garden. Pumpkins are available in multiple colors, from the traditional oranges to shades of white and grayish green. Choose several sizes for more impact in your display. To extend the life of jack-o'-lanterns, be sure to keep them out of direct sunlight. If you do not want to carve your pumpkins, you can paint all kinds of faces on them instead with the same great results.

October notes:

Tip of the Month

Here's a way to keep squirrels out of your bird feeder. Hang the feeder from a coat hanger that you've straightened out, leaving the hook to place over a tree limb and a curl at the other end to hold the feeder. Coat the wire with solid shortening. Hang the feeder at eye level, away from the trunk or nearby limbs. After some very funny attempts, squirrels will learn your feeder is for birds only.

BEVERLY WHITE

Magical Japanese Maples

When Mother Nature waves her seasonal wand,
these trees explode in fiery colors.

BY CHARLIE THIGPEN / PHOTOGRAPHY VAN CHAPLIN

Each fall as the weather cools, Japanese maples ignite the landscape. Their delicate green foliage turns intense shades of orange, red, and yellow. These trees, backlit by the autumn sun, glow as if on fire. Seasonal winds whip the limbs around, making the trees' branches flicker like dancing flames. This blaze of glory shows why these maples are one of the best choices for the fall garden.

Japanese maples *(Acer palmatum)* thrive in our Southern climate. These small, stylish trees prefer well-drained, fertile soils that are acid or neutral. They also need ample moisture, so use mulch around the bases of trees to keep their fibrous, shallow root systems from drying out. Newly planted trees should be watered frequently. Japanese maples will tolerate poor, dry soils, but they will have less vigor, resulting in slow growth rates. (In areas where the soils are too alkaline, try growing them in large pots.)

In the Upper and Middle South, plant these trees in full sun. Not only does this bring about more intense fall color, but it also keeps selections with red summer foliage from turning green. Partial shade is better for Japanese maples in the Lower and Coastal South. However, intense summer heat in these areas may burn the foliage. It may also cause selections with red summer foliage to turn green. Avoid planting them in locations that receive hot western sun.

Size and Shape

There are more than 100 named selections of Japanese maples, ranging in height from 3 to 30 feet. Tall selections tend to grow in a wide vase or a rounded crown shape. The branches spread outward from the center trunk, forming strong horizontal lines. These sculpted limbs create layers of wispy, cloudlike foliage.

Japanese maples may be purchased in a single- or multi-trunked form. Single-trunked trees are often used in formal settings. Multi-trunked ones, which have a loose, spreading form, look good in an informal or natural setting. There are dwarf and weeping selections of Japanese maples that are low growing. 'Crimson Queen' (*A. palmatum dissectum* 'Crimson Queen') has a cascading habit, accentuating its slender foliage.

Year-round Appeal

These trees may produce exceptional fall color, but they truly are perfect for all seasons. In the spring, new foliage can be red to bronze. In the summer, the delicate palmate leaves add fine texture to the garden with their light and airy look. While the trees are leafless in the winter, their sculpted, graceful shapes add a special beauty. Some selections even sport brightly colored branches. Coral bark maple (*A. palmatum* 'Sango-Kaku') has coral red stems that are striking in the winter garden.

Versatile Tree

Some low-growing selections look great in containers near high-traffic areas where they can be easily seen. Weeping selections are often planted next to fountains or pools, where their billowy forms seem to drip into the water. Taller, upright selections work well on a terrace. Bigger trees may also be used to line the sides of a walkway, creating an allée.

'Crimson Queen' is a small, slow-growing cut-leaf selection, perfect for this container. Variegated ivy softens the edge of the pot.

JAPANESE MAPLES

- Japanese maple *(Acer palmatum)*—This green-leaved tree grows 25 feet tall and wide and has great fall color.
- *'Bloodgood' (*A. palmatum* 'Bloodgood')—Red foliage in spring and summer turns scarlet in fall. It grows 15 feet tall and wide.
- *'Crimson Queen' (*A. palmatum dissectum* 'Crimson Queen')—This dwarf weeping tree with red fernlike foliage grows 10 feet tall and wide.
- *coral bark maple (*A. palmatum* 'Sango-Kaku')—Green leaves turn gold in fall. Grows 15 to 20 feet tall.
- *'Waterfall' (*A. palmatum dissectum* 'Waterfall')—This dwarf weeping tree has lacy green leaves. It grows 8 to 10 feet tall and 10 to 12 feet wide.

*These selections are in the *Southern Living* Plant Collection from Monrovia.

Unlike red and sugar maples, Japanese maples' roots aren't invasive, so they can be planted as close to a house as 8 feet. They respond well to careful pruning, making them good for tight situations.

Cost Will Vary

Some rare or hard-to-find selections of Japanese maples can be expensive. Red-foliaged and cut-leaf selections *(A. palmatum dissectum)* cost more but give added interest. Green-leaved seedling selections *(A. palmatum)* are cheaper; their leaves are green most of the year but turn yellow, orange, and red in fall. If you like Japanese maples but don't have a lot of money, a green-leaved seedling offers beauty on a budget.

If you want a small tree, plant a magnificent maple. Don't let their delicate looks fool you. They have few problems with pests or diseases. Once established, they're fairly drought tolerant and virtually carefree. Easy yet elegant, Japanese maples can make your garden glow.

Simple Seasonal Arrangements

PHOTOGRAPHS: JEAN ALLSOPP

left: Pumpkins, squash, and Indian corn combine well with ornamental cabbage and kale. **above:** Circled by small white pumpkins, cockscomb, and green Osage oranges, an urn hosts cabbage and kale. **below, left:** Asters, mums, and beautyberry are showstopping.

There are two faces of autumn. The first is flamboyant, with flaming orange pumpkins, calico Indian corn, and garish gourds. The other personality is mellow. Its spectrum moves toward gray-blue squash, alabaster pumpkins, and jewel-like asters. This palette of gentle colors reflects the softer side of the season.

Outdoor Style

Use different-size benches and stools nestled together as a setting for pumpkins and squash. Bushel baskets or an old wheelbarrow also make a good starting point. Look at farmers markets and roadside stands for intriguing squash and pumpkins in shades of gray, white, and putty. You'll find them in a variety of sizes, shapes, and colors. 'Hubbard' squash and hard-shelled winter selections are also good additions.

Let the largest item be the focal point, and cluster others around it, leaning some and stacking others. Use varying heights to give the arrangement depth. In addition to vegetables, use ornamental cabbage and kale. Their cool colors combine with the subtle palette already established. Place them in weathered clay pots, antique galvanized buckets, or wooden crates for an easygoing look.

Fall Flowers

The evening chill produces vibrant flower colors that capture the season's urgency. Asters in assorted shades of magenta, pink mums, royal purple beautyberries, and red celosia bring autumn to a memorable close. Gather them in a simple arrangement for indoors or out. Here, the color of an old galvanized sap bucket complements our bouquet. If you don't have a garden, check out your grocery store's floral department for bunches of asters and chrysanthemums. These blooming bunches are often seasonally available and reasonably priced.

Indoor Simplicity

A few beautiful elements artfully placed compose a striking seasonal collection with little effort. Choose small plants and miniature items to keep the scale appropriate for your container, and use an odd number of items, which is usually more visually pleasing than a pair.

Our arrangement begins with a weathered iron urn elevated on a marble stand. The container is filled with 4-inch pots of ornamental cabbage and kale. At the base, tiny white pumpkins mimic the creamy color in the cabbage leaves. Green Osage oranges, 'Red Strawberry' Indian corn, and cockscomb complete our harvest still life. ELLEN RUOFF RILEY

Plant a Pot Of Gold

This might look like an expensive garden project, but really it's a cheap way to get lots of impact. One bag of daffodil bulbs, one pot, and a couple of bags of topsoil can transform a corner of your yard into a garden focal point and turn an ordinary container into a bounty of blooms. Planted this autumn, daffodils will reward you with some of spring's most endearing flowers.

Daffodils, sprinkled in abundance all across the Southern landscape, officially mark the end of winter. Many colonies have naturalized from gardens planted long ago. There's no doubt they do well in the ground, but don't overlook their power to excel in containers, too.

PHOTOGRAPHS: VAN CHAPLIN

above: Golden daffodils growing in a pot with a few sprinkled around its base will put on a nice spring show. **left:** Space bulbs 3 to 4 inches apart to achieve a full look.

Most garden centers, nurseries, and mail-order catalogs offer daffodil bulbs each fall. You can usually buy them in bulk to reduce your costs. A bag of 50 bulbs will fill a big pot, and you'll still have several left to sprinkle around its base. They range in color from yellow to white, and some sport orange to pink or multicolored trumpets. Selections such as 'King Alfred,' 'Thalia,' 'Barrett Browning,' 'Ice Follies,' and 'Carlton' are all dependable bloomers.

When buying bulbs, make sure they're fat and fleshy like a ripe onion. Avoid dried out, hollowed, or moldy ones. Buy bulbs as soon as they arrive in stores, because those that sit on a shelf or in boxes for long periods may spoil.

If you don't have a large container, you can plant bulbs in several smaller pots to dress up a deck or front porch. Small pots can be moved around strategically once daffodils bloom. If you're in the market for a container, select one that will look nice with your house and garden. (For example, a white Chippendale container would look out of place around a rustic home or in a woodland garden.)

Use a good quality potting soil to fill the container, and make sure it has sufficient drainage holes. Cover the holes with pot shards, gravel, or a paper coffee filter to allow water to flow freely through the pot while holding the soil in.

In October or November, plant daffodils 3 to 4 inches deep with the pointed end up; space them 3 to 4 inches apart for a nice look. Mix a little Bulb Booster into the soil to give plants a head start. The bulbs will need little water until foliage begins to emerge; then keep them evenly moist until they bloom. If the flowers begin to lean in one direction, rotate the pot occasionally to keep them straight and upright. When the daffodils are through blooming, they can be planted in the yard or left in the pot. Don't cut any of the straplike foliage until it turns brown and is lifeless.

CHARLIE THIGPEN

PHOTOGRAPHS: VAN CHAPLIN

This Walk Works

Guide visitors gracefully from the curb to the door.

With most houses, getting people from the street or parking area to the front door seems relatively straightforward. But the home of Bill and Barbara Peel of Chevy Chase, Maryland, presented a special challenge. A portico added to the middle of their L-shaped home means that the front door faces the lot at a 45-degree angle. Which direction should the walk go?

Garden designer Dan Law of Garden Gate Landscaping in Silver Spring, Maryland, came up with the answer. "Running a walk straight to the door from either the street or the driveway would have looked awkward," says Dan. So he designed a curving walk that provides easy access to both. From the street, you step onto the brick walk and stroll beneath the gnarled limbs of a magnificent, old Yoshino flowering cherry. Azaleas and liriope planted on each side of the walk near the street clearly mark the entrance.

Take three or four steps down the walk, and you come to a landing that connects to the driveway. Azaleas and liriope mark this entry too. The landing is a mirror image of the floor of the portico and directs your eye to the front door. But instead of heading straight to the door, which would have sliced the lawn into two angular and unequal sections, the walk parallels the driveway for a bit, then curves gracefully around to the portico.

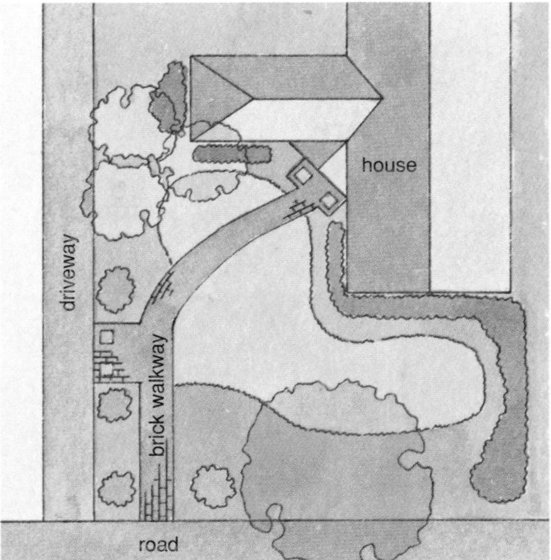

The foundation plantings are simple and easy to maintain. "Your goal in planting should always be to enhance the house, not hide it," comments Dan. That's just what he did here. Because the front windows are low, starting at about 15 inches from the ground, Dan was careful to use low-growing liriope beneath them. A sweep of liriope connects the house to the driveway landing. Dogwoods and English yews at the right front corner of the house screen the service area behind them from the street. The only other additions to the landscape are an espaliered euonymus to the right of the portico and a few carefully placed boxwoods.

As this example demonstrates, a straight line may be the shortest way between two points, but it isn't always the best way. This walk proves that, taking a turn for the better.

STEVE BENDER

top: You pass beneath the boughs of an old Yoshino flowering cherry as you enter the walk between azaleas and liriope. **above:** Dogwoods and English yews planted in a sweep of liriope screen a service area behind.

splendor of the grasses

BY STEVE BENDER / PHOTOGRAPHY SYLVIA MARTIN, VAN CHAPLIN

Ornamental grasses are beautiful, affordable, and easy to grow. And you never have to mow them. What more could you want?

Like most of you, I grew up thinking of grass as just something you cut. Letting it grow taller than 3 inches or so risked verbal abuse, a city citation, and an embarrassing picture of your lawn in the newspaper. Then I discovered ornamental grasses, and my outlook changed forever.

Suddenly, I saw grass as more than the makings of a lawn. It could bloom, it could billow, it could wave in the breeze. Grasses could have red leaves, yellow leaves, blue leaves, or purple leaves. They could top out at 4 inches or tower more than 16 feet tall. And they could do all of these things in sun or shade, in wet or dry soil, with very little input from me. What a deal.

That was 20 years ago. Nowadays, ornamental grasses are considered mainstream plants. Dallas landscape architect Rosa Finsley includes them in many of the gardens she designs. "One of the things I like most about them is that they put on a great show in fall and then really carry the garden through winter, when few other plants look like much," she says. Rosa especially favors muhly grasses (*Muhlenbergia* sp.), Southern natives that thrive in dry, alkaline, and sunbaked soils. But noting the plethora of grasses available, she adds, "There are good ornamental grasses for wherever you are."

DESIGN: MOLLY KISCADEN, ABINGDON, VIRGINIA

Like beams of sunlight, the green-and-white leaves of ribbon grass illuminate a corner of this garden.

Nothing To Fear

So then why are some people *afraid* of ornamental grasses? Maybe they're still antsy about discovering their yard on the front page of the *Daily Scandal*. More likely, they're just not sure how to work these plants into their gardens. Sound like you? Worry no longer. Here are some attractive ways to incorporate ornamental grasses.

- Grasses look great beside any body of water, be it pool, marsh, stream, or ocean. Wind whipping through the leaves and plumes brings motion and sound to the garden.
- Plant a sweep of a midsize grass, such as pennisetum, beside a walk or sitting area.
- Mix ornamental grasses into herbaceous borders. Let their slender, graceful leaves contrast with the coarser, stiffer foliage of other plants.
- Tuck smaller grasses, such as blue fescue, into decorative pots or niches between rocks.
- Use variegated or golden-leaved grasses as color accents to brighten shady spots or contrast with deep green plants.
- Plant tall, sculptural grasses, such as pampas grass *(Cortaderia selloana)*, ravenna grass *(Erianthus ravennae)*, and giant reed *(Arundo donax)* at the corner of the house or against a large, bare wall. Or use them for screens and windbreaks.

Growing Great Grasses

Most ornamental grasses prefer full sun and well-drained soil (although some grow in shade and wet soil). Most grow quickly, tolerate heat and drought, and have no serious pests. About the

left: Pampas grass is an excellent choice for coastal gardens where its plumes and leaves constantly wave in the breeze. Give it plenty of room—it gets big.

only regular maintenance needed is trimming back old foliage in late winter. To get more plants, dig and divide clumps in early spring prior to the emergence of new growth. Be aware that some grasses, notably river oats *(Chasmanthium latifolium)*, seed themselves with abandon. So either remove the seedheads before they mature, or plant such grasses in naturalized areas where they can spread to their hearts' content. Other grasses, such as giant reed, 'Picta' ribbon grass (*Phalaris arundinacea* 'Picta'), and blue lyme grass *(Leymus arenarius)* spread aggressively by underground runners. To control them, dig and discard unwanted new shoots in the springtime.

A Grass for Every Garden

Still wondering which grass is right for you? The following lists should help you decide.

Tall grasses (above 10 feet)—giant reed, pampas grass, ravenna grass, giant Chinese silver grass *(Miscanthus giganteus)*

Short grasses (below 2 feet)—blue fescue *(Festuca glauca)*, 'Hameln' Chinese pennisetum (*Pennisetum alopecuroides* 'Hameln'), sweet flag (*Acorus* sp.), sedge (*Carex* sp.)

Grasses for shade—river oats, *(Chasmanthium latifolium)*, sweet flag, sedge, ribbon grass, Japanese forest grass *(Hakonechloa macra)*, feather reed grass (*Calamagrostis* x *acutiflora*)

Grasses for moist soil—river oats, sweet flag, switch grass *(Panicum virgatum)*, sedge, ribbon grass, giant reed

Grasses for colorful fall foliage—Chinese pennisetum, switch grass, river oats, ravenna grass, flame grass (*Miscanthus sinensis* 'Purpurascens')

Grasses for the beach—pampas grass, river oats, ribbon grass, switch grass, blue lyme grass

Grasses for containers—sweet flag, blue fescue, 'Hameln' Chinese pennisetum, purple fountain grass (*Pennisetum setaceum* 'Rubrum'), river oats, sedge, Japanese forest grass, Oriental fountain grass *(P. orientale)*

1: Gulf muhly grass *(Muhlenbergia filipes)* glistens in the afternoon light. **2:** The soft mounds of maiden grass (*Miscanthus sinensis* 'Gracillimus') contrast wonderfully with the coarser texture of black-eyed Susans.

Selections of pennisetum, pampas grass, miscanthus, sedge, sweet flag, and Japanese forest grass are in the *Southern Living* Plant Collection from Monrovia (1-888-752-6848).

3: The plumes of Chinese pennisetum resemble foxtails. **4:** Reddish plumes of purple fountain grass (*Pennisetum setaceum* 'Rubrum') appear from spring until fall. **5:** A sweep of Oriental fountain grass guides visitors along this walk. **6:** A native grass, Lindheimer's muhly tolerates heat, drought, and poor soil. Upright silvery spears seem to catch fire in the afternoon sun.

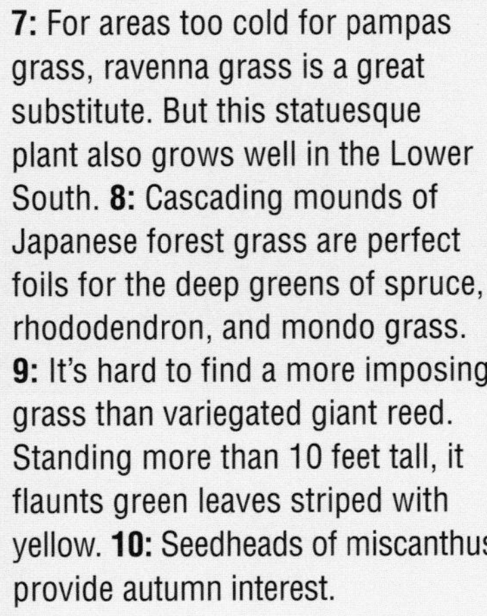

7: For areas too cold for pampas grass, ravenna grass is a great substitute. But this statuesque plant also grows well in the Lower South. **8:** Cascading mounds of Japanese forest grass are perfect foils for the deep greens of spruce, rhododendron, and mondo grass. **9:** It's hard to find a more imposing grass than variegated giant reed. Standing more than 10 feet tall, it flaunts green leaves striped with yellow. **10:** Seedheads of miscanthus provide autumn interest.

pumpkin **alley**

On Halloween, Gloucester Avenue in Middlesboro, Kentucky, looks like Mayberry painted orange.

Several homeowners located on and around Gloucester Avenue take Halloween quite seriously. The tidy homes are rather ordinary until the southeast Kentucky air becomes chilled and fallen leaves crackle underfoot. As the days lead up to the magical 31st of October, lawns become seas of pumpkins. Front porches and steps abound with festive decorations. Middlesboro locals commonly refer to this little residential area as Pumpkin Alley.

It all began 19 years ago when Paul and Wanda Lee started filling their yard with jack-o'-lanterns. Paul, who had a small farm, would pick pumpkins and bring them home. Wanda liked being creative and carving faces in the different-size pumpkins, while Paul enjoyed seeing the children gather and get excited about the upcoming holiday. Soon kids began to huddle around their picnic table to help with the carving.

Before long, neighbors wanted in on the action. Now, 15 homes in a one-block area participate. Everyone pools money, and Paul purchases truckloads of pumpkins from local farmers. Last year, farmers delivered close to 2,000 to the neighborhood. Children, pushing wheelbarrows, work like little ants moving the piles to distribute the basketball-shaped produce around the block. Some 100 to 200 pumpkins are delivered to each home, depending on the lot size.

At first, homeowners were responsible for carving their own pumpkins, but as the event grew, the task became impossible. Today a high school ROTC unit, church

BY CHARLIE THIGPEN
PHOTOGRAPHY
VAN CHAPLIN

groups, sororities, Japanese exchange students from nearby Lincoln Memorial University, and others gather to clean and carve the orange globes. Some pumpkins are sculpted into traditional jack-o'-lanterns, while others sport unique designs.

About five nights before Halloween, the show begins. Everyone scrambles around at dusk to light the votives. Thousands of the small candles are used each year—so many, in fact, that Paul once had to drive as far as Knoxville to find enough.

Witnessing Pumpkin Alley in the daytime is one thing, but experiencing it at night is another. As the sun sets and darkness falls,

Top: Pumpkins come to life at night as the flames flicker in the luminous globes. **Above:** On the days before Halloween, this sleepy town bustles with activity as neighbors work to carve and set out almost 2,000 pumpkins.

The plethora of pumpkins will be etched in the memories of these children forever.

Right: By the time the carving is done, each pumpkin has a singular, new identity.

scary music echoes down the street. Howling cats, creaking doors, rattling chains, and eerie moans greet visitors who congregate along the sidewalks. The air gives off the scent of pumpkin pie as the candles heat up inside the glowing orbs.

When Halloween night finally arrives, busloads of people from all over the community and nearby towns roll in. Local police block off the streets, and families walk hand in hand down the sidewalks. Children dressed in colorful costumes knock on doors, yell "trick or treat," and open their candy bags wide. As the evening winds down, everyone stops to take one last look. The plethora of pumpkins will be etched in the memories of these children forever.

The morning after the big event, burned-out pumpkins, slumping after five nights of candle-burning, are carted off by a farmer. His livestock will feast on these leftovers throughout the winter. Nothing is wasted, and the cleanup is quick.

Paul and Wanda planted a seed in this little Southern community and watched it grow. That seed made pumpkins sprout throughout the neighborhood, creating a wholesome event for children and their families. If you are traveling around Middlesboro at Halloween, look for the orange glow, and you'll know you've found Pumpkin Alley. ◆

DIRECTIONS

In Kentucky, take U.S. 25E into Middlesboro. Take a right onto Cumberland Avenue, and then take a right onto 29th Street, which turns into Gloucester Avenue. For more information call the Bell County Chamber of Commerce at (606) 248-1075.

A resting spot underneath the vibrant leaves of a dogwood tree (See page 209.)

November

Garden Checklist 204

The Camellia for Fall 206
sasanqua produces beautiful foliage and gorgeous blooms

Benchmarks of Fall 209
a perfectly placed bench offers a handsome resting spot

Red Hot for Cold Weather 210
easy to grow and colorful, pyracantha is a nice choice for a winter landscape

A Pair of Early Risers 210
plant Lenten rose and dwarf iris for January and February blooms

Old Pumpkins, New Look 211
use these heirloom favorites for fall decoration

Tried-and-True Tulips 212
try these bulbs for a fantastic spring show

Parking in Style 213
a planted Florida driveway

Autumn's Last Harvest 214
nature provides a bounty of seasonal decorations

Foolproof Bromelaids 216
this plant provides a long-lasting centerpiece for the holidays

Editor's Notebook

PHOTOGRAPH: LACY KERR ROBINSON

Ever wonder why local newscasters use the word deadly at least four times a minute? Because they know that, with the possible exception of Pat Boone singing "Layla," nothing will keep you glued to the set like the feeling of mortal danger. Even in safe neighborhoods, folks install alarm systems. But if you'd rather not go to the trouble or expense, I have the perfect answer—thorny plants. Yes, just plant something with thorny stems or spiny leaves (such as pyracantha, barberry, yucca, or hardy orange) beneath your windows, and you'll never again have to worry about somebody climbing in at night. Of course, using pyracantha this way can be risky. Because orange-red berries completely smother its branches in fall, its thorns could be considered concealed weapons. I'm not overly concerned at the moment though. Pat Boone's singing "Layla" on TV. That always eases my worried mind. —STEVE BENDER

Pansies

Plant in full sun, 10 inches apart, for flowers lasting from now until March. Mulch the bed with pine straw or bark chips. Fertilize lightly once a month with a general-purpose fertilizer such as 12-6-6 or 10-10-10. Avoid bloom-booster fertilizers that have more phosphorus (the middle fertilizer number) than nitrogen or potassium. Many Florida soils already have sufficient phosphorus, and the excess from fertilizers is picked up by rainwater and carried into lakes where it can stimulate heavy algae growth. Water every other day until pansies are established and then twice a week during dry periods. There are many excellent series from which to choose, including Majestic Giants, Accord, Crown, Imperial, Crystal Bowl, Maxim, and Universal.

TIPS

- **Citrus—**In the Coastal and Tropical South, oranges and some early tangerines and grapefruits are ripening. Pick oranges when they reach mature size, even though the skin on the outside may not be dark orange.
- **Decorative materials—**Harvest plants as they mature for fall and winter arrangements. Collect gourds, okra pods, and ears of corn. Cut flowering stalks of ornamental grasses such as miscanthus, pennisetum, little bluestem, and muhly grasses as their blooms open. Cut and dry bachelor's buttons (gomphrena), cockscomb, zinnias, and statice. Gather green grapevines (muscadine), and bend them into wreaths before drying.
- **Leaves—**Regularly rake them from your grass throughout the fall. Piles of leaves become wet blankets after it rains and can suffocate your lawn. Use them as a mulch around trees and shrubs, or add to your compost pile to improve your garden soil in the spring.
- **Perennials—**Now is a great time to divide perennials in the Lower and Coastal South. Use a fork to lift and divide summer phlox, bearded iris, hostas, daylilies, and coneflowers. When lifted, some will fall apart easily while others may need to be gently coaxed apart. Set divided plants back into the soil at the original growing depth, water well, and then mulch with leaves, pine straw, or finely ground pine bark.
- **Winter lawns—**Keep part or all of your lawn green this winter by overseeding with ryegrass. Use no more than 5 to 10 pounds of seed per 1,000 square feet. Water the area lightly every day until seeds sprout and start growing. Then water once a week if there is no rain.

PLANT

- **Colorful trees—**Plant trees that have good autumn color, such as dogwood, sweet gum, hickory, crepe myrtle, Chinese pistache, Florida maple, Japanese maple, red maple, 'Bradford' or other ornamental pears, Shumard oak, sourwood, and ginkgo.
- **Daffodils—**Now is the time to select and plant daffodil bulbs. Mail-order bulbs are readily available if you cannot find local sources. Plant bulbs in well-drained beds that receive at least a half-day of direct sunlight. Selections include 'Ice Follies,' 'Carlton,' 'Erlicheer,' 'February Gold,' and 'Barrett Browning.'

■ Holiday amaryllis—This is one of the easiest bulbs to force, and it is captivating to watch the flowers open. Amaryllis bulbs should be potted at least six weeks in advance for holiday use. Larger bulbs usually have larger flowers and more bloom spikes. They prefer to be crowded, so select a pot that is a little larger than the bulb. Plant in a potting mix that is rich in organic matter, such as peat moss. Water well, and place potted bulb in a warm, sunny room. Amaryllis blossoms come in singles, doubles, and miniatures.

■ Peonies—In the Upper, Middle, and Lower South, plant peonies *(Paeonia lactiflora)* now. When buying, select rhizomes that have three to four eyes. The most reliable peony for the South is the white-flowering 'Festiva Maxima.' Pink-flowering 'Sarah Bernhardt' and red-flowering 'Philippe Rivoire' are also good selections. Incorporate organic matter, such as composted manure, into a bed that has well-drained soil and receives at least four hours of sun a day; late-afternoon shade is best.

■ Shrubs—Fall is actually a better time than spring for planting new shrubs. Roots will be better established when next year's heat stress arrives. For the first month, water at least every third day when there is no rainfall. After that, water twice a week. Don't fertilize at planting. Wait until late February or early March.

■ Spring flowers—In the Lower and Coastal South, sow seeds of larkspur, bachelor's buttons, sweet peas, and California poppies in a bed with full sun now, and you'll make neighbors jealous early next spring. Keep soil moist with daily waterings until seeds sprout and plants are more than an inch tall.

■ Sweet peas—Choose a sunny, well-drained site that is protected from north winds, and prepare the soil thoroughly prior to planting seeds. Traditionally sweet peas are planted in shallow trenches (4 to 6 inches deep) to protect them from frost. Plants will gradually grow and fill the trench. Provide strings or trellises so the vines can climb. Early-flowering types are best for our area. Frequent cutting of flowers encourages more blooms and provides fragrant bouquets.

Violas

Add them to your borders and containers for masses of flowers that will last through the spring. These fragrant prolific bloomers come in many colors. Set transplants in a sunny location with rich, well-drained soil. Mix with ornamental cabbage or kale, parsley, alyssum, or red mustard for a great combination. Popular selections include Penny Series 'Orange' and Sorbet Series 'Blue Heaven,' 'Lemon Chiffon,' 'Coconut,' and 'Purple Duet.'

■ Vegetables—Plant successive crops of mustard and turnip greens, radishes, beets, carrots, kale, and lettuce from seed every 4 to 6 weeks. Transplants of cabbage, broccoli, cauliflower, and collards thrive in cool weather. Onions, celery, Swiss chard, cilantro, fennel, arugula, and parsley may be planted now.

FERTILIZE

■ New beds—Add several inches of organic material, such as soil conditioner (composted pine bark), sphagnum peat moss, or compost, along with 2 to 3 pounds of balanced fertilizer per 100 square feet of bed area. Till to a depth of 8 to 10 inches.

November notes:

Tip of the Month

I have an arbor with climbing 'Don Juan' roses that I hated tying up with twine. So this year I took grapevines, stripped off the leaves, and wound them around the roses. They look beautiful and natural—much better than string or twine.

JANICE SAULS
TIFTON, GEORGIA

The Camellia for Fall

Easy-to-grow sasanquas combine stunning autumn flowers with handsome foliage.

left: Trained against a brick wall, this 'Mine-No-Yuki' sasanqua blooms for weeks every fall and wows passersby.
above: An evergreen rosebush? No, a 'Bonanza' sasanqua blooming in November.

Imagine spending life as Cleopatra's sister. Each morning, you don the most exquisite gown and have your hair coiffed and your nails gilded, yet no one ever notices. That's how it is to be a sasanqua. Though it's one of the classic plants that define our region and its beauty can dominate autumn, to those enamored with the ostentatious flowers of its winter- and spring-blooming sibling, a sasanqua will always be "the other camellia."

What an injustice to a shrub that has been cultivated in its native Japan since the 14th century and in the American South for nearly 200 years. *Camellia sasanqua* may lack the grapefruit-size blooms of *Camellia japonica,* but in many respects, it's a better plant for your garden.

Smaller, Easier, More Versatile

Let's start with size. The common camellia *(C. japonica)* begins as a shrub but usually ends up as a tree, 15 to 25 feet high and wide. So it takes up a lot of space—not exactly the perfect choice for planting under eaves and windows or between the sidewalk and curb. A mature sasanqua is smaller. Upright selections can grow 10 to 12 feet high and wide. Mounding types, popularly called dwarf sasanquas, grow only 2 to 5 feet tall and wide. Therefore, when you plant one of these, you won't have to worry that your house with a camellia out front will morph into a camellia with a house in back.

Now examine the foliage. A sasanqua's leaves are simply beautiful, with many types emerging coppery-bronze and maturing to glossy, deep green. These leaves are about half the size of a common camellia's and much less coarse. "Sasanquas have this delicate quality about them, almost like a child," notes landscape architect Steve Dudash of Design-Works in Charleston, South Carolina. "Their leaves aren't big and thick like those of a [common] camellia."

Sasanquas also boast a laxity, grace, and airiness unmatched by common camellias. In the landscape, a common camellia looks as dense as a bowling ball and as stiff as a guard at Buckingham Palace. But a sasanqua's branches reach up and out, leaving spaces in between, and its

BY STEVE BENDER / PHOTOGRAPHY JEAN ALLSOPP, ALLEN ROKACH

DESIGN: SHEILA WERTIMER, WERTIMER & ASSOCIATES, CHARLESTON, SC

Cold-hardy 'Cleopatra' grows into a small multitrunked tree with lavender-pink blooms and a shape similar to a crepe myrtle.

stems are much more pliable. Combine smaller size and beautiful foliage with a graceful form, and you wind up with a plant you can use in many different ways.

Sue and Reid Crider of Vestavia Hills, Alabama, know this well. In 1972, their family began training a pair of 'Mine-No-Yuki' (aka 'White Doves') sasanquas to grow flat against a brick wall—an art known as espalier. They carefully pruned each spring and summer to limit size and also tied stray branches to the wall. Now a flurry of white blossoms powder the foliage for weeks each fall. Neighbors take notice. "When people find out where we live, they'll say, 'Oh, you live at the house with the white camellias,' " says Reid.

If espalier isn't your style, though, relax—sasanquas are extremely versatile. For example, dwarf types are wonderful for foundation plantings, berms, low borders, or massing at the foot of taller plants, such as glossy privet *(Ligustrum lucidum)*. Upright forms can be clipped into hedges, used for tall screens, or pruned into tree form for use in courtyards, corner plantings, small yards, and formal beds.

Color and Fragrance Too

Depending on the selection and where you live, sasanquas can bloom any time from late summer through autumn and into winter. (A personal favorite, red-flowered 'Yuletide,' blooms around Christmastime.) Flowers may be single, semidouble, or double, usually with a central burst of bright yellow stamens. Some exude a pleasant tea scent—not surprising, as sasanqua is closely related to the tea plant *(C. sinensis)*. Colors range from cherry red to rose to shell pink to fairest white. Individual flowers live but a short time, shattering into a storm of falling petals. Abundant new flowers soon replace them, though, and the carpet of petals at the foot of the shrubs only adds to the spectacle.

Suited to all areas except the Tropical South, sasanquas are a cinch to grow. They love summer heat and can take full sun or light shade. Give them moist, acid, well-drained soil that contains plenty of organic matter. They're not quite as cold hardy as common camellias, though. In the Upper South, plant them in places sheltered from winter wind and sun, or keep them in pots in cool greenhouses over winter.

Sasanquas may lack the fame of common camellias, but you certainly couldn't call them weak sisters. Plant these classic beauties in your garden, and I guarantee that people will notice. ◆

A SASANQUA SAMPLER

* **'Bonanza'**—Compact, spreading, large, semidouble, deep red, dwarf type, can be kept low

'Cleopatra'—Tall, open, semidouble, lavender-pink, very cold hardy

* **'Mine-No-Yuki'** ('White Doves')—Upright, willowy, double, white, good for espalier, very floriferous

* **'Shishigashira'**—Low, spreading, semidouble, rose, dwarf type, good for foundation planting and massing

'Showa-No-Sake'—Low, spreading, double, soft pink, dwarf type, good for foundation planting and massing

** Belongs to the* Southern Living *Plant Collection from Monrovia. For a source near you, call 1-888-752-6848.*

PHOTOGRAPHS: VAN CHAPLIN

left: A path of green lawn leads to a pleasant destination—a simple bench placed beneath the limbs of a dogwood. **above:** Chosen for handsome foliage as much as for flowers, mounded *Chrysanthemum pacificum* adorns stone steps leading to the upper garden.

Benchmarks of Fall

Create a peaceful place to sit and enjoy the subtle beauty that autumn brings.

Cool, silky air caresses the skin. Rich smells of woodsmoke and moldering leaves tug at the nostrils. Trees and shrubs cloak themselves in harvest colors of red, yellow, and brown. It is autumn—a very special time in Amy Lamb's garden.

Fourteen years ago, when Amy and her husband, Bob, moved into their home in Bethesda, Maryland, they decided to transform a predictable backyard of azaleas into sweeping planting beds separated by a swath of lawn. To address a steep slope that ran up from the house toward the rear of the lot, garden designer Dan Law of Garden Gate Landscaping in Silver Spring, Maryland, suggested a stacked-stone wall that divides the yard into two tiers connected by stone steps.

With Dan's guidance, Amy dedicated the lower garden to flowers for birds and butterflies. It contains mainly summer-blooming plants such as butterfly weed, butterfly bush, sedum, coneflower, and bee balm. The upper garden, which screens the Lambs' yard from the neighbors', features dozens of different trees, shrubs, and perennials, including oaks, serviceberry, hostas, nandina, hydrangeas, hardy begonias, and ferns. Off in a corner, under the spreading arms of a scarlet dogwood, beckons a simple hideaway—a solitary wooden bench. What better place to enjoy an autumn afternoon?

The garden is the venue for Amy's passion. A former research biologist, she's now a still life photographer with works exhibited all over the country. Her subjects are the flowers, leaves, fronds, and seedheads from plants that she and Bob grow.

The subtleties of this season call to her. "So often, my photography highlights the brilliant color of a flower at its peak. But it's the muted colors of fall that I really love," she explains. For example, clipped hydrangea blooms slowly dry to pastel blues and pinks. She'll photograph them in the months ahead. Green hosta leaves mellow to soft golden brown. Even seeds are a treat to Amy's keen eye. In one of her photographs, the seedhead of a single clematis bloom stands boldly atop a long stem. It looks like the neck of a strutting ostrich crowned with a swirl of feathers.

But if there's one picture from her garden that I'll remember, it's that of a lone bench placed at the foot of a dogwood. What an easy way to enjoy the serenity of fall. "We love that bench," says Amy. "It's isolated, very peaceful. And autumn is a quiet time of life." STEVE BENDER

SMALL TREES FOR FALL COLOR

So you have the bench but have yet to decide on the tree? The following small trees (under 30 feet) look great in autumn.

- crepe myrtle—red, orange, and yellow leaves
- dogwood—scarlet and crimson
- fringe tree—yellow
- hawthorn—scarlet and orange
- Japanese maple—scarlet, orange, and yellow
- serviceberry—scarlet and orange
- sourwood—scarlet
- Yoshino flowering cherry—red, orange, and yellow

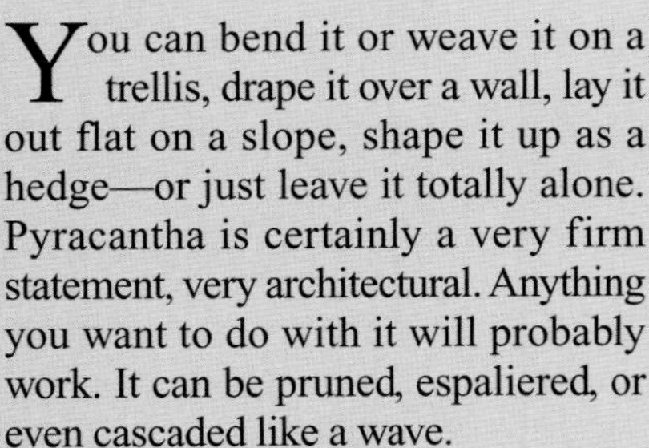

PYRACANTHA
At a Glance

Height: varies with species and selection
Growth rate: rapid
Light: full sun
Soil: any well drained
Water: Do not overwater.
Problems: aphids, scales, fireblight, and scab—pick disease-resistant selections
Range: evergreen in Middle to Coastal South, hardy in Upper South depending on selection

Easy to grow and colorful, pyracantha dominates a winter landscape.

Red Hot for Cold Weather

You can bend it or weave it on a trellis, drape it over a wall, lay it out flat on a slope, shape it up as a hedge—or just leave it totally alone. Pyracantha is certainly a very firm statement, very architectural. Anything you want to do with it will probably work. It can be pruned, espaliered, or even cascaded like a wave.

Pyracantha is one of those wonderful plants that grows more vigorously if rarely watered and produces more berries if never pruned. In fact, because it bears its colorful fruit on last year's wood, any clipping done to keep your pyracantha groomed as a hedge or espalier will reduce the number of berries produced.

Now there are tall, short, and prostrate selections available, so it is possible for you to choose a plant that will grow roughly the shape and size you desire without having to do any pruning except for the removal of an occasional contrary branch.

If you do choose to clip or otherwise train your pyracantha, don't let the common name, firethorn, put you off. It has true thorns from the woody core of the twig—nice, firm, widely spaced ones that are easy to spot and avoid, rather than nasty little prickles that snap off in your skin.

The thorns can even be seen as an asset if pyracantha is trellised under windows to deter intruders or planted between your yard and that of the neighbor with the rowdy children. It's also the thorns that make pyracantha perfect for the perimeter of a garden, because it's one of the few plants that browsing deer really don't like. For birds, however, because of both the protection factor and the abundant winter berries, pyracantha is the ideal habitat. ◆

A Pair of Early Risers

If you want early-season blooms in your yard, plant Lenten rose *(Helleborus orientalis)* and dwarf iris *(Iris reticulata)*. This combination will provide flowers for your garden in January and February while most plants are still too scared to brave the chilly weather.

Lenten Rose

Fall is a great time to plant, and if you set out Lenten roses now, they will add bold texture to your garden with their coarse, leathery foliage. Their large palmate leaves have a fine-toothed edge. These low-growing evergreen plants prefer loose, well-drained, fertile soil. They thrive in full to partial shade. When set out in sunny locations, their foliage will burn, especially when exposed to hot western sun.

These little blue iris make nice companion plants for the late-winter blooms of Lenten rose.

Plant them about 15 inches apart in large sweeps to make a wonderful, low-growing ground cover. Lenten roses nicely complement ferns or hostas in woodland settings or shade borders. Flowers appear as early as mid-January and will last a month or two. Blooms vary in color from ►

pink and purple to white with buttery yellow stamens. In the spring, flowers turn green and small seedpods form inside the old blooms. If you want plants to multiply, don't cut off old flowers until the seedpods have split open and dispersed their seeds. You can let the seeds drop naturally, or you can collect and scatter them in other areas.

Dwarf Iris

Many people are familiar with tiny, early-blooming crocus and have seen their small-cupped flowers sprinkled across the ground, but few have witnessed the beauty of dependable dwarf iris. Their little, brown, teardrop-shaped bulbs can be planted in the fall to produce a magical show in only a few months. Dwarf iris bulbs may be hard to find at your local garden center, so purchase them from a mail-order catalog.

Their small size makes them easy to plant. Just bury them about an inch or two below the soil surface, pointed end up. Space about 4 inches apart, and plant them in sweeps. Water them in, and you won't need to water any more unless you have lengthy dry periods.

Green shoots will begin emerging from the bulbs in mid- to late-January, and then it takes only a couple of weeks until blooms appear. The little iris blooms can last for two to three weeks. Flowers sit on strong 4- to 6-inch stems. Once the blooms are spent, the low, spiked foliage continues to grow to 12 to 14 inches in height. By summer the leaves die down and disappear. Dwarf iris will come back each year and multiply by sending out offsets from the bulb.

This petite iris will take full sun, but it also performs well in partial shade, positioned next to Lenten rose. These early bulbs and perennials can team up for a showy late-winter combination. Because there is so little color in the garden at this time of year, even small flowers really stand out; they give us hope and are proof that spring is returning. ◆

Use 'Jarrahdale,' 'Long Island Cheese,' and 'Valenciano' heirloom pumpkins to dress up your steps for the harvest season.

Old Pumpkins, New Look

Pumpkins have become pigeonholed. A fall favorite, they are loved by children and adults alike for home decorating and Thanksgiving pies. But there is more to pumpkins than holiday traditions.

Heirloom varieties that grow in unusual colors give a different twist to autumn decor indoors or out. People will do a double take when they notice the striking contrast provided by pairing these unconventional pumpkins with the deep hues of autumn flowers.

Blue-gray 'Jarrahdale' pumpkins (*Cucurbita maxima* 'Jarrahdale') are especially eye-catching with their unusual color. Amateur seed savers helped this plant survive, and seeds are now available through a few commercial outlets.

'Long Island Cheese' pumpkin (*C. moschata* 'Long Island Cheese') was named for its shape and color, which bring to mind a wheel of dairy-fresh cheese. In addition to its pleasing pale orange skin, this pumpkin also boasts sweet flesh that's good for baking.

The stark white 'Valenciano' (*C. maxima* 'Valenciano') adds an unusual twist to arrangements. Its pallid skin stands out against the rich, vibrant colors more common in autumn decorating.

Heirloom pumpkins are available this time of year in many farmers markets and some grocery stores. 'Jarrahdale' and 'Long Island Cheese' pumpkins are sometimes sold as squash.

If you can't find them in your area, however, consider growing your own crop for next year. Seeds can be sown in the ground in spring, about two weeks after the last frost, in loose, enriched soil. Plants require plenty of water and sun—and lots of space. They produce, on average, two fruits per plant, so if you're planning a big display, be sure to plant several. They'll be ready for harvest three to four months after planting. ◆

Tried-and-True Tulips

For surefire success next spring, plant the right bulbs now.

PHOTOGRAPH: JEAN ALLSOPP

You can always count on 'Pink Impression' for a magnificent performance.

People are created equal, but tulips aren't. Some put on a fantastic show every spring, while others are hit-and-miss. So which kinds should you buy this fall? We asked three experts—Sally McQueen Squire, author of *A Gardener's Guide to Growing Bulbs on the Gulf Coast*; Sandra Barnette, who supervises the planting of thousands of tulips at Agecroft Hall in Richmond; and *Southern Living*'s own Charlie Thigpen, who plans bulb displays at our *Southern Living* gardens.

They all have favorites. "One dependable tulip we use each year is 'Christmas Marvel,' " Sandra says. Sally recommends Darwin Hybrid tulips, which offer reliable color in the Coastal South. These plants feature big flowers atop long stems. Her favorite selections include 'General Eisenhower' and 'Jewel of Spring.' Charlie swears by 'Pink Impression,' 'Maureen,' 'Ivory Floradale,' 'Golden Oxford,' and 'Apricot Beauty.'

Buy Early, Prepare Well

"Try to get your bulbs as soon as possible," recommends Sally. "Some nurseries and garden centers don't treat their bulbs properly—they put them outside where it's hot." If you buy early, you'll likely get bulbs in top condition. Pick the largest bulbs you can find; bigger bulbs have bigger flowers. Look for firm, fat bulbs. Avoid soft, shriveled, or moldy ones.

Tulip bulbs need several months of cold temperatures each winter. This isn't a problem in the Upper and Middle South, but short, mild winters in the Lower, Coastal, and Tropical South can result in short stems, shrunken flowers, or no flowers at all. Sally suggests that people in areas with mild winters refrigerate their tulips for 8 to 10 weeks before planting. "Put them in a mesh bag or old panty hose, and store them on a refrigerator shelf," she says. "But don't put them in the freezer or in the crisper with vegetables or fruit." Ripening produce gives off a gas that harms bulbs.

Prepare soil before planting. "Good drainage is extremely important," states Sandra. "We fork compost into our beds about 10 to 12 inches deep before planting." Place these big-flowered tulips 4 to 6 inches deep and apart. Don't skimp on bulbs. Plant a sweep of at least 50 of a single color. Treat them as annuals, and replant every fall.

STEVE BENDER

TIME-TESTED TULIPS

SELECTION	TYPE	COLOR	HEIGHT	BLOOM TIME
'Apricot Beauty'	Single Early	salmon-rose	16-18 inches	early
'Arabian Mystery'	Triumph	purple and white	12-16 inches	midseason
'Christmas Marvel'	Single Early	cherry red	12-16 inches	early
'General Eisenhower'	Darwin Hybrid	red	28-30 inches	midseason
'Golden Oxford'	Darwin Hybrid	yellow	18-20 inches	midseason
'Hibernia'	Triumph	white	14-16 inches	midseason
'Ivory Floradale'	Darwin Hybrid	white	22-24 inches	midseason
'Jewel of Spring'	Darwin Hybrid	soft yellow	22-24 inches	midseason
'Maureen'	Cottage	white	28-30 inches	late
'Monte Carlo'	Double Early	double yellow	10-12 inches	early
'Mount Tacoma'	Double Late	double white	18-20 inches	late
'Pink Impression'	Darwin Hybrid	pink	22-24 inches	midseason
'Temple of Beauty'	Single Late	salmon-rose	34-36 inches	late

Parking in Style

This driveway is so attractive, it's like a patio for cars.

Let's face it. Most driveways are about as exciting as...well, as a slab of concrete. But Frank Koo and his wife, Sussanna Rehmann, wanted something with more style for their Orlando home. When they considered how much of their front yard was already consumed by their circular driveway and how much more would be taken up with the addition of a guest parking pad, they started thinking of ways to soften it a little.

Frank and Sussanna met with landscape architect Stephen Pategas and landscape designer Kristin Pategas of Hortus Oasis, in Winter Park, Florida, seeking advice on creating an attractive parking space. The two couples worked together to come up with a gridded parking area that matches the homeowners' contemporary tastes and is also environmentally friendly.

A Perfect Match

Stephen and Kristin envisioned a design of repeating geometric patterns. "Instead of installing just an expanse of concrete, we devised a grid of 3-foot-square concrete pads, interplanting them with dwarf mondo grass," Stephen says. Their design specified that the concrete contractor pepper the wet, pewter-colored surface with rock salt for texture.

Earth-Friendly Design

All new construction in drought-stressed Florida is scrutinized by building inspectors who ensure there is a balance between pavement and plantings. Because rain can seep into the ground through the planting strips, the parking pad has less runoff after a rain than a solid concrete parking area would.

This creative solution for Sussanna and Frank's dilemma added plenty of extra parking but did it with style. In fact, the strips of mondo grass make the new parking pad look so attractive that it resembles a patio. Now their only problem is convincing their visitors that it's okay to park there.

GLENN R. DINELLA

Although the mondo grass strips contain a system of drip irrigation, homeowner Frank Koo occasionally provides the plants with an extra refreshing drink from the hose.

PLANTING YOUR DRIVEWAY

- Use dwarf mondo grass (*Ophiopogon japonicus* 'Nana'), which grows about 2 inches tall, not the standard mondo *(O. japonicus)*, which grows 8 to 12 inches tall.
- Soaker hoses beneath plants provide water and encourage deep roots during the first year when plants are becoming established. Sprinklers may be needed too.
- Mondo grass spreads slowly, so place plants close together. Stephen used 2-inch potted plants spaced 3 inches apart.
- To prevent plants from being crushed, leave about an inch between the top of the mondo grass and the concrete surface.

To prevent the tarmac look, a grid of dwarf mondo grass visually breaks up the concrete in this guest parking pad.

PHOTOGRAPHS: ALLEN ROKACH

PHOTOGRAPHS: WILLIAM DICKEY

Autumn's Last Harvest

Use the season's bounty to decorate your home.

Nature lures us this time of year to hunt and gather the last lovely garden offerings before frost. Flower petals exude the sun's radiance while fluorescent berries and vivid vegetables blaze in autumn sunset colors. Make another sweep through the garden, bringing these enduring gems indoors; celebrate and decorate with the season's grand finale.

If you don't have a garden of your own, fear not; Indian corn, petite pumpkins, and dazzling fall fruit are all easily found in grocery stores, along with pomegranates, persimmons, pears, and gourds spanning the rich autumn palette. Look to farm stands for more unusual items including cockscomb, broomcorn, sunflower seedheads, and berry-covered branches.

Seasonal Greetings

An entryway is an excellent place to begin. A big basket overflowing with a harvest assortment is simply lagniappe. If your container is large, fill the bottom with an empty box or pinecones to reduce the amount of perishable materials by about half.

Wreaths are a wonderful way to bring the season indoors. Florist foam rings are the bases for our displays, providing moisture and keeping flowers fresh for several days. Soak the forms thoroughly, and stand them in the sink to drain. For the sunflower wreath, run florist wire

top: Let the sun shine with this fat sunflower wreath. It remains fresh for several days and with time will dry, becoming an everlasting arrangement. **above:** Fill a basket with a harvest of goodies from the garden, grocery store, and farm stand. It's easygoing in attitude and straightforward in assembly.

through the backs of three sunflower seedheads, and attach them in a triangle pattern. Push the flower stems, cut 3 to 4 inches below the bloom, into the foam, filling out the arrangement. Perch this sunny presentation on your mantel, or lean it on a wide windowsill—this ring is too heavy to be hung.

You can also place a wreath on your table as a centerpiece. Duplicate our flower-and-fruit arrangement (above, left) by setting a plate or saucer under the damp florist foam. Working from the bottom, start with a layer of broomcorn or corn tassels around the base; then add crimson cockscomb, leaving space for small pears. If the flower heads are too large, gently break them apart into smaller pieces. Cluster the fruit in groups of three; use florist picks to pierce each one, and gently push them into place on the form. The fruit will remain fresh for three to four days, while the flowers will dry and become a permanent arrangement.

Construct an easy-to-assemble Indian corn garland (below, left) beginning with a piece of sisal rope. If you like, dye it dark brown or a golden maize shade. Wrap it with broomcorn, corn tassels (stalks are available at farmers markets), or other dried grasses. Place corn along the rope single file or gathered in bundles of three. Wire corn securely in place, and then tie raffia on top for a finishing touch. Hang your garland across a door or from your mantel.

A flat-sided basket hanging on a door adds another dash of welcome. Filled with brilliant berries and a small pumpkin or two, this arrangement is splendid and quick.

The garden's last harvest lends itself to simplicity. Put these beautiful materials together in easygoing arrangements for supremely seasonal decorations. ELLEN RUOFF RILEY

top, left: Cockscomb, tiny pears, and broomcorn rest on a bamboo place mat, bringing autumn to the table. A clear saucer underneath, hidden from view, protects furniture from moisture. **center, left:** Simplicity is always a good policy when displaying beautiful materials. In this hen feeder, the garden's final roses, pears, and a few brightly colored dogwood leaves are the epitome of elegance. **left:** This garland adorns a screen door beautifully. A few well-paired elements personify the season with simplicity. **above:** A door basket filled with firethorn branches and one small pumpkin is all it takes to offer a warm welcome.

BY ELLEN RUOFF RILEY
PHOTOGRAPHY WILLIAM DICKEY

Bromeliads echo the colors of traditional Thanksgiving decorations. Group them with pumpkins, persimmons, pomegranates, and squash for an easy, long-lasting arrangement.

Foolproof Bromeliads

These beautiful blooms will give your holiday centerpiece a bold new look.

Harvest-colored flowers take many forms—some traditional and some unexpected. This year, take a break from using conventional chrysanthemums, and give your holiday centerpiece a twist with autumn-hued, easy-to-arrange bromeliads. These long-lasting plants partner beautifully with time-tested elements we love to include on a Thanksgiving table—pumpkins, gourds, colorful fruit, and brilliant leaves.

An old shoe-shine box houses a collection of small Vriesea and Guzmania bromeliads. Choose one large-flowered selection as the focal point, and position the smaller ones around it.

A small pie pumpkin becomes the focal point of each place setting when it holds a tiny bromeliad.

Caring for these plants is simple. Put your bromeliads in a bright location, avoiding direct sunlight. When dry, remove plants from decorative containers, water the soil well, and drain thoroughly. These tropical jewels are comfortable with high humidity, so mist the foliage each time you water. While pots must not sit in water, it is perfectly acceptable for moisture to remain on foliage where stems and leaves come together.

Center of Attention

Part of bromeliads' versatility comes with their size assortment. Small 2½-inch pots contain petite plants; larger 4- and 6-inch pots are also available. A collection of these containers nest together and arrange easily for a decorative centerpiece.

Begin with a large container or collection of smaller ones, complementing the style and attitude of your dining area and table setting. Place one as the focal point with smaller vessels surrounding it. For our Thanksgiving table, we used an old colander and tart pan to create a look that's compatible with the homespun cloth and casual atmosphere.

Line the container with foil to protect furniture from moisture. Leaving the bromeliads in their pots, snuggle them together, starting with the tallest plant and working toward the container edge with smaller ones.

Surround the plants with tiny pumpkins, persimmons, pomegranates, and gourds. Bring the arrangement onto the table by clustering large elements close to the containers and trailing smaller ones between.

Cascade a cornucopia of plants, fruits, and vegetables down a sideboard. This arrangement also works well as a table centerpiece.

On the Side

It's always fun to personalize the table, and a small bromeliad is a great way to mark each place setting. Carve a hole in a small pie pumpkin, making it slightly larger than the plant's 2½-inch container. Remove the plant from the pot, and gently slip the soil into the pumpkin, dressing the top with sunflower birdseed. Add a place card to the side, or inscribe a name on each pumpkin using a waterproof pen.

A sideboard holds a sprawling cornucopia of plants, vegetables, and fruits. Place a long, narrow basket on its side at the table's end. Tuck the bromeliads inside, with foliage flowing out and around the edges. Secure pots with crumpled newspaper or wedges of dry florist foam. Arrange

A SEASONAL SWITCH

Bromeliads bloom for months with proper care. Your Thanksgiving centerpiece will still be in full flower as the Christmas season arrives, so keep the display intact. Simply change out the seasonal elements, or choose a new decorative container. Replace pumpkins, gourds, and fruit with glass ornaments, and you're set for another season's arrangement.

the largest pumpkins and squash close to the plants, adding smaller elements around them. Cluster similar items together as they cascade to the top of the sideboard.

This type of arrangement lasts for weeks, provided plants are watered weekly. Check the fruits and vegetables frequently—don't allow them to mar furniture with moisture.

Bromeliads offer colorful blooms and an easy-care attitude. They bring a great look to Thanksgiving decorations and won't miss a beat as Christmas arrives. Give them a try—you'll feel like a pro making easy, stylish arrangements.

The addition of glass ornaments takes this arrangement into the Christmas holidays. How's that for easy?

A cedar wreath greets holiday guests
(See pages 224–226.)

December

Garden Checklist 222

Simple Wreaths 224
quick and easy holiday decorations
inspired by backyard materials

One Fine Vine 227
Jackson vine looks great in winter gardens

White Christmas 228
pristine bloomers with a festive touch

Fabulous Winter Pots 229
dazzling containers to liven up the season

Creative Lighting 230
glowing trees to greet guests

A Garden Under Glass 231
a greenhouse full of flowers for winter

Glorious Christmas Cactus 232
a traditional Southern plant for the holidays

Editor's Notebook

PHOTOGRAPH: VAN CHAPLIN

There are so many things to do to get ready for the holidays—baking cookies, checking the eggnog for salmonella, using caller ID to avoid phone calls from that annoying collection agency, and remembering exactly what your wife said she wanted for Christmas on Tuesday, July 16 at 9:31 p.m. But there is one more vital detail you must address—how to buy a beautiful poinsettia with blooms that will last until your visiting sister, her husband, and every one of the screaming banshees they call children have packed their minivan and headed home to Little Rock. To do that, you must realize that the brilliant red, pink, or white things you call poinsettia flowers aren't blooms at all but colorful leaves called bracts. The true flowers are tiny, budlike, and bunched at the top of the stalk. Choose poinsettias with true flowers that are tightly closed or just beginning to open. They'll stay colorful longer than those with fully open flowers. Well, here's hoping you have a nice Christmas. As for me, just pray my wife can't remember what she asked me for on July 16 either. (Not a chance.)

—STEVE BENDER

Cyclamen

Provide welcome winter color with pots of hooded white, red, rose, or purple cyclamen. Plants in 4- and 6-inch pots can be grouped in larger containers for holiday decorating. Because cyclamen are relatively cold hardy, they can also be set outside for winter garden color. Indoors, they prefer a cool location that is away from heat sources. Cyclamen thrive on little water. Apply a water-soluble fertilizer every few weeks, and place them in a bright location.

TIPS

■ **Arrangements**—If you are missing the wealth of fresh material you had in summer for centerpieces, don't overlook the dried seedpods and grasses that offer interesting shapes and textures. If cut now, they can be fashioned into wreaths, sprays, and bouquets that will last all winter.

■ **Citrus**—In the Coastal and Tropical South, if a hard freeze is predicted, mound soil around the base of citrus trees, or wrap insulation around the trunks. Leave fruit on the tree, because it may not freeze. If it does, you have several weeks after the freeze to make juice from the fruit.

■ **Holiday plants**—Extend the life of seasonal plants by carefully monitoring water, drainage, temperature, and light. Poinsettias can easily last a month or more in a cool room with plenty of light. Amaryllis and narcissus may need staking, because their bloom stalks extend out. Punch through the foil wrappings to allow drainage to occur, and make sure there is no standing water in saucers or decorative containers.

■ **Kalanchoes**—Poinsettias aren't the only holiday flowers out there. Try kalanchoes—and don't worry about mispronouncing the name, because there are several acceptable pronunciations. From winter into spring, these delightful succulents produce spectacular clusters of flowers in red, pink, orange, salmon, yellow, and lavender. Although most folks discard them after the holidays, they can make long-lived houseplants, needing only a sunny window and well-drained soil.

■ **Living Christmas trees**—Most Christmas trees that are bought live end up dead because they've been in the house too long. Plan to keep yours inside for only a week, and make sure the root ball stays moist. Spruce, hemlock, Douglas fir, and white pine are good choices for the Upper and Middle South. In the Lower and Coastal South, try Eastern red cedar, Leyland cypress, spruce pine, or Virginia pine.

■ **Mulching**—When's a good time to put a winter blanket of mulch around your shrubs, trees, roses, and evergreens? After a hard frost. If you mulch too early, heat held in the soil may delay the onset of dormancy, making plants susceptible to winter injury. Mulching at the proper time insulates roots and keeps them moist.

Possumhaw *(Ilex decidua)*

PLANT

■ **Bulbs—**If you haven't gotten around to planting your spring bulbs (tulips, hyacinths, daffodils), time's a-wasting. Don't wait until the ground freezes, or you'll need a jackhammer. Most spring bulbs require at least eight weeks of winter chilling to bloom well. Can't plant right away? Cover your future planting bed with straw or mulch to keep the soil soft until you can.

■ **Camellias—**In the Lower and Coastal South, select your favorite types of camellias while they're in bloom. Plant them in moderate shade or filtered sunlight, such as under pines. It is best to avoid full sun or heavy shade.

■ **Seasonal color—**If Christmas lights are the only source of color in your landscape right now, you obviously haven't met possumhaw (Ilex decidua). This easy-to-grow deciduous holly drops its leaves in fall, revealing thousands of bright red or orange berries that gleam for months in the winter sun. Only female selections, such as 'Warren's Red' and 'Council Fire,' bear fruit. To get berries, plant a male possumhaw, such as 'Red Escort,' or a male American holly (I. opaca) nearby.

PRUNE

■ **Frost-burned perennials—**Hardy hibiscus, Mexican bush sage, Mexican mint marigold, firebush, esperanza, chrysanthemums, and other fall-blooming perennials should be cut back to within a few inches of ground level after their tops have frozen. Mulch the crowns for extra protection during cold spells. Ornamental grasses such as miscanthus, muhlenbergia, and pennisetum should be allowed to remain unpruned until new growth begins to emerge next spring.

■ **Garden greenery—**Deck the halls (and walls too) with holiday greenery gathered from the garden. Favorites such as holly and Southern magnolia like to be pruned. They'll grow bushier as a result. Make sure you cut back to a leaf or branch, and don't leave a stub. You can harvest greenery from conifers, too. But don't cut back beyond a branch's innermost needles, or it will die.

December notes:

Tip of the Month

I drink herbal tea and save the bags. Once a week, I steep the old tea bags for several minutes in hot water, let it cool, and then water my potted plants with it. My plants are green and glossy, and they grow like mad.

CLARA NULL
OKLAHOMA CITY, OKLAHOMA

A fragrant cedar wreath graces this gate.

Simple Wreaths

These holiday decorations are quick and easy, and the inspiration is as close as your own backyard.

Wreaths provide an extra hello to the holidays, extending a bright welcome and reminding guests to take a moment to enjoy this time of year. The colors, fragrances, and textures of the ones shown here captivate the senses. So make a natural wreath to truly honor the spirit of the holidays.

With winter well on its way, nature offers many gifts to adorn the season. Eastern red cedar boughs, colorful berries, shells, and pinecones make beautiful wreaths. Inspiration also can be found in acorns, sweet gum balls, bark, pine needles, or leaves. Getting outside, enjoying the fresh air, and making a wreath will put you in the mood for the holidays. All the materials used here are placed on homemade grapevine wreaths. If you believe your skills lie more in the decoration, you can purchase a grapevine wreath ready-made.

Making a Grapevine Wreath

Muscadines *(Vitis rotundifolia)* grow throughout the South. Most Southerners are more familiar with muscadine or 'Scuppernong' grapes than they are with the vines. The fruit ripens in late summer and early fall when it can be eaten off the vine or turned into jams, jellies, and wine. The vines grow just about anywhere and have smooth, grayish-brown bark. Look for them in open areas, because they grow over the ground, onto fences, and up into trees. In the fall, leaves turn a bright yellow and drop, exposing the vines. Using hand pruners, cut the vines, and pull them clear of any obstacles. Then, go along the vines, and clip the side branches. Be sure to leave the vines' tendrils, as they will add interest to the wreath. Next, hold the large end (the end with the greatest diameter), and form a circle with the vine. It is important to size your wreath to the location you plan to hang it. When you make your first circle, hold it up as if you were going to hang it. Now is the time to adjust it, because as you add materials, it will continue to increase in size.Weave the vine through the circle, wrapping it around the initial circle. Continue wrapping the vine until it's about 3 inches wide. Using wire, make a hanger for the wreath. If you don't have time to make your own, ready-made grapevine wreaths are inexpensive and widely available.

FRAGRANT CEDAR WREATH

Easy, easy, easy. This wreath is made of materials available throughout the South. The fragrant green boughs and blue berries of Eastern red cedar *(Juniperus virginiana)* make it especially appealing. Starting at one point on the circle, push cut boughs through the grapevine wreath. Continue placing boughs until complete. Then use your clippers to trim and shape it. Add berries and pinecones, and hang your wreath.

Materials:

grapevine wreath
Eastern red cedar boughs
Eastern red cedar berries (Note: Berries are blue.)
pinecones
smooth sumac berries *(Rhus glabra)*

Note: You can substitute berries from American holly *(Ilex opaca)*, possumhaw *(Ilex decidua)*, nandina, *(Nandina domestica)*, or winterberry *(Ilex verticillata)*.

Tools:

hand pruners

Tips: Cut the boughs, and soak them in water overnight. The next day, let them air dry, and then begin building your wreath. This extra bit of hydration extends the life of the wreath. Also, remember that the brightest blue berries grow on the side of the tree that receives the most sun.

BY GENE B. BUSSELL / PHOTOGRAPHY J. SAVAGE GIBSON

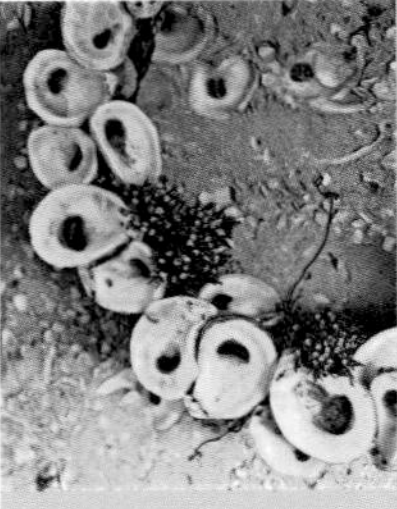

OYSTER SHELL WREATH

This simple wreath can decorate your home year-round; just add Eastern red cedar berries for the holiday season. The oyster shells used here were saved from a fall oyster roast. Clean and then soak shells in a hot water-and-bleach bath. Use four parts water to one part bleach. It may take a few soakings to thoroughly clean the shells. Do a final bath in hot water with dishwashing soap. Allow the shells to dry completely; then begin gluing them onto the grapevine wreath.

Materials:
grapevine wreath
oyster shells
Eastern red cedar berries

Tools:
glue gun

above: An oyster shell wreath seems to have emerged from the tabby wall.
below: A berry wreath finds a home on a porch.

BRIGHT BERRY WREATH

Insert clusters of nandina berries to cover the grapevine wreath. Use strips of florist wire to hold them in place; the berries will still hang a little loose. Once the berries are in place, use the same method to attach the kumquats, lemons, rose hips, and calamondin oranges (with stems still attached). If you can't find fruit with stems, insert florist picks into the fruit, and weave the picks into the wreath.

Materials:
grapevine wreath
nandina berries
(Nandina domestica)
calamondin oranges
(*Citrus* x *citrofortunella mitis*)
'Meyer' lemon (*C. limon* 'Meyer')
kumquats *(Fortunella margarita)*
rose hips (*Rosa* sp.)
florist wire
florist picks

Tools:
hand pruners

Tip: Place in a stationary position.

PHOTOGRAPHS: VAN CHAPLIN

A luxuriant bower of Jackson vine festoons the home of Pinkie and Bryan Chace. "It softens the architecture of the porch," Pinkie says.

JACKSON VINE
At a Glance

Size: 8 to 15 feet
Growth rate: moderate to fast
Light: sun or light shade
Soil: fertile, well-drained, tolerates drought
Pests: none serious
Range: Middle, Lower, Coastal South

One Fine Vine

How it got its name is a mystery, but this climber's good points are crystal clear.

Is it named for Stonewall Jackson? Kate Jackson? Jackson Pollock? Nobody seems to know. But when it comes to why people adorn their homes with Jackson vine *(Smilax smallii)*, there's no mystery. It's pretty, evergreen, and easy to grow.

Look closely as you drive through older neighborhoods in Birmingham, Atlanta, and other Southern cities, and you'll start seeing Jackson vine all over the place. People commonly use it to frame porches, doorways, and bay windows. If you have it at your house, chances are you inherited it from previous owners. It's hard to find at local nurseries because it grows from an enormous tuber that is usually dug from the wild in late winter and potted. But seedlings do sprout around an established vine, so you can also obtain it that way.

Birds gobble the berries that cluster beneath glossy, deep green leaves.

This native climber can look a little scary when it first emerges from the ground in spring. A stiff, snakelike stem ascends to a height of 3 feet or more before finally unfurling its leaves. Sharp thorns arm the base of the stem, but the remainder of the stem is thornless. Training it over a doorway or along the front of a porch is easy. Just run a sturdy wire where you want the vine to go. It'll use twining tendrils to attach itself. New stems will cling to older ones. Prune off any stray growth, or weave it back into the rest of the greenery.

Its lance-shaped leaves, 4 to 6 inches long and 2 to 3 inches wide, are deep green and glossy. Cut branches will last a long time indoors and out, which makes them favorite holiday decorations.

Clusters of blackish-blue or gray berries, which ripen in fall and last through winter, are magnets for birds. Pinkie Chace of Mountain Brook, Alabama, notes that nesting birds seem irresistibly drawn to the thick foliage and tasty berries on the vine growing above her porch. "I've had a mockingbird nest and a robin nest, and the purple finches just love it," she says. "They've made as many as three or four nests in a season." Sometimes when she walks out on the porch, the whole side of the house starts flapping.

While the usefulness of this vine is undeniable, one burning question still remains. Who the heck was Jackson vine named for? Janet Jackson? Bo Jackson? Inquiring minds want to know.

STEVE BENDER

White Christmas

Bring a fresh spirit to your home with these pristine bloomers.

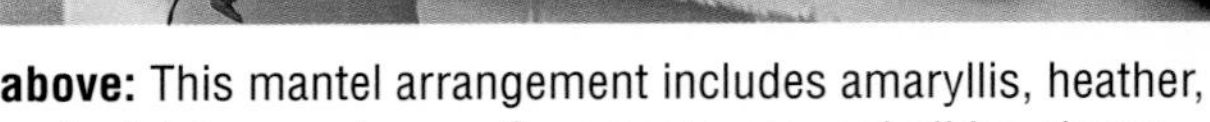

above: This mantel arrangement includes amaryllis, heather, and miniature cyclamen. Ornaments ensure holiday charm.

SIMPLE STATEMENTS

Dressing up white flowers is a fun study in color. Along with the plant materials you select, the shades you choose to finish the arrangement determine its mood and attitude. Use silver, gold, or cool metallic-tone containers and appointments for quiet elegance. Introduce traditional red, green, and vibrant jewel tones for an easygoing appearance.

Christmas is a feast for the senses, with blinking lights, pine-scented boughs, and flamboyant colors all part of the mix. Flowers are important ingredients in the decorating formula, and white blooms offer a refreshing look for holiday decor. Consider this color easygoing or elegant, depending on your style; the beauty of a white blossom is its versatility.

Growing plants produce long-lasting flowers throughout the holiday season. There is a grand assortment of white blooms. You can use them as single specimens or gather them in a composition. Our mantel arrangement sits in a narrow, old box lined with foil for moisture protection. Stately amaryllis reach toward the ceiling, while fluffy white heather fills in below. At the base, miniature cyclamen's airy blooms float above glossy foliage. Finishing touches include variegated ivy, maidenhair fern, and frosty green grapes tucked in the box and cascading over the edge. Shiny ornaments add a dash of color.

While cut flowers have shorter shelf lives than their rooted counterparts, they play a wonderful role in decorating. A single white blossom in a shiny red vase bursts with seasonal cheer. Spice-scented carnations, inexpensive and sturdy, adapt to casual and formal arrangements.

Snow-white Oriental lilies make a dramatic statement, and their fragrance perfumes a room. Purchase stems with a few buds still closed, and you'll have fresh blooms for more than a week. Other easy-to-find options include gerbera daisies, stock, roses, chrysanthemums, and calla lilies. Buy a stem or two of each, and place them in bud vases arranged on a table or tray. The striking simplicity is a welcome approach. ELLEN RUOFF RILEY

PHOTOGRAPHS: WILLIAM DICKEY

above: Small pots contain (clockwise from top) amaryllis, kalanchoe, viola, cyclamen, and calla lily.

Fabulous Winter Pots

Great plant combinations liven up the season.

Containers play an important role in the landscape, and winter plantings in them can be every bit as dazzling as summer's sizzling mixtures. If you consider this cool season lackluster, think again. Sunshine may be in short supply, but warm, colorful combinations abound.

The Nature of Texture

Conifers and evergreens can be woven together in a fabulous tapestry of foliage blending myriad shades of green. Choose plants for their individual personalities and also for how well they play with others. For example, the graceful blue-green branches of a Leyland cypress make a strong, slender spire. In a pot by itself, it appears lonely. Paired with a thick-leaved, leathery mahonia (shown at left), it presents a striking contrast. Introduce a dwarf nandina, dressed in winter's brilliant red leaves, a golden arborvitae, and ivy for a container filled with interesting partners.

Or fill a pot with silver plants. In the one shown at left, Arizona cypress is the focal point, and 'Powis Castle' artemisia fills out the pot's midsection. Lamb's ears accent the edge with big, fuzzy leaves, appropriate foils to the other delicate textures. If this combo appears a bit too cool, add gazing balls. Tucked in among the plants, whimsical garden ornaments inject unanticipated color.

PHOTOGRAPHS: VAN CHAPLIN

Simplicity is always a winner. A large boxwood is surrounded by colorful pansies and ivy in a plastic pot that resembles fine terra-cotta.

above: Leyland cypress, mahonia, dwarf nandina, ivy, and golden arborvitae greet visitors. **right:** Silver plants, such as Arizona cypress, 'Powis Castle' artemisia, and lamb's ears suggest winter. Pots of acorus and evergreen fern complete the effect.

Simply Colorful

Containers in sunny locations are prime candidates for winter's best bloomers—pansies and violas. The simple combination above features a portly boxwood in a classic pot. Pansies surround the lustrous foliage, and ivy tumbles over the edge. A weekly watering with a blossom-boosting fertilizer keeps this feature at its best.

Life's Short—Plant Big

A cold truth: Most shrubs don't do much growing in winter. Plant your container to be full from the beginning. There is a wide range of materials available in 1-gallon-size pots, so you can fit a nice assortment in a 12- or 14-inch container. Make your selections, and snuggle them tightly in the vessel. ELLEN RUOFF RILEY

Creative Lighting

Illuminate your porch with seasonal decorations for a warm holiday welcome.

PHOTOGRAPHS: VAN CHAPLIN

MAKE A GLOWING FABRIC TREE

Hang Christmas lights from the center of a pyramid-shaped metal topiary frame. Wrap the burlap around the frame, and use florist wire to attach it. Any visible seam can be positioned on the back of the tree. Place the burlap-covered frame in a terra-cotta pot for a simple and sturdy base.

Foliage and fabric, backlit by Christmas lights, can make your front porch shine for the Yuletide season. Here, a topiary frame wrapped in fabric gives a warm red glow for a neat nighttime effect, while tiny lights illuminate a wreath of beech leaves. These simple projects will help you use lights for a different, festive look.

Lit From Within

This twinkling decorated topiary form resembles a miniature Christmas tree. Filled with a swag of red lights and draped in burlap, the metal frame emits an inviting glow from dusk till dawn. The small rays of light shining through the cloth look like tiny red stars.

Topiary frames come in all shapes and sizes. This project calls for one with a pyramid shape. (The metal frame used here is topped with a decorative finial.) Start by attaching the red lights to the inside of the frame. Then wrap a piece of burlap around the outside, and attach with florist wire. (We used burlap, but any sheer fabric will do.)

Place the covered frame in a short, wide container, stuffing excess material down out of sight. (The container is also a good place to hide the electrical cord.) Finally, hang sweet gum balls by their stems from the cloth, and cluster magnolia leaves and pinecones around the base.

A Sparkling Wreath

This foliage wreath looks good during the day, but as night falls, it turns into a circle of gold accented by clear lights. It's simple to make, and you don't have to use beech leaves. Evergreens, such as holly or magnolia, work just as well. In fact, leftover clippings of greenery from your Christmas tree can also be used to wrap the circular form.

First, make or purchase a simple vine wreath. Wrap a string or two of lights around the wreath's frame. You may need to use thin-gauge wire to secure the lights to the wreath. Next, clip 16- to 18-inch branches with nice foliage, and layer them over the lights. Freshly cut branches are flexible and can be bent to conform to the circular shape. Use wire to secure branches to the form. A small pair of pliers with wire cutters comes in handy for cutting and bending the wire. You'll need hand pruners to trim and shape branches as you work them onto the wreath. CHARLIE THIGPEN

A Garden Under Glass

There's more than one way to beat the winter blahs.

PHOTOGRAPHS: VAN CHAPLIN

Not a day passes for Mary LaLone that she isn't surrounded by flowers. Though Blacksburg, Virginia, winters can be long and hard for a woman who grew up in balmy California, she has the pleasure of gardening year-round with a greenhouse.

"When it's all gray and yucky outside, it's beautiful inside," she says. In her work teaching anthropology at nearby Radford University, Mary spends hours each week reviewing her students' papers. Thanks to her greenhouse, that time is delightful. On those days, her desk chair is wicker, her lamp the sun, and her bookshelf holds only orchids, tropical foliage, and a few carnivorous plants.

In fact, orchids are her specialty. "They are addicting to grow," Mary says. "I got a few and started wanting more." At last count she had 350. "People ask how long it takes to water all these," she says, "but if you're just going through quickly with a hose like you would outdoors, it's not bad."

Her secret is foresight. She had a faucet installed in the house wall and a drain placed in the tile floor. So she can water with a hose and a nozzle that gives a gentle mist or shower. The excess runs onto the floor.

With all that moisture combined with the warmth of the sun, it seems as if the greenhouse would grow mold faster than an unvented shower and plant diseases would abound. But vents allow the air to change, so fungal spores are sent out into the cold. "Having a lot of air circulation helps," Mary says. "I discovered that extra fans really made a difference."

There's no need to worry about this gardener's spirit lagging during a long winter. She reminds us, "It's really a pleasant place to be. I can't imagine living without a greenhouse." In fact, her husband, Kim Knight, was so envious of her greenhouse that he built his own for his collection of cacti.

LINDA C. ASKEY

MARY'S SECRETS TO GREENHOUSE SUCCESS

- Double-pane glass insulates plants from extremely cold temperatures and contains both the warmth of the sun and any supplemental heat.
- Choose about a 30% tint for the glass on the ceiling. This keeps the room from becoming too hot.
- Learn about air circulation and where to put the greenhouse for maximum sun. Read books, and talk to people who have greenhouses.
- Use benches that allow the air to flow around the plants. Mary made her own from stackable shelving available at a local home-center store.

Glorious *Christmas* CACTUS

The bright flowers of this pass-along plant rekindle holiday traditions.

The Christmas season is centered around remembrance and sharing. No holiday plant exemplifies this spirit quite so well as Christmas cactus (*Schlumbergera* x *buckleyi*), a traditional Southern plant. Gently arching branches with bright blooms in fuchsias, reds, pinks, whites, or yellows provide cheerful color for the holiday. And the simple act of giving a plant provides a way to remain close to someone though you may be apart. That gift establishes a lasting bond that you both can nurture. Year after year, when the blossoms begin to swell and the colorful flowers open, that special gift is once again remembered and shared.

BY GENE B. BUSSELL
PHOTOGRAPHY JEAN ALLSOPP
STYLING CARI SOUTH

'Gold Charm' Christmas cactus glows as the centerpiece for this holiday table.

Name Game

Christmas cactus originated way down South—South America, that is—growing on the branches of trees in the jungles of Brazil. Although happy in trees, it was equally content in pots. Taken to Europe and crossed by breeders, it now boasts many selections and colors. You can also find this plant sold as Thanksgiving cactus *(Schlumbergera truncata* or *Zygocactus truncatus)*. It is commonly known as crab cactus, because the stems resemble crab claws. But it's not crabby. Confused? Don't be. Sometimes, as with people, it's easier just to remember the first name, the genus *Schlumbergera*.

Just Add Water

This plant is beautiful and easy to grow. It looks especially good in hanging baskets or footed pots where its graceful branching habit is best displayed. Although its name suggests otherwise, Christmas cactus prefers moist, well-drained soil. If it stays too wet, the roots will rot; if too dry, the roots will die. It needs bright, indirect light, so a window with an eastern exposure is ideal. It also likes to be outside in the summer in a lightly shaded spot. Hang it, or put it on a plant stand (not on the ground); slugs love its stems as much as you do.

Christmas cactus begins to set its buds in the fall as the days become shorter and the nights cooler. In the Upper and Middle South, bring your plant inside in early fall, and let it set buds. In the Lower, Coastal, and Tropical South, allow it to stay outside to set buds. Watch this plant carefully, and bring it in if it gets too cold. Indoors, don't place it in drafty situations or in too much sun, as this can cause the buds to drop or the flowers to develop too fast.

After your plant has finished blooming, reduce watering and allow it to rest for several months. Then resume a regular watering and feeding schedule. It is still a nice houseplant when it's not in bloom; the pendulous green foliage remains attractive. Remember that it prefers to be potbound, so you may only need to add a

top: The salmon flowers of 'Christmas Fantasy' warm the entry to this front hall. **above:** The soft colors of 'White Fantasy' find a home near the family Christmas tree. **right:** A collection of red pots echoes the vivid flowers of 'Sunburst.'

HOW TO ROOT

Once your Christmas cactus has finished flowering, take cuttings that are about 5 inches long and have several branches. Because it is a succulent, allow the cut to dry before potting. You can use a rooting hormone to speed things up, but it is not necessary. Use a soil mix that has some organic matter, such as peat, and drains quickly. Put two to three cuttings in a small clay pot. The clay breathes, so there is less chance that the cutting will rot from overwatering. Place the pot in bright, indirect light, and keep the soil moist. Your cuttings should root in several months. Christmas cactus loves to be potbound, so it can remain in the clay pot until you are ready to move it to a larger container. Pass a few along to your friends and family, because these plants will become happy memories.

Note: You can also divide your plant if you do not want to root a new one. Gently separate several leaf stems from the mother plant, keeping the roots intact. Reset into a new pot, and you'll have a new plant.

topdressing of soil early in spring. Christmas cactus is often the first plant people succeed with, because you don't need a green thumb. That's reason enough to love it.

When next Christmas rolls around and the flowerbuds of your Christmas cactus return, let the blooms spark memories of shared plants and a season of joy.

Index

Acer palmatum, 188–190
Acer rubrum 'October Glory,' 186
Acorus gramineus, 50, 180
African violet, 24–26
Agapanthus sp., 50
Ajuga reptans, 50
Alyssum, sweet, 17
Amaryllis, 144, 187, 205, 222
Amethyst flower, 50
Anemone, 18, 166, 168
Angel's tears *(Lindernia grandiflora),* 180
Angel's trumpet, 50, 58
Annuals. *See also* specific annuals.
- drought-tolerant, 108
- fall, 186
- fertilizing, 15
- growing from seed, 62
- planting, 23
- pruning, 131
- shade-loving, 50, 84
- sun-loving, 50, 84, 108, 130
- winter, 186

Aphids, 131
Apple, 164
Apricot, 22
Arrangements, 120, 153, 186, 204, 222. *See also* Cut flowers, Decorations, Wreaths.
- fall, 191, 214, 215
- holiday, 216–219, 228

Arrowhead vine, 12, 13
Arum, Italian, 50
Arum italicum, 50
Aster, 165, 166–168
Aucuba, Japanese, 50
Aucuba japonica, 50
Azalea, 17, 30–31, 33, 34–36, 171

Bachelor's buttons, 42
Backyards, 51–53, 64–66, 121. *See also* Gardens.
Banana shrub *(Michelia figo),* 181
Basil, 84, 122, 130, 144, 164
Baskets, hanging, 123
Bay, culinary *(Laurus nobilis),* 182
Beans, 116
Beech, 22
Begonia, 50, 73
Berry plants, 11, 50
Bignonia capreolata 'Tangerine Beauty,' 89
Bird feeders, 187
Birdhouses, 140, 141
Birds, 10, 131, 149, 227
Black-eyed Susan *(Rudbeckia hirta),* 130
Black spot, 144
Blanket flower *(Gaillardia sp.),* 164
Blazing star, spike *(Liatris spicata),* 55
Bluebonnet, 'Texas Maroon,' 37
Blue star *(Amsonia tabernaemontana),* 67
Bok Tower Gardens, 56–59
Borders, 55, 102–104
Bougainvillea, 144
Boxwood, 'Wintergreen' *(Buxus micro-phylla koreana* 'Winter-green'), 181
Bromeliads, 216–219
Browallia sp., 50
Brugmansia sp., 50
Buddleia sp., 38, 50, 55, 166–167
Bulbs, 18–19, 84, 109, 187, 223. *See also* specific bulbs.
Bush daisy, African *(Gamolepis chrysanthemoides),* 38
Butterfly bush, 38, 50, 55, 130, 166–167
Butterfly gardens, 38

Cactus, 232–235
Caladium, 50, 72, 84
Camellia, 10, 33, 50, 206–208, 223
Camellia japonica, 10, 50, 207
Candlelit gardens, 146–148
Candlestick plant *(Cassia alata),* 177
Cardinal flower *(Lobelia cardinalis),* 67
Carpet bugleweed, 50
Cast-iron plant *(Aspidistra elatior),* 14
Cedar, Eastern red *(Juniperus virginiana),* 225
Celosia, 85
Centipede grass, 131
Chaste tree *(Vitex* sp.), 144–145
Cherry, Okame, 20–21, 28–29
Chinch bugs, 131, 165
Chives, 122
Christmas decorations, 216–220, 222, 223, 224–226, 228, 230
Chrysanthemum, 85, 164, 167, 209
Chrysanthemum pacificum, 209
Chrysogonum virginianum, 50
Cigar plant *(Cuphea ignea),* 144, 164
Citrus, 10, 62, 145, 165, 204, 222
Clematis, 17, 32, 50, 115
Clematis armandii, 50
Clematis terniflora, 17, 115
Cleome, 42, 88
Cleome hasslerana, 88
Clivia, 32
Club moss, golden *(Selaginella kraussiana* 'Aurea'), 180
Cockscomb, 85
Coco-fiber, 123
Coleus, 50, 152
Coneflower, 42, 50, 130
Containers, 26. *See also* specific containers.
- combining plants in, 229
- growing plants in, 118–119
- plants suitable for, 50
- saucers for, 11
- watering plants, 71, 119, 223

Convolvulus tricolor, 117
Coreopsis, 50, 55, 67
Cosmos, 42
Cottage gardens, 175–177
Courtyards, 14, 86–88, 169
Crabgrass, 32
Creeping Jenny *(Lysimachia nummularia),* 87
Crepe myrtle, 45, 50, 110–112, 130, 145
Crocus, 'Ruby Giant' *(Crocus tomasinianus* 'Ruby Giant'), 19
Crossvine, 'Tangerine Beauty,' 89
Cucumbers, 116
Cucurbita sp., 187, 198–201, 211
Cut flowers, 63, 130, 133, 134, 161, 165. *See also* Arrangements.
Cyclamen, 18, 222

Daffodil, 18, 19, 192, 204. *See also* Narcissus.
Dahlia, 186
Daisy, 38, 42, 127, 131
Daphne odora, 16, 50
Daphne, winter, 16, 50
Datura metel, 50, 58
Daylily, 50, 55, 84, 108
Decks, 118–119
Decorations, 215. *See also* Arrangements.
- Christmas, 216–220, 222, 223, 224–226, 228, 230
- Thanksgiving, 214–219

Doctor Dirt, 174–177
Dogwood, flowering, 45
Doors, front, 44
Driveways, 52, 54
Drought-tolerant flowers, 50, 108
Drying flowers, 153, 186

Echinacea purpurea, 130
Elaeagnus, 17
Elephant's ear, 'Illustris' *(Colocasia esculenta* 'Illustris'), 88

Elm, Chinese or lacebark *(Ulmus parvifolia),* 45
Entryways, 44, 46–47, 52, 54. *See also* Walkways.

Fall arrangements, 191, 214, 215
Fall color, trees with, 204, 209. *See also* specific trees.
Fall plants, 17, 131, 144, 145, 164, 165, 186, 223. *See also* specific plants.
Feather reed grass *(Calamagrostis* x *acutiflora),* 196
Fences, 43
Fern, sensitive *(Onoclea sensibilis),* 67
Fertilizing, 205
Fescue, blue *(Festuca glauca),* 196
Firebush, 149
Firespike *(Odontonema strictum),* 144
Firethorn, 204, 210
Fishponds, 90, 91
Flame grass *(Miscanthus sinensis* 'Purpurascens'), 196
Florida lawn care, 96–98
Flowers
- cut, 63, 130, 133, 134, 161, 165
- drought-tolerant, 50, 108
- drying, 153, 186
- fall, 17, 186
- growing from seed, 42
- spring, 17, 18–19, 22, 205
- summer, 17
- white, 228
- winter, 10, 186

Follies (structures), 151
Forcing, 22
Forest grass, Japanese, 50, 196, 197
Fothergilla, 62
Fountain grass, 50, 196, 197
Fountains, 80, 87–88
Four o'clock, 17
Fragrant plants, 10–11, 16–17, 50
Fringe tree *(Chionanthus virginicus),* 32
Frogs (flower holders), 120
Fruit plants, 22. *See also* specific plants.
- fertilizing, 145
- harvesting, 204
- pest control, 165
- planting, 10, 62
- protecting from cold, 222
- pruning, 11, 23
- watering, 165

Gardenia, 17, 50
Gardenia jasminoides, 50
Gardens, 100–105, 124–127, 178–183. *See also* Backyards, Yards.
- at night, 146–148
- border, 102–103, 104
- butterfly, 38
- candlelit, 146–147, 148
- cottage, 175–177
- cut flower, 63
- disasters in, 84
- herb, 170
- kitchen, 170
- makeover, 86–88
- native plant, 67
- parterre, 60–61, 67, 78–81, 104, 105
- public, 55–59, 137
- rock, 100, 103, 104, 105
- shady, 136
- shared, 64–66
- sloping, 90–91, 209
- small, 136, 150–151, 170
- terrace, 14, 104, 105
- tropical, 154–157
- vegetable, 64–66, 138, 140, 141
- water, 14, 145

Gazing balls, 108
Giant reed *(Arundo donax),* 195, 196, 197
Ginger lily, 17, 50, 165
Globe amaranth *(Gomphrena* sp.), 88, 130
Glorybower, Harlequin, 17
Goldenrod *(Solidago* sp.), 67
Golden star, 50
Goldsberry, Leon, 174–177
Grapevines, 205, 225
Grasses, 40, 50, 97, 98, 194–197. *See also* Lawns, specific grasses.
Grass, keeping out of flowerbeds, 145
Greenhouses, 231
Greens
- holiday, 223
- leafy, 11, 164

Ground covers, 50, 108, 131. *See also* specific ground covers.
Groundsel, golden *(Senecio aureus),* 67

Hakonechloa macra, 50, 196, 197
Hamelia patens, 149
Harry Lauder's walking stick *(Corylus avellana* 'Contorta'), 118
Heart rot, 75
Hedychium sp., 17, 50, 165
Helianthus angustifolius, 168, 177
Helianthus salicifolius, 168
Helleborus orientalis, 50, 210–211
Herb gardens, 170
Herbicides, 27
Herbs, 22, 62, 122. *See also* specific herbs.
Hibiscus, 50, 108
Holiday decorations, 214–220, 222, 223, 224–226, 228, 230
Holly, 50, 223
Hollyhock, 42
Honeysuckle, 11, 16, 17, 32, 67
Hosta, 'Royal Standard,' 17
Houseplants, 12–13, 23, 71, 84, 223. *See also* specific houseplants.
Hyacinth, 16
Hydrangea, 82–83, 101, 102–103
Hydrangea macrophylla, 50

Ilex decidua, 223
Impatiens, 50, 92–93
Ipomoea alba, 17, 87, 109
Iris
- bearded, 17, 144
- dwarf, 210, 211
- 'Harmony,' 8–9, 19
- Japanese *(Iris ensata),* 55
- Japanese roof, 73, 144
- Siberian *(Iris sibirica),* 47

Iris reticulata, 210, 211
Iris tectorum, 73, 144
Iris x *germanica,* 17, 144
Iron deficiency, correcting, 109

Jack-o'-lanterns, 187, 198–201
Jackson vine, 227
Jacobinia, 62
Jasmine, 50, 181, 182
Jessamine, Carolina *(Gelsemium sempervirens),* 44
Joe-pye weed *(Eupatorium purpureum),* 67
Journals, garden, 10, 108
Justicia carnea, 62

Kaffir lily, 32
Kalanchoe, 222
Kitchen gardens, 170
Kumquat *(Fortunella margarita),* 226

Labels, plant, 63
Lady-slipper, tropical, 172–173
Lagerstroemia indica, 45, 50, 110–112, 130, 145
Landscaping, 39–42, 46–49, 51–53, 55
Lantana, 50, 63, 130
Lantana sp., 50, 63, 130
Lawns. *See also* Grasses.
- aerating, 27
- care, 27, 96–98, 165

Lawns *(continued)*
fertilizing, 27, 33, 63, 98, 109, 145, 165
mowing, 27, 49, 97–98, 130
mulching, 131
seeding, 10, 27, 63, 204
small, 49, 121
sodding, 27, 63
watering, 97, 98
weed control, 23, 27, 32
Leaves, fallen, 186, 204
Lemon, 'Meyer' *(Citrus limon* 'Meyer'), 226
Lenten rose, 50, 210–211
Lighting, 146–147, 148, 230
Lilac, 50
Lilium formosanum, 135
Lilium lancifolium or *tigrinum,* 114
Lily, 17, 49, 101, 114, 135
Lily-of-the-Nile, 50
Lily-of-the-valley, 17
Lime, 11
Liriope, 11, 50
Liriope muscari 'Big Blue,' 50
Lupinus texensis 'Texas Maroon,' 37
Lyme grass, blue *(Leymus arenarius),* 196

Magnolia, 17, 45, 50
Magnolia grandiflora, 17, 45, 50
Mahonia bealei, 50
Mahonia, leatherleaf, 50
Maiden grass *(Miscanthus sinensis* 'Gracillimus'), 196
Mailboxes as planters, 87
Maple, 45, 186, 188–190
Marigold, 42, 131
Mazus, 50, 73
Mazus reptans, 50, 73
Mealybugs, 71
Mites, 71, 165
Moisture meters, 71
Mondo grass, 11, 213
Moonflower, 17, 87, 109
Morning glory, dwarf, 117
Mosaics, 74
Mosaic virus, 114
Moss, 123
Mother-in-law's tongue, 12, 13
Mountain laurel, Texas, 70
Mowing, 27, 49, 97–98, 130
Muhly grass *(Muhlenbergia* sp.), 195, 196, 197
Mulch and mulching, 41, 186, 222
Muscadine, 225

Nandina, 33, 50
Nandina domestica 'Monum,' 50
Narcissus, 222. *See also* Daffodil.
Native plant gardens, 67
Nematodes, 97
Night, gardens at, 146–148

Oak, 45
Obedient plant, 168
Ophiopogon japonicus, 11, 213
Optical illusions, 94–95
Orange, 177, 226
Osmanthus, 17
Osmanthus fragrans, 50

Paeonia lactiflora, 16, 17, 205
Palm, 13, 85
Pampas grass *(Cortaderia selloana),* 194–195, 196
Pansy, 15, 16, 204
Paperwhite, 16
Paphiopedilum sp., 172–173
Par-cel, 122
Parking areas, 52, 54, 213
Parrot's feather *(Myriophyllum aquaticum),* 14
Parsley, 122
Parterres, 60–61, 67, 78–81, 104, 105
Paths. *See* Walkways.
Patios, 14, 86–88, 169
Peace lily, 12, 13, 50
Peas, 23, 116
Pennisetum, Chinese *(Pennisetum alopecuroides),* 196, 197
Pennisetum setaceum 'Rubrum,' 50, 196, 197
Pentas, 32
Pentas lanceolata, 32
Peony, 16, 17, 205
Perennial borders, 55
Perennials, 62, 166–168. *See also* specific perennials.
dividing, 204
fall, 131, 144, 145, 164, 165, 223
planting, 33
pruning, 145, 165, 223
spring, 165
sun-loving, 108, 130
Pergolas, 115
Periwinkle, common, 50
Petunia, 17, 80
Philippine violet *(Barleria cristata),* 144
Phlomis fruticosa and *russelliana,* 99
Phlox, blue, 68–69
Physostegia virginiana, 168

Piepans as flowerpot saucers, 11
Pipe cleaners, use with plant supports, 109
Pistache, Chinese, 45
Planters. *See* Containers.
Poinsettia, 222
Poison ivy, 109
Ponds, garden, 90, 91
Pools, 14, 105, 113, 154–155, 156, 157
Poppy, 42
Porches, 44, 54
Porterweed *(Stachytarpheta* sp.), 38
Possumhaw, 223
Pothos, 12, 13
Potpourris, 153
Pots. *See* Containers.
Primrose, 16
Privet, glossy *(Ligustrum lucidum),* 208
Pruners, 71
Pumpkins, 187, 198–201, 211
Pyracantha, 204, 210

Ravenna grass *(Erianthus ravennae),* 195, 196, 197
Ribbon grass *(Phalaris arundinacea),* 195, 196
River oats *(Chasmanthium latifolium),* 196
Rock gardens, 100, 103, 104, 105
Roots, matted, 71
Rosa sp. *See* Rose.
Rose, 17, 50, 55
disease control, 85
fertilizing, 23, 85, 145
Noisette, 76–77
pest control, 85
planting, 22, 164, 187
pruning, 23, 33, 109, 145
supporting, 205
Rose campion *(Lychnis coronaria),* 115
Ryegrass, 187

Sage. *See also* Salvia.
autumn *(Salvia greggii),* 33, 84
bog *(Salvia uliginosa),* 84–85
Brazilian *(Salvia guaranitica),* 131
Jerusalem, 99
mealy-cup *(Salvia farinacea),* 33
Mexican bush, 162–163
pineapple *(Salvia elegans),* 144
Russian *(Perovskia atriplicifolia),* 55
scarlet *(Salvia splendens),* 130

Salt-tolerant grasses, 97
Salvia, 33, 84–85. *See also* Sage.
Salvia leucantha, 162–163
Sansevieria trifasciata, 12, 13
Saucers, flowerpot, 11
Saxifraga stolonifera, 73
Scarlet bush, 149
Schlumbergera x *buckleyi,* 232–235
Sculptures, garden, 137
Sedge *(Carex* sp.), 50, 196
Sedum, 50, 73, 168
Sedum sieboldii, 73
Seeds, 10, 144, 164
growing from, 22, 42, 62, 164, 187
Shade-loving plants, 50, 84
Shady gardens, 136
Shasta daisy, 'Becky' *(Chrysanthemum* x *superbum* 'Becky'), 115
Sheds, 128–129, 140, 141, 150–151
Shrubs. *See also* specific shrubs.
fertilizing, 23, 85, 145
fragrant, 10–11
mulching, 84
planting, 11, 22, 32, 187, 205
pruning, 11, 23, 33
Silver grass, giant Chinese *(Miscanthus giganteus),* 196
Skimmia, Japanese, 50
Skimmia japonica, 50
Sky vine, 63
Slopes, landscaping on, 51–54, 90–91, 209
Smilax smallii, 227
Snowdrop, 18, 19
Soil preparation, 10, 11, 22, 32, 42
Sophora secundiflora, 70
South Carolina Botanical Garden, 137
Spathiphyllum sp., 12, 13, 50
Spider flower, 42, 88
Spinach, Malabar, 116
Spittlebugs, 131, 165
Spring plants, 17, 18–19, 22, 63, 84, 165, 187, 205, 223. *See also* specific plants.
Squirrels, 85, 187
Stakes, 33, 116
St. Augustine, 84, 131
Strawberry jars, 73
Sumac, smooth *(Rhus glabra),* 225
Summer plants, 17, 109. *See also* specific plants.
Sunflower, 42, 50, 109, 142, 158–161
Mexican, 42
swamp, 168, 177
willowleaf, 168
Sun-loving plants, 50, 84, 108, 130
Supports, plant, 33, 66, 84, 116
Sweet flag, 50, 180
Sweet pea, 17, 205
Sweet potato, 'Blackie' *(Ipomoea batata* 'Blackie'), 88
Sweet William, 17
Switch grass *(Panicum virgatum),* 196
Syringa sp., 50

Tables, garden, 74
Taxus cuspidata, 50
Tea bags, use in watering, 223
Tea olive, 50
Tea plant *(Camellia sinensis),* 208
Tepees (plant supports), 116
Terrace gardens, 14, 104, 105
Thanksgiving decorations, 216–219
Thryallis, yellow *(Galphimia glauca),* 180
Thunbergia grandiflora, 63
Thyme, 85, 122
Tithonia rotundifolia, 42
Tobacco, flowering, 17
Tomato cages, 84
Tomatoes, 63, 116
Toolsheds, 128–129, 140, 141
Torenia fournieri, 50
Towers, bell, 56–58, 59
Trachelospermum jasminoides, 50
Transplant roots, matted, 71
Trees. *See also* specific trees.
Christmas, 222
fertilizing, 23, 85, 145
flowering, 32. *See also* specific trees.
fruit, 10, 11, 23, 62, 145, 165, 204, 222
mulching, 84
planting, 10, 11, 22, 45, 62, 187
pruning, 11, 23
removing, 53
with fall color, 204, 209.
Trellises, 116
Tropical gardens, 154–157
Trumpet creeper, hybrid *(Campsis tagliabuana),* 115
Trumpet honeysuckle *(Lonicera sempervirens),* 67
Trumpet vine, common *(Campsis radicans),* 131
Tubers, 109. *See also* specific tubers.
Tulip, 10, 212
Tulip poplar, 45
Turk's turban *(Malvaviscus arboreus drummondii),* 177

Vegetable gardens, 64–66, 138, 140, 141
Vegetables. *See also* specific vegetables.
fertilizing, 85
growing from seed, 22, 187
growing vertically, 116
harvesting, 108, 144
planting and transplanting, 11, 22, 33, 85, 187, 205
Verbena bonariensis, 47
Viburnum carlesii, 50
Viburnum, Korean spice, 50
Vinca minor, 50
Vines, 10, 32, 62. *See also* specific vines.
Viola, 15, 205
Vitis rotundifolia, 225

Walkways, 46–47, 48, 54, 94–95, 193. *See also* Entryways.
Waterfalls, 90, 91
Water gardens, 14, 145
Watering, 108, 130, 164, 186–187
Watering cans, 71
Weeds, 23, 27, 32
White flowers, 228
Wildflowers, 164
Willow, desert *(Chilopsis linearis),* 144–145
Windbreak plants, 11
Winterberry *(Ilex verticillata),* 225
Winter plants, 10, 16, 50, 186, 229. *See also* specific plants.
Wintersweet *(Chimonanthus praecox),* 11
Wishbone flower, 50
Witch hazel, common, 17
Wreaths, 214–215, 220, 224–226, 230

Yards. *See also* Backyards, Gardens, Lawns.
front, 40–41, 46–47, 52–53
makeover, 39–41, 46–48, 51–53, 54
side, 14, 48
sloping, 51–53
Yarrow *(Achillea* sp.), 165
Yellow bells *(Tecoma stans),* 145
Yew, Japanese, 50
Yucca, 50, 145, 181

Zinnia, 42, 50, 66, 109, 132–133, 134
Zinnia angustifolia, 50
Zone map, plant hardiness, 240
Zoysia, 40

Plant Hardiness Zone Map

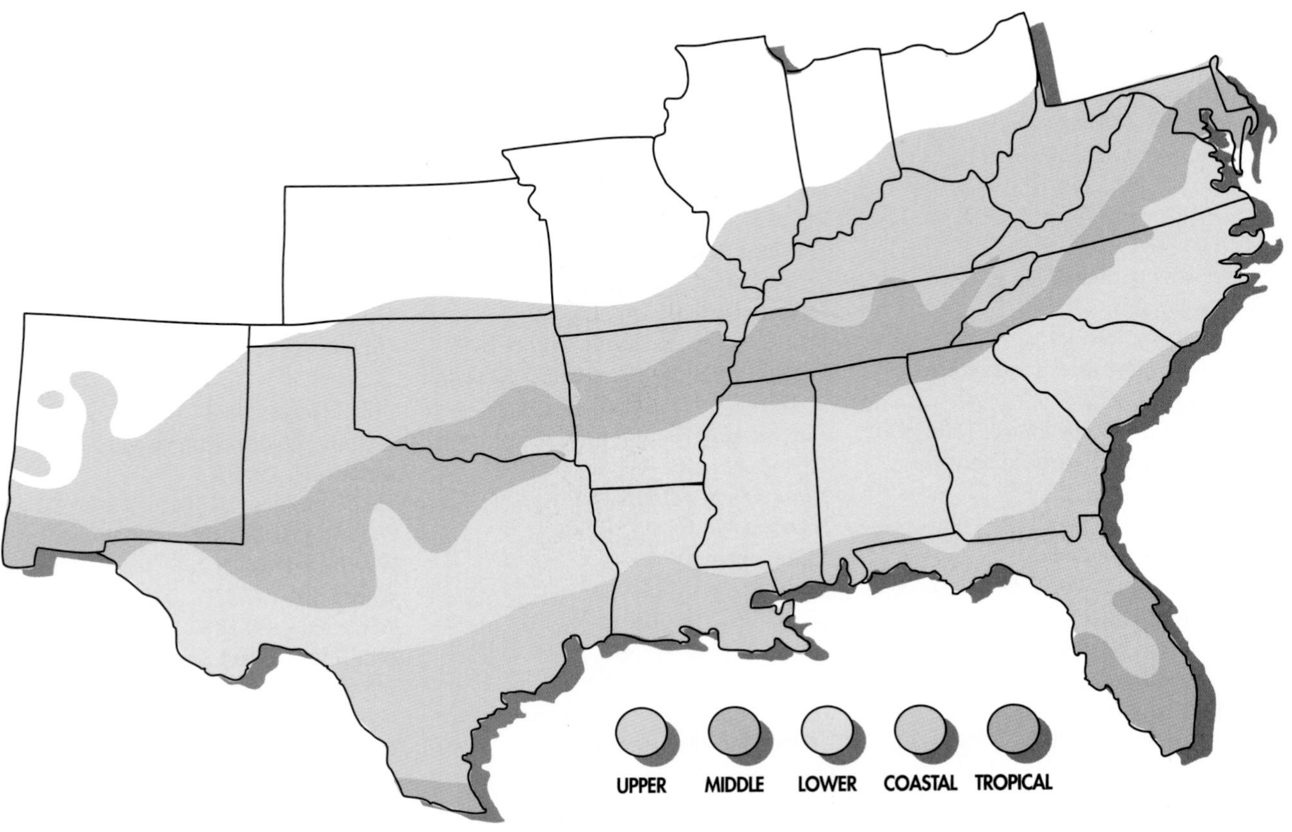

The United States Department of Agriculture has charted low temperatures throughout the country to determine the ranges of average low readings. The map above is based loosely on the USDA Plant Hardiness Zone Map, which was drawn from these findings. It does not take into account heat, soil, or moisture extremes and is intended as a guide, not a guarantee.

The southern regions of the United States that are mentioned in this book refer to the following:

Upper South: -10° to 0°F minimum
Middle South: 0° to 5°F minimum
Lower South: 5° to 15°F minimum
Coastal South: 15° to 25°F minimum
Tropical South: 25° to 40°F minimum